G000153695

Microsoft Team Foundation Server 2015 Cookbook

Over 80 hands-on DevOps and ALM-focused recipes for Scrum Teams to enable the Continuous Delivery of high-quality Software... Faster!

Tarun Arora

BIRMINGHAM - MUMBAI

Microsoft Team Foundation Server 2015 Cookbook

Copyright © 2016 Packt Publishing

All rights reserved. No part of this book may be reproduced, stored in a retrieval system, or transmitted in any form or by any means, without the prior written permission of the publisher, except in the case of brief quotations embedded in critical articles or reviews.

Every effort has been made in the preparation of this book to ensure the accuracy of the information presented. However, the information contained in this book is sold without warranty, either express or implied. Neither the author, nor Packt Publishing, and its dealers and distributors will be held liable for any damages caused or alleged to be caused directly or indirectly by this book.

Packt Publishing has endeavored to provide trademark information about all of the companies and products mentioned in this book by the appropriate use of capitals. However, Packt Publishing cannot guarantee the accuracy of this information.

First published: January 2016

Production reference: 1250116

Published by Packt Publishing Ltd.
Livery Place
35 Livery Street
Birmingham B3 2PB, UK.

ISBN 978-1-78439-105-8

www.packtpub.com

Credits

Author

Tarun Arora

Reviewers

Mohamed Aboelqasem

Mike Branstein

Michael Jurek

Sudheer Mohan Mirampally

Commissioning Editor

Douglas Patterson

Acquisition Editor

Vinay Argekar

Content Development Editor

Shali Deeraj

Technical Editor

Prajakta Mhatre

Copy Editor

Charlotte Carneiro

Project Coordinator

Sanchita Mandal

Proofreader

Safis Editing

Indexer

Tejal Daruwale Soni

Graphics

Kirk D'Penha

Jason Monteiro

Abhinash Sahu

Production Coordinator

Aparna Bhagat

Cover Work

Aparna Bhagat

About the Author

Tarun Arora is obsessed with high-quality working software, continuous delivery, and Agile practices. He has experience managing technical programs, implementing digital strategy, and delivering quality @ scale. Tarun has worked on various industry-leading programs for fortune 500 companies in the financial and energy sector.

He is one of the many geeks working for Avanade in the United Kingdom. Avanade helps clients and their customers realize results in a digital world through business technology solutions, cloud, and managed services that combine insight, innovation, and expertise in Microsoft technologies.

For the past 5 years, Tarun has been a Microsoft Most Valuable Professional in Visual Studio and Development Technologies. His core strengths are enterprise architecture, .NET, WPF, SQL, and PowerShell. He was awarded the MVP of the year award by Microsoft in 2014 for going over and above in supporting the product teams and the community with his contributions. He is also an ALM Ranger and has contributed to key guidance and tooling projects focused on Azure, Team Foundation Server, Visual Studio Team Services, and Visual Studio Extensibility. Tarun is an active open source community contributor, speaker, and blogger. Follow him on twitter at `@arora_tarun` and his blog at `http://www.visualstudiogeeks.com` for the latest and greatest in technology trends and solutions on DevOps and ALM.

Tarun loves photography and travel. He is a very active traveler and has travelled to more than 21 countries in the last few months. Parts of this book have been written on his journeys across three continents. While some chapters were written on the beaches of Mauritius, others were written in transit, airport lounges, and taxis. Follow his adventures on his travel blog (`https://outofofficetraveller.wordpress.com`).

Acknowledgments

This book is dedicated to my mother, Mrs. Raj Rani Arora, and my father, Mr. Inder Jit Arora, without whom I wouldn't be what I am today. This book would never have been complete without the support of my lovely wife, Anuradha Arora. I would also like to thank my family and friends for their encouragement throughout the process.

The Microsoft Product Team, especially Brian Harry, Buck Hodges, Aaron Bjork, Chris Patterson, Gopi Chigakkagari, Ravi Shanker, Karen Ng, Charles Sterling, and Will Smyth, have been extremely helpful in guiding the direction of this book.

I would also like to thank ALM Champs and ALM Rangers for their technical inputs and review on the book, especially Josh Garverick, Utkarsh Shigihalli, and Willy Peter Schaub.

About the Reviewers

Mohamed Aboelqasem is a solution architect in Kuwait Finance House Bank—development department, where he engages with leading and designing different enterprise on-premises and cloud solutions. He brings over 12 years of deep technical experience to Microsoft technologies. He has deep practical experience in the government, financial, and oil and gas industries. M.Aboelqasem works mainly in the Middle East, Egypt, KSA, and Kuwait. He currently resides with his family in Kuwait.

He is working in the KFH bank, which is one of the biggest Islamic banks in the Middle East and is the Islamic bank leader in Kuwait. KFH owns groups of banks in different countries such as Bahrain, Turkey, Malaysia, Saudi, and Germany.

> I would like to thank my wife for helping and supporting me in my social and professional life, which always increases my moral to share in professional communities.

Mike Branstein is a developer and leader, who is passionate about systems architecture, team building, application life cycle management, and technology. Mike lives in Louisville, KY, and is the director of application development at KiZAN Technologies. As a consultant, he enjoys working with clients to improve development and project management processes using Team Foundation Server.

Mike blogs with his brother, Nick Branstein, at http://brosteins.com, where they are known as "The Brosteins". You can find Mike on Twitter at @mikebranstein.

Michael Jurek is a senior professional with over 15 years of experience in the IT industry. He likes learning new technologies and enjoys addressing technological challenges. He sees himself as a strong and creative personality with very good communication and presentation skills and a great sense of humor.

Michael worked for 13 years for Microsoft as a software architect focused on solution architecture, databases, ALM (Application Lifecycle Management), and cloud adoption. Since 2013, he has been a freelance consultant with the same focus.

Michael is married and has two children. His hobbies are using a giant astronomical telescope, playing volleyball, reading about the history of the Second World War, and manually working at his weekend house located deep in the forest.

Sudheer Mohan Mirampally is a senior solution architect for Yash Technologies, where he is responsible for the technology and architecture across US and Middle East (Dubai, Saudi Arabia, Bahrain). He is currently in the Yash Technologies Global presales team and supports sales and customer/prospect engagements.

As a solution architect at Yash, he is responsible for building and presenting customized business solutions with Microsoft Dynamics CRM and Office 365, in addition to integrating CRM and Dynamics Marketing, Dynamics NAV, and Dynamics AX, he is also well poised in SQL Server DQS and MDM.

Sudheer completed his MCA degree from Osmania University, and has a total of 11 years of experience in CRM and Microsoft Stack consulting, implementing, and supporting solutions that have diverse technologies and capabilities. He worked as a consultant and implemented the business solutions with Intac, Cyquent FZ LLC, Source Edge, and HCL (ADHAAR).

I would like to thank my parents, my siblings, my wife, and all my colleagues for their continuous support every day. I would also like to thank the Team Foundation Server community.

I would like to thank Packt Publishing for giving me the opportunity to review this book. My special thank goes to my guru, Mr. Sunil Kumar Benny, and my best friends, Vivek Patil (Compusoft India) and Ahmad Saad, for their continuous help and support in my life.

www.PacktPub.com

Support files, eBooks, discount offers, and more

For support files and downloads related to your book, please visit www.PacktPub.com.

Did you know that Packt offers eBook versions of every book published, with PDF and ePub files available? You can upgrade to the eBook version at www.PacktPub.com and as a print book customer, you are entitled to a discount on the eBook copy. Get in touch with us at service@packtpub.com for more details.

At www.PacktPub.com, you can also read a collection of free technical articles, sign up for a range of free newsletters and receive exclusive discounts and offers on Packt books and eBooks.

https://www2.packtpub.com/books/subscription/packtlib

Do you need instant solutions to your IT questions? PacktLib is Packt's online digital book library. Here, you can search, access, and read Packt's entire library of books.

Why subscribe?

- ▶ Fully searchable across every book published by Packt
- ▶ Copy and paste, print, and bookmark content
- ▶ On demand and accessible via a web browser

Free access for Packt account holders

If you have an account with Packt atwww.PacktPub.com, you can use this to access PacktLib today and view 9 entirely free books. Simply use your login credentials for immediate access.

Instant updates on new Packt books

Get notified! Find out when new books are published by following @PacktEnterprise on Twitter or the *Packt Enterprise* Facebook page.

Table of Contents

Preface

Visual Studio is a suite of Microsoft Developer Tools and Services, a few key ones being Visual Studio IDE, Visual Studio Code, Visual Studio Team Services, and Visual Studio Team Foundation Server (TFS). Back in November 2004, Microsoft released its first version of integrated Application Lifecycle Management (ALM) tool, called "Microsoft Visual Studio Team Systems". Over the last 15 years, the product has gone through several evolutions, each enriching the developer experience and the scope of tooling:

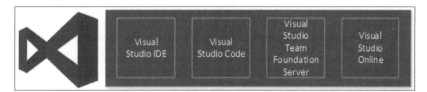

Visual Studio – Any App Any Developer

The Visual Studio family of tools and services now enables heterogeneous software development across various platforms. The experience of using open source tooling within the product has improved tremendously. Open source solutions are being given first class citizen status, and more of these solutions are being pre-packaged into the product. This gives us a clear indication that Microsoft wants to become the platform of choice for every developer, independent of the technology or platform. There is a huge overlap between the tools and services within the Visual Studio family of tools. This book focuses entirely on Visual Studio Team Foundation Server 2015.

Microsoft Visual Studio Team Foundation Server 2015 is at the center of Microsoft's ALM solution, providing core services such as version control, Work Item tracking, reporting, and automated builds. TFS helps organizations communicate and collaborate more effectively throughout the process of designing, building, testing, and deploying software, ultimately leading to increased productivity and team output, improved quality, and greater visibility of an application's life cycle.

Software delivery itself has gone through a revolution in the last decade. The introduction of Agile practices and lean frameworks, such as Scrum, Kanban, XP, and RUP, among others, have demonstrated that iterative feedback-driven development helps to cope with changes in the marketplace, business, and user requirements. Lean processes also help minimize waste and maximize value delivery to end users. Better DevOps practices encouraging continuous integration, continuous deployment, continuous delivery, and continuous feedback along with better tooling are enabling organizations to break the silos between teams. Mission-critical applications may still choose to deliver using Waterfall, while a line of business applications may find more success choosing lean methodologies. There is no right or wrong in this; choose the process and tools that are most appropriate to your delivery scenario. Visual Studio TFS supports most processes out of the box, and gives you the flexibility to customize and define processes that work best for your organization.

Visual Studio Team Foundation Server 2015, henceforth referred to as TFS in this book, is Microsoft's on-premise offering of ALM Tooling. Microsoft also offers a cloud-hosted service called Visual Studio Team Services (VSTS). Do not confuse VSTS for being Visual Studio IDE in the cloud; it is instead a collection of developer services comparable to TFS that run on Microsoft Azure and extend the development experience in the cloud. Microsoft is really committed to its hosted service, and has moved it into a 3-week cadence. All features are released in VSTS first, and then, most features are rolled into TFS via quarterly updates. A timeline of features released and those planned in the future releases can be found at `https://www.visualstudio.com/en-us/news/release-archive-vso.aspx`. The product teams solicit new feature requests via user voice. If you have a burning idea for a feature, be sure to log your request at `https://visualstudio.uservoice.com/forums/121579-visual-studio-2015/category/30925-team-foundation-server-visual-studio-online`. VSTS now offers a lot of enterprise features such as guaranteed uptime, single sign on using ADFS and AAD, and compliance to US, European, and Australian data sovereignty laws by offering tenants hosted in those regions. Though VSTS boasts of having over 3 million active users, organizations that need more control of the environment and their data will still prefer TFS over VSTS.

 All recipes in this book are designed for TFS; however, because of the overlap between VSTS and TFS, most of what you learn in this book is applicable to VSTS.

The various clients that can be used to connect to TFS can be broadly divided into two groups—primary clients, and task-specific clients, as shown in the following screenshot. A full list of the functions that can be performed using these clients can be found at `https://msdn.microsoft.com/en-us/library/ms181304.aspx`.

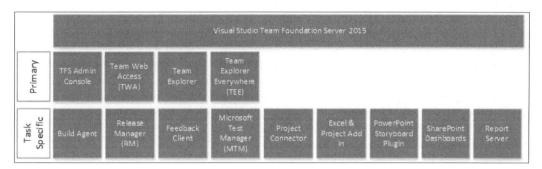

If you're setting up TFS for personal use, or to evaluate the core features, such as version control, build, and Work Item tracking, use TFS Express. It's free, it's simple to set up, and it can be installed on both client and server operating systems. Express does not support integration with SharePoint or Reporting Services. If you are setting up TFS for your organization, use the standard version of TFS. You can set up TFS on a single computer, in a dual server configuration, or in a multi-server configuration. Use the following handy reference to check the compatibility matrix for TFS 2015:

`https://msdn.microsoft.com/Library/vs/alm/TFS/administer/requirements`

The TFS architecture setup and network and port requirements can be found at `https://msdn.microsoft.com/en-us/library/ms252473(v=vs.120).aspx`. The product setup documentation can be found at `https://msdn.microsoft.com/en-us/Library/vs/alm/TFS/setup/overview`. The planning and disaster recovery guidance (`http://vsarplanningguide.codeplex.com/`) from ALM Rangers is very useful when planning an enterprise grade TFS setup. TFS 2015-specific license updates will be covered in the *Assigning a license, adding users, and auditing user access* recipe in *Chapter 1, Team Project Setup*. To learn more about the license requirements for TFS, please read through the Visual Studio and MSDN Licensing white paper at `http://www.microsoft.com/en-gb/download/details.aspx?id=13350`.

The recipes in this book require a standard one machine setup of TFS. You can set up a standalone single server using the preceding installation instructions, or, alternatively, use a preconfigured TFS 2015 Virtual Machine. Instructions to download and set this up can be found at `http://vsalmvm.azurewebsites.net/`.

What this book covers

Chapter 1, Team Project Setup, covers Team Project, which is a logical container isolating all tools and artifacts associated with a software application together in a single namespace. Features such as Welcome pages, Dashboards, Team Rooms, and many more enable better collaboration within Teams, whereas the ability to rename Team Projects and scripting Team Project creation empowers you to better administer a Team Project. In this chapter, we'll learn the different features of a Team Project and how to set up these features to leverage them to their full potential.

Chapter 2, Setting Up and Managing Code Repositories, introduces TFS, which is the only product to offer a centralized as well as distributed version control system. In this chapter, we'll learn how to set up both TFVC and Git repositories in a single project and how to tackle technical debt by enforcing code reviews and code analysis into the development workflows.

Chapter 3, Planning and Tracking Work, explains the requirements that are implemented but never used, or those that are used just long enough to identify that they don't satisfy the needs of the users cause and waste, re-work, and dissatisfaction. In this chapter, we'll learn how to set up and customize multiple backlogs, Kanban, and Sprint Task Board. We'll also learn how to integrate with external planning tools using Service Hooks, and how to improve the feedback loop by leveraging the feedback features in TFS.

Chapter 4, Building Your Application, introduces the new build system (TFBuild), which is a cross platform, open, and extensible task-based execution system with a rich web interface that allows the authoring, queuing, and monitoring of builds. In this chapter, we'll learn how to set up and use TFBuild for continuous integration. We'll also learn how to integrate TFBuild with SonarQube and GitHub. We'll also review features that help lay the foundations for continuous delivery of software.

Chapter 5, Testing Your Application, states that low quality software just isn't acceptable. But you may ask "what is the right level of quality?" In this chapter, we'll learn how to plan, track, and automate using the testing tools available in TFS. We'll also learn how to leverage the new build system to integrate non-Microsoft testing frameworks, such as Selenium and NUnit, into the automation testing workflows.

Chapter 6, Releasing Your Application, explains the new web-based Release Manager in TFS that uses the same agent and task infrastructure offered by TFBuild. In this chapter, we'll learn how to set up, secure, and deploy to multiple environments using release pipelines. We'll also learn how to track and report on releases delivered through the release pipeline. The techniques in this chapter enable you to set up your software for continuous delivery.

Chapter 7, Managing Team Foundation Server, teaches you how to update, maintain, and optimize your TFS, enabling high availability for geo-distributed Teams and reducing the administration overheads.

Chapter 8, Extending and Customizing Team Foundation Server, explains that it is not uncommon for organizations to have different tools to manage different parts of the life cycle, for example, Jira for Agile project management, TeamCity for builds, Jenkins for release management, and ServiceNow for service management. In this chapter, we'll learn about the TFS object model and TFS REST APIs to programmatically access and integrate with systems. In this chapter, we'll also cover how to customize Team Projects by leveraging Process Template customization.

What you need for this book

The recipes in this book are based on Team Foundation Server 2015. All recipes have been tested with the TFS 2015 Update 1 setup. To work through the recipes, you'll need a working setup of Team Foundation Server 2015 with Visual Studio 2015.

Who this book is for

This book is for all software professionals, including developers, testers, architects, managers, and configuring analysts, using or planning to use TFS.

The book covers the functions of Team Foundation Server 2015, including Team Projects, Source Control, Work Items, Build, Test, Release, Administration, Extensibility, and Customization with focus on DevOps and ALM-centric topics.

This book provides hands-on recipes to leverage new and existing features of TFS for Scrum Teams to enable continuous delivery of high quality software, faster. Rather than just covering the theoretical concepts, each recipe uses a cookbook format that presents a problem, solution, and explanation, taking you directly into real-world practical usage scenarios.

The book assumes you have a working setup of Team Foundation Server 2015 and basic knowledge of TFS, Software Development Lifecycle, and Scrum framework.

Sections

In this book, you will find several headings that appear frequently (Getting ready, How to do it, How it works, There's more, and See also.)

To give clear instructions on how to complete a recipe, we use these sections as follows:

Getting ready

This section tells you what to expect in the recipe, and describes how to set up any software or any preliminary settings required for the recipe.

How to do it...

This section contains the steps required to follow the recipe.

How it works...

This section usually consists of a detailed explanation of what happened in the previous section.

There's more...

This section consists of additional information about the recipe in order to make the reader more knowledgeable about the recipe.

See also

This section provides helpful links to other useful information for the recipe.

Conventions

In this book, you will find a number of text styles that distinguish between different kinds of information. Here are some examples of these styles and an explanation of their meaning.

Code words in text, database table names, folder names, filenames, file extensions, pathnames, dummy URLs, user input, and Twitter handles are shown as follows: "The `tfsdeleteproject` command carries out the deletion in two phases."

A block of code is set as follows:

```
# User-specific files
*.suo
*.user
*.sln.docstates
# Specific files
*.txt
# Build results
[Dd]ebug/
[Rr]elease/
```

Any command-line input or output is written as follows:

```
refs/heads/master, TF402455: Pushes to this branch are not permitted; you
must use pull requests to commit changes.
```

New terms and **important words** are shown in bold. Words that you see on the screen, for example, in menus or dialog boxes, appear in the text like this: "From the **Projects and My Teams** submenu, click on **New Team Project....**"

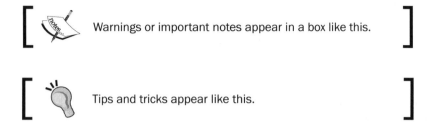

Warnings or important notes appear in a box like this.

Tips and tricks appear like this.

Reader feedback

Feedback from our readers is always welcome. Let us know what you think about this book—what you liked or disliked. Reader feedback is important for us as it helps us develop titles that you will really get the most out of.

To send us general feedback, simply e-mail feedback@packtpub.com, and mention the book's title in the subject of your message.

If there is a topic that you have expertise in and you are interested in either writing or contributing to a book, see our author guide at www.packtpub.com/authors.

Customer support

Now that you are the proud owner of a Packt book, we have a number of things to help you to get the most from your purchase.

Downloading the example code

You can download the example code files from your account at http://www.packtpub.com for all the Packt Publishing books you have purchased. If you purchased this book elsewhere, you can visit http://www.packtpub.com/support and register to have the files e-mailed directly to you.

Errata

Although we have taken every care to ensure the accuracy of our content, mistakes do happen. If you find a mistake in one of our books—maybe a mistake in the text or the code—we would be grateful if you could report this to us. By doing so, you can save other readers from frustration and help us improve subsequent versions of this book. If you find any errata, please report them by visiting http://www.packtpub.com/submit-errata, selecting your book, clicking on the **Errata Submission Form** link, and entering the details of your errata. Once your errata are verified, your submission will be accepted and the errata will be uploaded to our website or added to any list of existing errata under the Errata section of that title.

To view the previously submitted errata, go to https://www.packtpub.com/books/content/support and enter the name of the book in the search field. The required information will appear under the **Errata** section.

Piracy

Piracy of copyrighted material on the Internet is an ongoing problem across all media. At Packt, we take the protection of our copyright and licenses very seriously. If you come across any illegal copies of our works in any form on the Internet, please provide us with the location address or website name immediately so that we can pursue a remedy.

Please contact us at copyright@packtpub.com with a link to the suspected pirated material.

We appreciate your help in protecting our authors and our ability to bring you valuable content.

Questions

If you have a problem with any aspect of this book, you can contact us at questions@packtpub.com, and we will do our best to address the problem.

1

Team Project Setup

"It is not the beauty of a building you should look at; it's the construction of the foundation that will stand the test of time."

–David Allan Coe

In this chapter, we will cover:

- ▶ Connecting to TFS using Team Explorer
- ▶ Setting up your user profile in TFS
- ▶ Creating a Team Project using the Scrum Template
- ▶ Assigning a license, adding users, and auditing user access
- ▶ Configuring Dashboards in Team Project
- ▶ Setting up a welcome page for a Team Project
- ▶ Creating and setting up a Team Room
- ▶ Renaming a Team Project
- ▶ Creating a new Team Project through the command line
- ▶ Deleting a Team Project

Introduction

Microsoft Visual Studio Team Foundation Server provides a set of integrated tools enabling Teams to effectively manage the life cycle of their software project. The Team in Team Foundation Server is encapsulated within the container of a Team Project. Simply put, **Team Project** is a logical container isolating all tools and artifacts associated with a software application together in a single namespace.

The conceptual boundary introduced through Team Project eliminates the problem of having access to unrelated artifacts such as code, Work Items, or release information not relevant to your applications development. Related Team Projects can be grouped together into a Team Project Collection. It can be used to introduce a physical separation between the groups of related Team Projects by hosting them in separate databases.

Team Foundation Server supports multiple Team Project Collections, each of which can internally host multiple Team Projects. Resources such as build pools are scoped at the Team Project Collection level. A Team Project can host multiple Teams; certain resources are set at the Team Project level and others at the Team level. As illustrated in the following screenshot, the selection of a source control repository (TFVC or Git) is made at the Team Project level; however, Teams have autonomy on the level of backlogs they choose and the workflows on the Kanban board. The delivery framework of choice is applied through the Process Template; this in turn applies the delivery framework-specific terminology, artifacts, and workflows to the Team Project and all Teams within the Team Project:

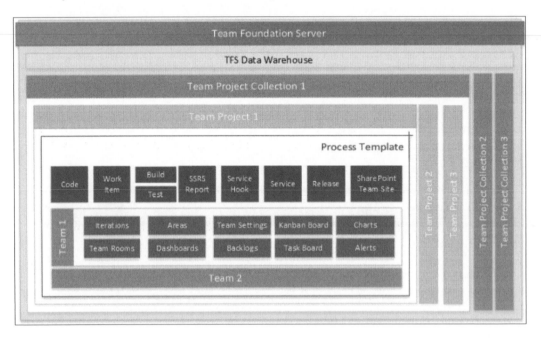

TFS Reporting warehouse is a traditional data warehouse consisting of a relational database organized in an approximate star schema and an SQL Server Analysis Services cube built on top of the relational database. All Team Projects, irrespective of the Team Project Collection they belong to, are aggregated into a single data warehouse.

Team Foundation Server provides a hierarchical security model. Permissions can be set through TFS Groups or AD Group membership through every level, right from the server through to the object level. Groups can be nested and set to inherit permissions through the hierarchy. Inheritance of permissions can be set to **Denied** where you want to control access to selected resources. A more in-depth breakdown of precreated groups with details of access and permissions can be found at `http://bit.ly/1PPaU6l`.

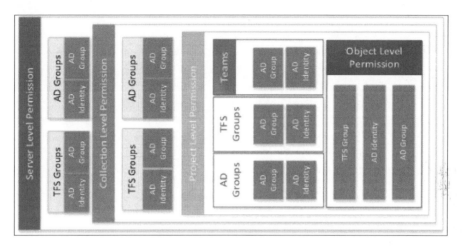

Permissions can be used to limit access to resources within or between Team Projects, Team Project Collections provide an isolation altogether. Team Project Collections also provide other functional and technical benefits such as:

- The usage of a single TFS instance across multiple departments while still providing a level of isolation. Collections can be used to reflect an organizational structure too.

- Flexibility in backup and restore. This can reduce downtime as restoring one collection will not impact users of other collections.

- Scalability and load balancing by moving collections on separate SQL Server instances.

In this chapter, we'll touch on Administration and Process Templates; these topics are discussed at length in future chapters. The focus of this chapter is on creating and setting up various elements of a Team Project.

Connecting to TFS using Team Explorer

To build, test, track, or release your software, you'll need to connect the client of your choice to Team Foundation Server. As a software developer, you'll spend a lot of time in the Visual Studio IDE. Whether you store the code in the TFS Git repository or TFVC source control, you'll need to connect the IDE to TFS to interact with the code. In this recipe, you'll learn how to connect to TFS using Team Explorer.

Getting ready

If you have any Visual Studio 2015 SKU installed, you already have Team Explorer. With TFS 2015, a separate install of Team Explorer is no longer available; you will need to install Visual Studio Community at the very least to get Team Explorer.

 To connect to TFS via any of the office products, you can install the TFS Office Integration Installer: `http://bit.ly/1k3wh7p`. You can read more about the benefits of the TFS Office Integration Installer at `http://bit.ly/1Grh3DS`.

When you start Visual Studio for the first time, you'll be asked to sign in with a Microsoft account, such as Live, Hotmail, or Outlook, and provide some basic registration information. Choose a Microsoft account that best represents you. If you already have a MSDN account, it's recommended that you sign in with its associated Microsoft account. If you don't have a Microsoft account, you can create one for free. Logging in has various benefits such as the synchronization of Visual Studio settings across multiple machines. While logging in is advisable, it is not mandatory.

How to do it...

1. Open Visual Studio 2015.

2. Click on the **Team** toolbar and select **Manage Connections...**:

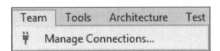

3. From within Team Explorer, click on the **Manage Connections** hyperlink and choose **Connect to Team Project**:

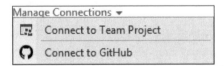

4. In the **Connect to Team Foundation Server** window, the drop-down shows a list of all the TFS Servers you have connected to before. If you don't see the server you want to connect to in the drop-down, click on **Servers...** to enter the details of the Team Foundation Server. Click on **Add...** and enter the details of your TFS Server. You may be required to enter the login details to authenticate with the server.

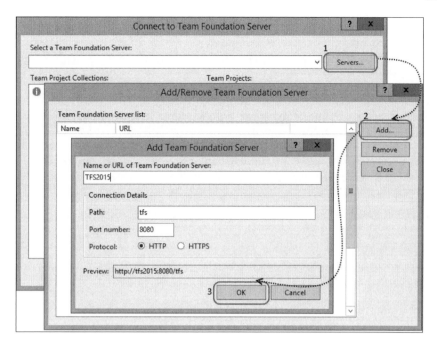

5. The authenticated user details along with server details will update on the **Connect to Team Foundation Server** window. Click on the **Connect** button to complete the operation.

6. You should be successfully connected to TFS via Team Explorer now:

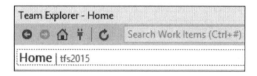

How it works...

Visual Studio now ships with a GitHub connector. Now, the **Manage Connections** dialog within the Team Explorer allows you to connect not only to TFS and VSO, but also GitHub. This is a great example of how Microsoft is embracing open source by enabling seamless integration for non-Microsoft products.

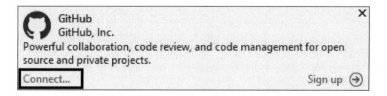

If you are a GitHub free account user, you will be limited to just one account in Visual Studio; this is a limitation posed by GitHub. GitHub Enterprise users have the ability to map multiple accounts from Team Explorer 2015.

If you are in two minds whether to log in to Visual Studio with Microsoft account, weigh these benefits:

> ▸ **Synchronizes your Visual Studio settings**: Visual Studio settings such as key bindings and color theme, apply immediately when you sign in to Visual Studio on any another device.

> ▸ **Extends the trial period**: If you do not have a Visual Studio license, by logging in you can extend the trial period on Visual Studio Professional or Enterprise from 30 to 120 days.

> ▸ **Unlocks Visual Studio**: If your Microsoft account is associated with your MSDN account, your copy of Visual Studio is automatically unlocked.

If you do not want to synchronize the settings, this feature can be disabled. In the **Tools** menu, chose **Options**. Look for **Synchronized Settings** under **Environment** and uncheck the option as shown in the following screenshot:

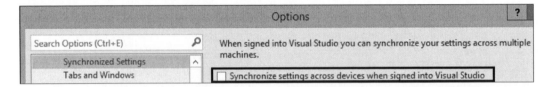

Setting up your user profile in TFS

Team Foundation Server gives you the ability to personalize your experience by choosing your own settings. Every TFS user has a profile by virtue of a login. In this recipe, you'll learn how to customize your profile in TFS.

How to do it...

1. Open Team Portal by navigating to `http://tfs2015:8080/tfs/`.

2. The top right-hand corner contains the name of the logged-in user. Click on the name to open the user profile control as shown in the following screenshot:

3. Click on **My profile** to view and customize your profile. Let's go through the general settings first.

4. To change your profile image, click on the **Change picture** hyperlink, choose an image less than 4 MB and click on **Save Changes**.

5. To change the display name, click on the **Edit** hyperlink, change the name from **Tarun** to `Tarun Arora`, and click on *Enter*.

6. To change the preferred e-mail, click on the **Edit** hyperlink, change the e-mail address to `tarun.arora@outlook.com`, and click on *Enter*.

7. The **UI SETTINGS** field can be changed from default to high contrast by selecting the **High contrast** theme from the drop-down:

8. Switch over to the locale settings by clicking on the **LOCALE** tab. The language and time zone settings can be changed from here.

How it works...

User profile settings only apply to the individual; these settings will not impact other users. Your profile should now have an image, display name, preferred e-mail address, and a theme of your choice. Any alerts you may configure for Work Item, build, and code review will be delivered to your preferred e-mail address.

The time zone settings in TFS will override the time zone settings of the machine. For example, if your machine is in the UTC + 1 time zone, but your profile is configured to UTC + 5:30. On creating a new Work Item, the created time in the Work Item will be UTC + 5:30 and not UTC + 1.

> There are certain functions in the Team Foundation Server that are influenced by the time zone settings of where the Team Foundation Server is hosted. For example, if your Team Foundation Server is hosted in Washington, USA, and part of your distributed Team is in Delhi, India, the current sprint would end based on when the day ends in Washington.

When the profile is opened within the scope of a Team Project, you'll see the **My alerts** option in the **Profile** menu. Alerts allow you to configure e-mail notifications when certain events occur within a Team Project. For example, build completion, Work Item assignment, and so on.

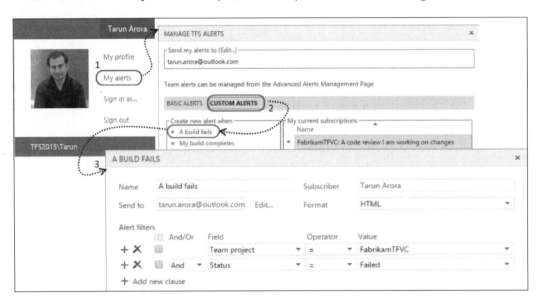

Clicking on **My alerts** will launch the window to manage your TFS Alerts. Basic and Custom Alerts can be managed from within this window. Alerts can be customized with clauses. The window also contains a link to the advanced alerts management page that can be used to manage the Team Alerts.

Creating a Team Project using the Scrum Template

In TFS, a Team Project is a logical container that stores artifacts such as Work Items, code, builds, and releases. Different Teams follow different processes to organize, manage, and track work. TFS allows process specification via Process Templates. The Scrum, Agile, and CMMI template are offered out of the box. The Process Template defines the set of Work Item types, queries, and reports that can be used to plan and track the project. In this recipe, you'll learn how to create a new Team Project using the Scrum Template.

Getting ready

Team Projects cannot be created from the Team Portal; in this recipe, we'll be using Team Explorer to create a new Team Project. If you haven't already, connect Team Explorer to TFS. Refer to the *Connecting to TFS using Team Explorer* recipe for more information on how this can be done.

In order to create a new Team Project, you will need the following permissions:

- **Create new projects permission**: You inherit this permission by being a member of the **Project Collection Administrators** group. The **Team Foundation Administrators global group** also includes this permission.

- **Create new Team sites permission**: This permission is granted by adding the user to a SharePoint group with full control rights on the SharePoint site collection. You don't need this permission if you decide not to create a SharePoint site as part of the Team Project creation.

  In order to use the SQL Server Reporting Services, you must be a member of the Team Foundation Content Manager role in Reporting Services.

 To verify whether you have the correct permissions, you can download the Team Foundation Server Administration Tool from CodePlex available at `https://tfsadmin.codeplex.com/`. TFS Admin is an open source tool available under the Microsoft Public license (Ms-PL).

How to do it...

1. Open Visual Studio 2015 and connect Team Explorer to TFS:

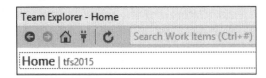

2. From the **Projects and My Teams** submenu, click on **New Team Project...**. This will bring up the new Team Project creation wizard:

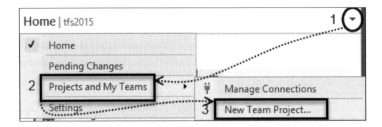

3. Enter the Team Project name and description, and click on the **Next** button:

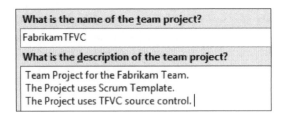

4. Select the **Scrum** Process Template and click on **Next**. This is possibly the single most important decision you make as part of the Team Project creation process. Learn more about the differences between Process Templates at `https://msdn.microsoft.com/library/vs/alm/work/guidance/choose-process`.

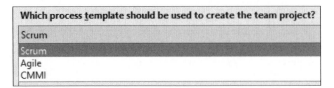

5. Choose the **Create a new SharePoint site** option. Click on **Configure...** to specify the location for the new site. If you do not have SharePoint integration, chose the option to not configure a SharePoint site. ·

6. This source control selection screen presents the second most important decision that you'll be asked to make as a part of the Team Project creation process. TFS supports both centralized (TFVC) and distributed (Git) source control systems. In *Chapter 2, Setting Up and Managing Code Repositories*, we'll go deeper into both source control types. Choose **Team Foundation Version Control** and click on **Next**:

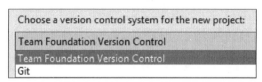

7. Once you have reviewed the settings, click on **Finish** to start the Team Project creation process:

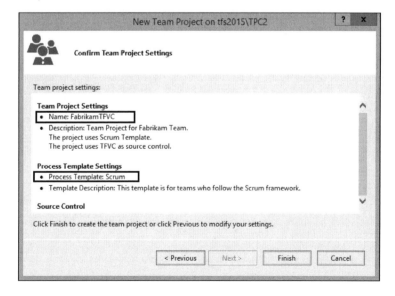

8. Once the Team Project creation completes, you'll see a completion status on the form. Click on the **View the team project creation log** hyperlink (we'll discuss the contents of logs in the *How it works...* section).

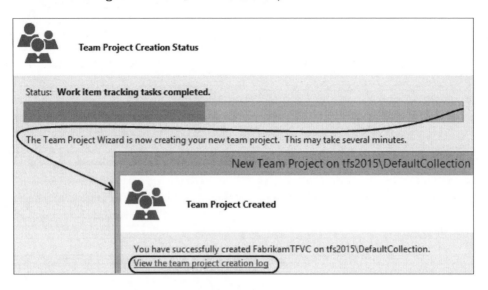

9. Team Explorer is now updated with the details of the newly created Team Project:

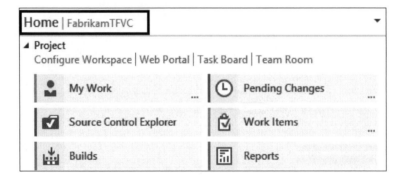

How it works...

The Process Template defines the set of Work Item types and reports that will be used to plan and track the project. The Process Template also applies the Work Item workflows and state transitions. Let's look at how the out-of-the-box templates differ broadly from one another:

- ► The Scrum Template is designed to support the Scrum framework as defined by the Scrum organization. This Process Template tracks bugs at the same level as Product Backlog items and tracks estimates using an Effort field.

- ► The Agile Template is designed to support Agile development for Teams that don't want to be restricted by Scrum. It supports estimating User Stories by using Story Points. Tasks contain fields to track the Original Estimate, Remaining, and Completed work fields. While originally the Agile Template didn't allow bug tracking on any backlog page, this can optionally be configured through Team settings in Team Portal.

- ► The CMMI Template is designed to support formal change management processes. This template supports the estimated requirements using a **Size** field. Tasks contain fields to track original estimate, remaining, and completed work fields.

The out-of-the-box templates are designed to meet the needs of most Teams. All of them support using the Agile planning tools to create the Product Backlog and work in sprints with the task board. If your Team has different needs, you can customize a template and then create the Team Project, or you can create a Team Project from a template and then customize the project.

You can download the Process Template by going into the Process Template Manager from the **Settings** view in Team Explorer. Refer to `https://msdn.microsoft.com/Library/vs/alm/Work/guidance/manage-process-templates` for further instructions on how to download the Process Template.

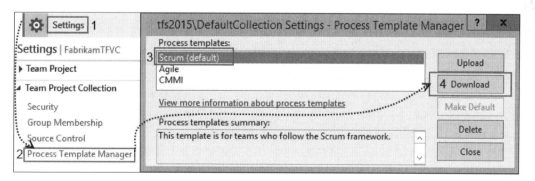

Open `ProcessTemplate.xml` from the earlier download location; you'll note that it follows an XML structure that constructs a sequence of plugins and instructions for setting up the plugins. The Main Template is linked to sub modules that are defined by other XML structures. In the following representation, you'll see the correlation between these XML Templates and the instrumentation generated from the project creation workflow. Process Template customization is discussed in detail in *Chapter 8, Extending and Customizing Team Foundation Server*.

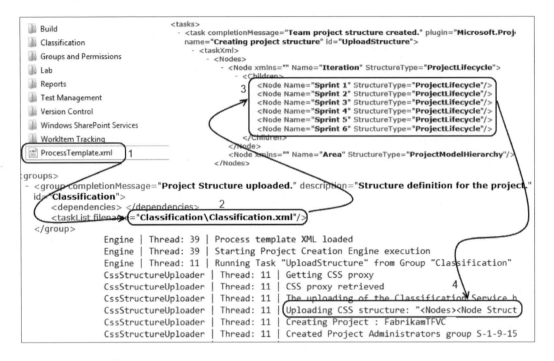

The following items are created for you as part of the Team Project creation process:

▶ **Code Repository**: A code repository based on your selection is provisioned.

▶ **Team**: A default Team with the same name as the Team Project is provisioned.

▶ **Area Path**: A default Area Path with the same name as the name of the Team is provisioned. The Teams backlog is configured to show Work Items assigned to this Area Path.

▶ **Iteration Path**: The set of iterations is precreated for the Team.

▶ **Team Portal**: The Team Portal allows the Team members to connect to TFS to manage source code, Work Items, build, and test efforts.

▶ **Team Room**: A room with the same name as the Team is provisioned. Team room is meant to be used for collaboration.

If your Team Foundation Server is configured to support SharePoint project portal and reporting, you'll see the **Documents and Reports** hub in Team Explorer. The **Documents** view offers deep integration with the SharePoint project portal. This allows you to create document libraries and organize and share documents with your Team members. The **Reports** view gives you a collection of precreated SSRS reports that you can use to track and manage the progress of work in your Teams:

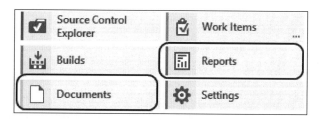

Assigning a license, adding users, and auditing user access

A Scrum Team consists of a product owner, a development Team, and a Scrum master. While your stakeholders aren't part of the Scrum Team, they will need visibility into the product backlog. The Scrum Team is cross-functional and will have the skills to cover design, development, testing, and deployment of the increment. From a tooling point of view, not everyone in the Team may need the same access to TFS.

TFS offers three access levels: Stakeholder, Basic, and Advanced. The TFS license required for the access levels is listed here:

Access level	License required
Stakeholder	No license required.
Basic	TFS client-access license (CAL) or Visual Studio Professional with MSDN subscription.
Advanced	One of these MSDN subscriptions: Visual Studio Enterprise with MSDN, MSDN Platforms, or Visual Studio Test Professional with MSDN.

The product licensing has been significantly simplified over the last year. A few key licensing changes have been introduced in TFS 2015 and now in TFS 2015 Update 1:

- The TFS CAL license has been changed to include access to even more TFS features:
  - **Agile planning**: All backlog management and sprint planning capabilities in TFS 2015 web access are now available to any user with a TFS CAL.
  - **Chart authoring**: Chart authoring and the ability to pin/share charts to your project home page are now available in the CAL.

- ❏ **Team Rooms**: Team Rooms are now available with a CAL in TFS 2015.
- ❏ **Test Hub**: With TFS 2015, the web-based test experience for executing test cases (for User Acceptance Testing such as scenarios) is now available in the TFS CAL.

- ▸ Buying Visual Studio Team Services, Professional, or Advanced license gives you a free TFS CAL for that named user with it. This provides several advantages:
    - ❏ You can now "rent" a TFS CAL. Rather than having to pay a onetime $499 (list price) license cost, you can pay a much lower monthly cost for as long as you need it.
    - ❏ Companies using vendors/contractors now have a simple way to manage people who need temporary access to their TFS.
    - ❏ The CAL is "always up to date". Because it is a subscription rather than a onetime purchase, you don't have to deal with buying/renewing your CALs when new TFS versions come out. The CAL that comes with a VS Online license works with any TFS version, whereas a traditionally purchased CAL supports only a given TFS version and earlier.

Access Level and Role are two separate things in TFS. Access Level dictates the features you have the right to use, the Role dictates the permissions. For example, with the basic license, the Access Level includes grants for source control use; however, if you are in the reader role, you will not have permissions to edit the source code.

The Team Foundation Server Access Levels are closely related to the typical roles in a software project and the activities carried out in those roles. The following table summarizes the feature to access level mapping. So a project supporter will only need a stakeholder license, a project manager or developer will need a basic license, and a tester or portfolio manager will need an advanced license.

Feature	Stakeholder	Basic	Advanced
View and edit all Work Items	Yes	Yes	Yes
Standard features	Yes	Yes	Yes
Agile boards	Yes	Yes	Yes
Basic backlog and sprint planning tools	Yes	Yes	Yes
Chart viewing	Yes	Yes	Yes
Chart authoring		Yes	Yes
Code		Yes	Yes
Build		Yes	Yes
Request and manage feedback			Yes
Web-based Test execution		Yes	Yes

Feature	Stakeholder	Basic	Advanced
Web-based Test case management			Yes
Team rooms		Yes	Yes
Administer account		Yes	Yes
Advanced home page		Yes	Yes
Advanced backlog and sprint planning tools		Yes	Yes
Advanced portfolio management		Yes	Yes
Analyze test results and manage machine groups		Yes	Yes

With stakeholder access, users can create and modify all Work Items, and create and save queries on all Work Items under their `My Queries` folder. (This is a change from limited access, in which users can create and modify only those Work Items that they created, and query and view Work Items they created.) Also, stakeholders can create and modify Work Items using Team Foundation clients such as Microsoft Excel, Microsoft Project, and Microsoft Feedback Client.

- ▶ Standard features include access to the home and work hubs.
- ▶ Can view backlog pages and Kanban boards and add Work Items through the **Quick Add** panel, which appear at the bottom of the list. It can't move items on the page or use other features.
- ▶ Can view sprint pages and task boards and add Work Items, but can't use other sprint planning tool features.

To set up new users in TFS, the user first needs to be assigned a license and then added to a Team. In this recipe, you'll learn how to allocate licenses and add members to a Team, you'll also learn how to audit user access in TFS.

Getting ready

In this recipe, we'll be allocating the license and permissions to the following users in the FabrikamTFVC Team Project.

Name (username)	Access Level	Comments
John Smith `TFS2015\JohnS`	Stakeholder	John usually provides feedback via the feedback client and creates Work Items in the product backlog.
Brian Miller `TFS2015\BrianM`	Basic	Brian is a developer and spends most of his time programming and unit testing.
Aaron Cook `TFS2015\AaronC`	Basic	Aaron is a developer and spends most of his time programming and unit testing.

Name (username)	Access Level	Comments
Willy Peter `TFS2015\WillyP`	Basic	Willy is a scrum master and developer on the Team. Willy mostly focuses on integration and SQL Server report development.
Annu Arora `TFS2015\AnnuA`	Advanced	Annu is a tester and spends most of her time functional and performance testing.
Tom Hacker `TFS2015\TomH`	Advanced	Tom is a business analyst and spends most of his time programming and integration testing.
Chris Wang `TFS2015\ChrisW`	Advanced	Chris is the product owner. He manages the product vision and portfolio.

In order to add new users to the Access Levels, you'll need to be a collection administrator. To add new users to a Team Project, you need to be a project administrator; if you aren't already, arrange to be added to these groups.

How to do it...

Assigning a user license:

1. Log into Team Portal and navigate to the Access Level administration screen by browsing to `http://tfs2015:8080/tfs/_admin/_licenses`:

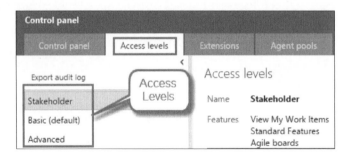

2. From the left panel, click on the **Stakeholder** access. From the right panel, click on the **Add** button and choose **Add Windows user or group**. In the **Add new user or group** window, enter the user details as **TFS2015\JohnS** and click the **OK** button:

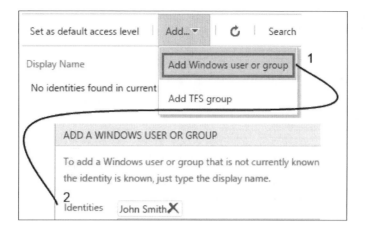

Repeat this step to add all users into the Access Levels as specified in the user table in the *Getting ready* section of this recipe. At this point, you should have one Stakeholder, three Basic, and three Advanced users.

Adding users to the project:

1. There are two ways to add users to the Team Project. One way is to navigate to the FabikamTFVC project security screen in Team Portal by browsing to `http://tfs2015:8080/tfs/DefaultCollection/FabrikamTFVC/_admin/_security`. From the left panel, click on the **Contributors** group, from the right panel, click on the **Members** tab and the **Add...** button to add Windows user or group. Enter the user details and click on **OK**:

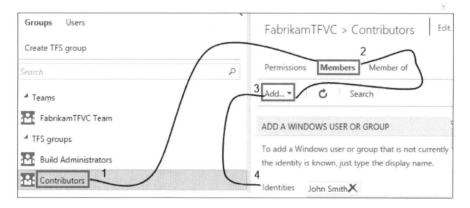

2. The other option is to navigate to the FabrikamTFVC project home page by browsing to `http://tfs2015:8080/tfs/DefaultCollection/FabrikamTFVC`. From the **Members** widget, click on **Manage...**, in the **MANAGE MEMBERS OF FABRIKAMTFVC TEAM** window enter the user details and press **OK**. Repeat these steps to add other users listed in the user table in the getting started section.

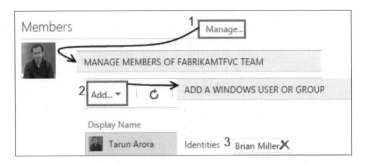

 Managing users in TFS is much easier if you create Windows or Active Directory groups for them. If you decide to use Active Directory groups in TFS, consider creating specific ones whose purpose is dedicated to user management in TFS.

Auditing user access

In the next few steps, you'll learn how to extract an audit log to track the last login of users and groups and their access type:

1. Navigate to the Access Level screen in Team Web Access by browsing to `http://tfs2015:8080/tfs/_admin/_licenses`.

2. From the left navigation, click on **Export audit log**. Open the downloaded CSV file; we'll explore this in depth in the *How it works...* section.

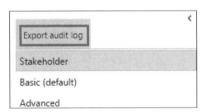

How it works...

The default Access Level is assigned to a user that is directly added via the Team Project security or members screen. It is recommended that the default Access Level be set to Basic. If a user is assigned to multiple Access Levels, the highest always takes precedence.

Next, let's review the audit log, import the `data.csv` into Excel. You should see a view similar to the following screenshot. The **Last Accessed (UTC)** column tells you whether the user has accessed TFS or not; you don't need to pay for a license for users that have not accessed TFS.

Display Name	Unique Name	Server	Last Ac	IsGroup	Stakeh	Basic	Advanc	IsDefau
Willy Peter	TFS2015\WillyP	TFS2015	8/24/2015	0	0	1	0	0
Chris Wang	TFS2015\ChrisW	TFS2015	8/24/2015	0	0	0	1	0
Harry Miller	TFS2015\HarryM	TFS2015	8/24/2015	0	0	0	0	1
Aaron Cook	TFS2015\AaronC	TFS2015	8/24/2015	0	0	1	0	0
John Smith	TFS2015\JohnS	TFS2015	8/24/2015	0	1	0	0	0
Annu Arora	TFS2015\AnnuA	TFS2015	8/24/2015	0	0	0	1	0
Brian Miller	TFS2015\BrianM	TFS2015	8/24/2015	0	0	1	0	0
Tarun Arora	TFS2015\Tarun	TFS2015	8/24/2015	0	0	0	1	0

Configuring Dashboards in Team Project

The Team Portal home page was traditionally used to pin charts, Work Item counts, and build status tiles to provide an at-a-glance view of the project to the Team members and stakeholders. The approach did not work well because the home page had hard-coded tiles that you were forced to have on the page. In addition, the page did not support grouping of the tiles or adding commentary to complement the visuals in the tiles. In TFS 2015 Update 1, the home page has been replaced by a new feature called **Dashboards**. The new feature comes with a library of widgets that can be used to create multiple Dashboards for your Team. In this recipe, you'll learn how to create a Dashboard using the widget catalog.

Getting ready

For permissions, you need to be a Team Administrator to create Dashboards. Only Team Administrators can create, customize, and move around widgets on a Dashboard. You don't need any special permissions to view the Dashboards. All Team members that have access to the Team Portal can view and interact with Dashboards.

The Team Portal home page has been replaced by the **Overview** Dashboard. All existing tiles from the home page have been migrated over into the **Overview** Dashboard. To see the **Overview** Dashboard, navigate to the FabrikamTFVC Team Portal by browsing to `http://tfs2015:8080/tfs/DefaultCollection/FabrikamTFVC/_dashboards`.

How to do it...

1. In the FabrikamTFVC Team Portal, click on the **+** icon to create a new Dashboard. Name the Dashboard `Team Updates`:

2. From the bottom-right of the page, click on the big green circle to launch the Dashboard widget gallery. From the widget gallery, add the code tile:

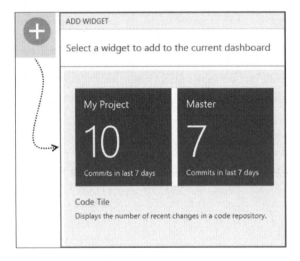

3. Once the tile is added to the Dashboard, click on the tile to configure it. Set the name as `All Code Changes` and set the code path to `$/FabrikamTFVC`. The tile will show the count of code changes under the source path `$/FabrikamTFVC` from the last 7 days. To commit the configuration changes, and click on **Save**:

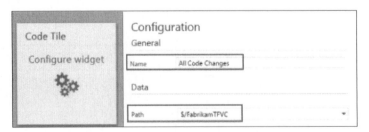

4. Next, add the **Query** tile widget from the widget gallery. Select the **Blocked Tasks** query to map the query results to be displayed in the tile. Configure the background color to red if the count is greater than or equal to 1:

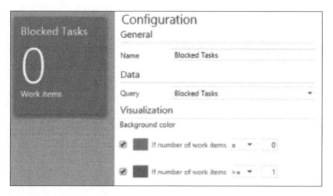

Format the background color of the tile based on the count of Work Items returned by the Work Item query

5. Add the **Markdown** widget. The widget is capable of render markdown; the tile can be scaled to different sizes. Choose the **3 x 2** size and add some commentary as indicated in the following screenshot:

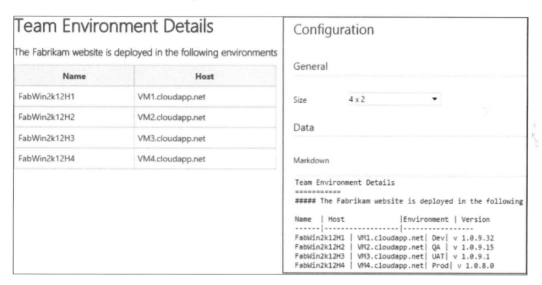

6. The gallery has other widgets such as Work Item Query Results, New Work Item, Team Rooms, Sprint Capacity, Burndown, and other links; these can also be added to the Dashboard. There are no widgets for charts. Charts can be added from the charts view in the work hub, and this is covered in detail in the *Creating charts using Work Item Queries* recipe in *Chapter 3, Planning and Tracking Work*.

How it works...

Dashboards provide a great way to create information radiators for sharing information internally with Team members and externally with stakeholders. Widgets are rendered as tiles in the Dashboard, the tiles use the TFS REST API to retrieve information from TFS. The information is loaded into the tiles using the template provided by the widget. The tiles can be moved around on the Dashboard and scaled to different sizes. The tiles support interactivity, for example clicking the **Query** tile would take you straight into the **Work Item Query** window. The tiles don't support cross-tile interaction yet. While it's possible to create multiple Dashboards, it is currently not possible to apply permissions for access to individual Dashboards. It is expected that in the long term more widgets will be added to the widget gallery and the API's will be made available to extend and create new widgets.

Setting up a welcome page for a Team Project

It is hard to summarize the objective of the Team Project by just its name or description. Software Teams are usually found creating introduction documents or README files to summarize the purpose of the project with references to other useful material. Traditionally, Teams would store these files in SharePoint. This information is all the more useful when seen in context with the Team Project. A new feature called **project welcome** pages provides the perfect solution here. In this recipe, you'll learn how to set up welcome pages using markdown files.

Getting ready

Project welcome pages are created using a very simple convention-based approach. The welcome page simply renders the markdown files checked into the source control of the project.

 For TFVC-based source control, the `readme.md` file needs to be at the root of the Team Project folder. For Git-based source control, the `readme.md` file needs to be at the root of the repository in the default branch.

Team project welcome pages require the underlying file to be written in a markdown format. Markdown is intended to be easy to read and easy to write with the main emphasis on readability. TFS offers a markdown editor in Team Portal to help you author the welcome pages. You can alternatively choose to author your markdown files using a desktop editor.

How to do it...

1. Open Team Web Access and navigate to the FabrikamTFVC Team Project `http://tfs2015:8080/tfs/DefaultCollection/Recipes`.

2. From the home hub, select the welcome view and click on **Edit** to start editing the `readme.md` markdown file.

3. Copy the markdown snippet into the editor:

```
# Welcome to the FabrikamTFVC
----------
The team project contains the resources for the Fabrikam
Software & Services.

## Contacts
---
* Project Owner - Tarun Arora [@arora_tarun](https://twitter.com/
arora_tarun)

## Definition of Done
  All product backlog items need to abide to the
definition of done before they can be marked done
  1. All source code is checked in
  2. All code passes CI & no failing unit tests
  3. Business services code coverage of > 60%
  4. All changes have been tested
  5. Deployment script added & updated
  6. Demo to Product Owner
     7. All associated tasks must be completed
## Definition of Bug
*Work in progress*
```

4. In the toolbar at the far right corner, you'll see the **Show Content Preview** icon. Click on the preview icon, the welcome page will now be rendered using the markdown:

5. Click on the **Save** icon to check in the `readme.md` file into version control.

How it works...

TFS supports common markdown conventions and GitHub-flavored extensions.

You can learn more about the Markdown syntax at `http://bit.ly/1jJjRlI`.

You can find out more about the **GitHub-Flavored-Markdown** at `http://bit.ly/1jJl38D`.

To simplify creating and editing markdown content, Team Foundation Server lets you link to other markdown files through both absolute and relative paths. When markdown is rendered as HTML, all headings automatically get IDs, so you can link to the headers by using the following convention `[text to display](#heading id)`.

TFS also allows you to refer to a markdown page that does not yet exist; the engine is smart enough to give you the option to create the page when you click on the referred link. You can use the following format in markdown to do so: `[new page](./newpage.md)`.

Creating and setting up a Team Room

Collaborating is key to the success of any project delivery. While there are lots of ways to collaborate with your Team members, it is very difficult to track those conversations back to the context of the work. TFS offers a collaboration hub called Team Room and that makes tracking work, project updates, and Team collaboration easy. In this recipe, you'll learn how to create, set up, and use a Team Room.

Getting ready

Permissions required: Project Administrators groups can create and administer Team Rooms that they've created. Team administrators can only manage Team Rooms for Teams they're administrators of.

License required to access Team Rooms: Only Basic and Advanced license users have access to Team Rooms. Stakeholders cannot access Team Rooms and need to be upgraded to Basic to participate in Team Rooms.

A Team and Team Room are created as part of the Team Project creation process. The Team Room has the same name as the name of the Team.

How to do it...

1. Navigate to the Team Web Access home page by browsing `http://tfs2015:8080/tfs/_home`.

2. From the top panel, click on the **Rooms** tab, this will navigate you to the Team Room's hub. In this page you'll see a list of all available Team Rooms. A Team Room is created along with the creation of a Team Project:

3. Click on the **New** button to create a new Team Room. Enter the name as `FabrikamShipRoom`. Click on **OK** to navigate to the `FabrikamShipRoom`:

4. Click on the **Manage events...** link to choose which TFS events are visible in the `FabrikamShipRoom`:

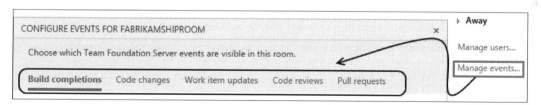

5. From the **Code changes** tab, add a Team Project. The Team Room is not Team Project-specific, so you can select multiple Team Projects. You also have an option to select if you want all changes or changes specific to the users in the Team Room. In this case, choose the **FabrikamTFVC**, select **By a room member**, and click on **Save** and close.

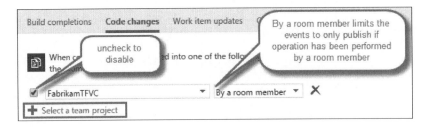

6. Repeat these steps to enable events for Work Items, build, code reviews, and pull requests.

 By unchecking the checkbox next to **FabrikamTFVC**, you can stop receiving the alerts for this Team Project in the Team Room.

7. Click on the **Manage users...** link and choose **Add TFS group** to select **FabrikamTFVC**. This will add all FabrikamTFVC Team members to the `FabrikamShipRoom`. To commit your changes click on **Save**:

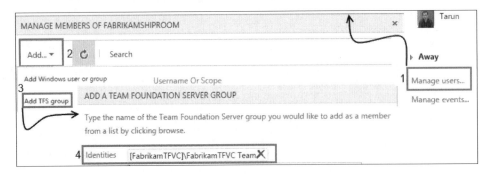

8. In the post a message textbox, copy the following text: `Welcome @Aaron Cook @Annu Arora @Brian Miller @Chris Wang @John Smith @Tom Hacker @Willy Peter to the #FabrikamShipRoom :):`

How it works...

Increase Team productivity by discussing work in progress, asking questions, sharing status, and clarifying issues that arise. Your Team Room provides an area for fostering and capturing communication among Team members, both near and far. Team Rooms are not scoped to a Team Project collection, so you can track multiple projects in a Team Room. Team Rooms allow you to see conversations by date, to see historic conversations, click on the left arrow in the top bar in the Team Room. You can alternatively select a date from the calendar.

The manage events give you access to various events as follows:

- ▸ **The build events**: When any of the following build definition is complete, an event will appear in the room indicating the status of the build.

- ▸ **Code changes**: When code is pushed or checked into one of the following Team Projects, an event will appear in the room. You can opt to scope this to just members in the Team Room or anyone.

- ▸ **Work item updates**: When a Work Item is created or an existing Work Item has the state or assignment changed in/under one of the following area paths, an event will appear in the room.

- ▸ **Code reviews**: When a code review is created in/under one of the following area paths, an event will appear in the room.

- ▸ **Pull requests**: When a pull request is created, approved, rejected, or completed in one of the following repositories, an event will appear in the room.

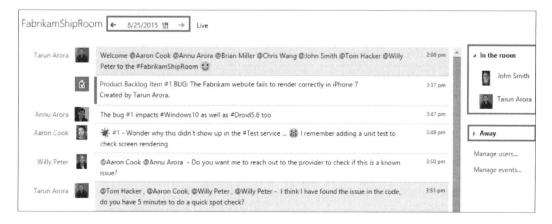

As you can see in the preceding screenshot, since the `FabrikamShipRoom` has a subscription for Work Items an alert gets published in the Team Room when product backlog ID 1 is created. The Team collaborates to figure out the root cause and fixes the issue.

 By prefixing a Work Item ID with #, TFS fully qualifies it. Clicking on **#3** in the Team Room navigates you directly into the Work Item form for Work Item ID 3.

By clicking on the audio icon on the right panel, you can optionally mute and unmute the sound on new messages in the Team Room. The data for the Team Rooms is saved in Team Foundation Server. It is possible to retrieve the Team Room data using the TFS REST API's, we'll be covering this in *Chapter 8, Extending and Customizing Team Foundation Server*.

There's more...

By default, a Team Room gets created with every Team or Team Project you create. Team Rooms can be renamed. It is also possible to delete a Team Room. However, once a Team Room has been deleted, it is not possible to recover the Team Room or any conversations from the Team Room. You'll see the **Rename** and **Delete** option in the context menu by clicking on the left of the Team Room name from the left panel in the Team Room hub.

 Interested in seeing which Team Rooms are most vibrant? The most recently accessed Team Rooms show up in the Team web access landing page.

 It is possible to manage Team Room permissions at a granular level. Choose **Security...** from the **FabrikamShipRoom** context menu. Both **Chat** and **Administer** permissions can be set to **Allow** or **Deny** from here. By setting the chat to **Deny** you limit the user to being a read only participant in the Team Room.

Renaming a Team Project

As your software evolves, at times you may find that the Team Project name you chose at the outset doesn't quite lend itself to the purpose of your project any more. Up until TFS 2015, it was fairly impossible to rename a Team Project once it was created. Team Project Rename has been the most voted feature on the Visual Studio User Voice website with over 6,000 votes. TFS 2015 now allows you to rename a Team Project. While the product has made it very simple to rename a Team Project, it is still a very disruptive process. In this recipe, you'll learn how to rename a Team Project and also go through the nuances of how to do so and what to watch out for when renaming a Team Project.

Getting ready

A Team Project Rename updates all of your version control paths, Work Items, queries, and other Team Project artifacts to reflect the new name. Team Projects can be renamed multiple times and older names can be reused as well. It is recommended to perform this action during off hours to minimize any impact. Things to consider are as follows:

- In order to rename a Team Project, you need to be a member of the project administrator group.
- Builds running during the rename might fail.
- All users will need to restart Visual Studio.
- Git remotes will need to be updated with the new project name.
- Version control workspaces will need to be corrected by running the latest get version command.

If individuals in the Team are using local workspaces then it is recommended to upgrade to Visual Studio 2013 update 5 or Visual Studio 2015 (release candidate or newer) to have the workspaces auto corrected for them at the next get. If they continue to use an earlier version of Visual Studio, then they will need to shelve any pending changes, create a new workspace, and unshelve their changes.

How to do it...

There are two entry points to the Project Rename feature through Team Web Access.

Option 1

1. Navigate to the administration page for the Team Project by browsing `http://tfs2015:8080/tfs/DefaultCollection/FabrikamTFVC/_admin/`.

2. On the left where the project name and description for the project are listed, you can click on the project name textbox to amend the name:

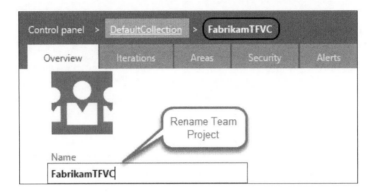

Option 2

1. Navigate to the collection administration page by browsing `http://tfs2015:8080/tfs/DefaultCollection/_admin`.

2. Rename the Team Project from the context menu:

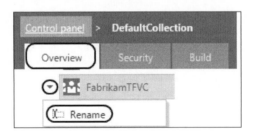

3. Change the name of the project from `FabrikamTFVC` to `Fabrikam` and proceed. You will receive a project rename warning message. Please read the warning message carefully and make sure that the users of the Team Project are aware of the rename.

When a Team Project is being renamed, any browsers with the Team Project opened may encounter some errors. These errors are due to caches held by the browser, which include the old Team Project name.

RENAME PROJECT

⚠ Warning: Please read the following carefully before proceeding!

Renaming team project "FabrikamTFVC" to "Fabrikam" will be disruptive to the project. It's recommended that renames be performed during off hours.

- Builds running during the rename might fail.
- All users will need to restart Visual Studio.

4. Tick the checkbox to acknowledge the warning and click **RENAME PROJECT**. The dialog will show the status. Click on **Close** once the rename is complete.

RENAME PROJECT

Renaming project "FabrikamTFVC" to "Fabrikam"

Renaming team project...

 Any default artifacts created in the Team Project get renamed along with the project if they share the same name as the Team Project. This includes artifacts such as the default Team, Team Room, and Git repository.

How it works...

In this section, we'll focus on actions that need to be performed by the Team once the Team Project rename has been completed.

- ▶ **Restarting the editor**: The editor you used to connect to the Team Project needs to be restarted. Be it Team Explorer, Eclipse, Office, Microsoft Test Manager, or any additional clients using the TFS Object Model.

▶ **Updating query-based test suites**: Unlike Work Item queries, query-based test suites are stored differently and can't update the Team Project name after rename. If you have any query-based test suites, open those suites in the browser and update the queries to use the new Team Project name.

▶ **Updating SharePoint Team Sites and Reporting Integrations**: Both SharePoint and Reporting Services Integrations continue to work, but some reports will not work as expected until the new Team Project name is populated. The old project name is still present until caches are updated with the new name. The reporting and SharePoint server administrator can manually run these jobs to immediately populate the new name.

A Team Project name can't be reused if there are still workspace mappings addressing it. This is done to avoid the ambiguity case where a workspace can be mapped to two projects. You will need to reach out to the users that have these mappings and either delete them or update them to use the new name.

Creating a new Team Project through the command line

As a Team Foundation Server administrator, you'll find yourself creating Team Projects over and over again. Team Project creation process can be scripted thanks to Team Foundation Server Power Tools. A Team Project is a container that can host multiple Teams and simplifies sharing of various artifacts such as processes, master backlogs, build definitions, and code artifacts. More often than not, you'll find that a new Team Project has been requested in ignorance simply because the requestor doesn't fully understand how multiple Teams can be accommodated in a Team Project. It is always beneficial to have a conversation to fully understand why a new Team Project has been requested. In this recipe, you'll learn how to script the creation of a new Team Project using the command line.

Getting ready

Microsoft Visual Studio Team Foundation Server Power Tools are available through the Visual Studio Gallery. Power Tools are a set of tools, enhancements, and command-line utilities that can make a TFS administrator more productive. Download and install the Power Tools by browsing to `http://bit.ly/1jJkEmt`:

Download the Microsoft Visual Studio Team Foundation Server 2015 Power Tools
from the Visual Studio Extensions Gallery

Installing TFS Power Tools installs the command-line utility **Tfpt.exe**. Tfpt.exe is a companion tool to **tf.exe** that offers additional version control commands, Work Item tracking, and Team Project manipulation. Open up a new command line and type `tfpt.exe /?`. If you do not see a list of available commands as shown in the following screenshot, the Power Tools haven't been installed correctly. Verify the installation before proceeding.

How to do it...

1. Create a new folder `TFSCookbook\Chapter01` in the `C:\` drive. Copy the text as follows in Notepad and save it to `C:\TFSCookbook\Chapter01` as `settings.xml`:

   ```xml
   <?xml version="1.0" encoding="utf-8"?>
   <Project xmlns="ProjectCreationSettingsFileSchema.xsd">
       <TFSName>http://tfs2015:8080/tfs</TFSName>
   <LogFolder>C:\TFSCookbook\Chapter01</LogFolder>
       <ProjectName>ScriptedTeamProject01</ProjectName>
       <ProjectReportsEnabled>true</ProjectReportsEnabled>
       <ProjectSiteEnabled>true</ProjectSiteEnabled>

   <ProjectSiteTitle>ScriptedTeamProject01</ProjectSiteTitle>
       <SccCreateType>New</SccCreateType>
       <ProcessTemplateName>Scrum</ProcessTemplateName>
   </Project>
   ```

2. In command prompt run the following command:

   ```
   tfpt createteamproject /settingsfile:"C:\TFSCookbook\Chapter01\
   settings.xml" /validate /verbose
   ```

3. You should receive a message confirming whether the validation is successful. If not, check the error message against the information in the settings file:

```
C:\Program Files (x86)\Microsoft Visual Studio 14.0>tfpt.exe createteamproject /
settingsfile:"c:\TFSCookbook\Chapter01\settings.xml" /validate
All provided settings are valid.
```

4. To create the Team Project, run the earlier command by removing the `/validate` switch.

   ```
   tfpt createteamproject /settingsfile:"C:\TfsCookbook\Chapter01\
   settings.xml" /verbose
   ```

5. Wait for the Team Project creation process to complete.

> Note that `tfpt createteamproject` does not support scripting a new Team Project with Git as the source control repository.

How it works...

The Team Project creation command takes the `settings.xml` file as an input; let's review the information that was provided in `settings.xml`:

- **`TFSName`**: This tag is used to specify the connection details of the TFS Server where you want the new Team Project to be created.

- **`LogFolder`**: This tag is used to specify the folder directory for the log file. This path should exist on the TFS application tier.

- **`ProjectName`**: The Team Project name. If you specify a Team Project name that already exists, the Team Project creation process will fail during the validation process.

- **`ProjectReportsEnabled`**: Certain default project reports are created as part of the Team Project creation process. This tags accepts a Boolean value; pass `false` to skip the default reports from being added.

- **`ProjectSiteEnabled`**: If your Team Foundation Server installation has SharePoint services enabled, you can pass a value of `true` in this tag to have a SharePoint Team site created for the new Team Project.

- **`ProjectSiteTitle`**: This tag is ignored if the value of `ProjectSiteEnabled` is `false`. This tag is used to specify the name of the SharePoint Team site you have chosen to create as part of the Team Project creation process.

- ► `SccCreateType`: If a `true` value is passed in this tag, a new TFVC source control is created, alternatively an existing TFS source control path can be passed to create a TFVC source control from the contents of the specified TFS path.

- ► `ProcessTemplateName`: This tag is used to pass the name of the Process Template that the Team Project should be based on.

> A list of all Process Templates available on your Team Foundation Server can be seen from Process Template Manager. To access Process Template Manager, open Visual Studio and connect to Team Foundation Server. From Team Explorer choose **Settings**. From the **Settings** view, click on **Process Template Manager**.

Now, let's review the `createteamproject` command:

```
tfpt createteamproject /settingsfile:"C:\TFSCookbook\Chapter01\settings.
xml" /validate /verbose
```

The `/settingsfile` path is used to specify the location of the settings file. TFPT parses the settings file and triggers the Team Project creation process by connecting to the Team Foundation Server using the details specified in the settings file. The Team Project isn't created when the `/validate` switch is used; the whole process is run as a validation to identify any potential issues. The `/verbose` flag is used to log details of the operations being performed during this process. The verbose option can be very useful when troubleshooting issues.

There's more...

The `tfpt.exe` command-line tools also provide many other useful commands. The two worth mentioning are `addprojectportal` and `addprojectreports`.

- ► `addprojectportal`: Over time, one may recognize the need for creating or moving the project portal. This command supports both operations in an existing Team Project.

  ```
  tfpt addprojectreports /collection:http://tfs2015:8080/tfs /
  teamproject:"Fabrikam" /processtemplate:"Scrum" /webapplication:""
  /relativepath:"pathfromwebapp" /validate /verbose
  ```

- ► `addprojectreports`: The add reports operation creates the reports in the chosen Team Project. This command overwrites the reports if they already exist.

  ```
  tfpt addprojectreports /collection:"http://tfs2015:8080/tfs" /

  teamproject:"Fabrikam" /processtemplate:"Scrum" /validate /verbose
  ```

Deleting a Team Project

Deleting a Team Project permanently removes data associated with that project from the database. The data cannot be recovered later. Therefore, you should save Team Project data that you might want to access later. In this recipe, you'll learn how to delete a Team Project using the TFS Admin Console and the command line. We will also review the difference between the two approaches.

Getting ready

In order to delete the Team Project, you should be a member of the following groups:

- ▶ Team Foundation Administrators group
- ▶ SQL Server Administrators group
- ▶ Farm Administrators group for SharePoint products (this is only required if TFS has been configured to integrate with SharePoint)

In this recipe, we'll review the two available options to delete a Team Project. The first option is to delete it from the TFS Admin Console, and the other option is to delete it from the command line. When a project is deleted from the admin console, any associated reports and SharePoint portal projects need to be manually deleted. The TFSDeleteProject command-line tool deletes all artifacts.

How to do it...

Option1

First let's look at how to delete the Team Project from the Team Project Administration Console:

1. Log into the server that hosts your Team Foundation Application Tier.

2. Open the **Team Foundation Administration Console** window and, from the left panel, click on **Team Project Collections**. Click on the **Team Projects** tab to see projects in the default collection:

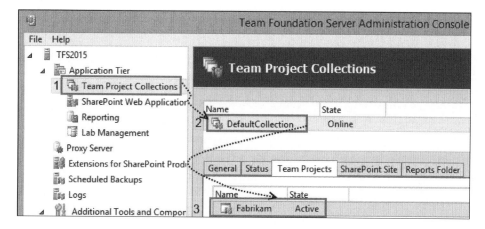

3. Select the **Fabrikam** Team Project and click on **Delete**:

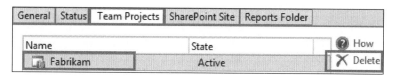

4. In the **Delete Team Project** window, select **Delete external artifacts** and **Delete workspace data**. Click on **Delete** button to continue.

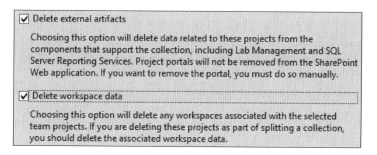

5. The deletion workflow is triggered, flip to the **Status** tab to track the progress:

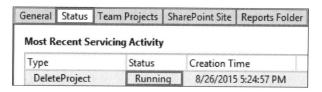

6. While all links to the project portal will be removed from Team Web Access, the SharePoint site that acts as the portal will need to be deleted manually from SharePoint Central Administration.

Option 2

Now, let's look at how to delete the Team Project using the `tfsdeleteteamproject` command-line tool:

1. Open the Visual Studio 2015 Command Prompt. Alternatively you could open up a command prompt and change the directory to `%programfiles(x86)%\ Microsoft Visual Studio 14.0\Common7\IDE`.

2. Run the following command:

   `tfsdeleteproject /q /force /collection:http://tfs2015:8080/tfs/ Fabrikam`

The command-line utility offers a few more switches:

▶ `/q`: This is an option switch; it enforces quite mode wherein no prompts are raised for confirmation during the deletion process.

▶ `/force`: This is an optional switch; it enforces that the deletion process should continue even if some components cannot be deleted.

▶ `/excludewss`: This is an optional switch. If you do not want to delete the SharePoint site associated with the Team Project, use this switch.

How it works...

The `tfsdeleteproject` command carries out the deletion in two phases. The first phase deletes the project data that includes data in version control, build and test manager, components of the Team Project in Team Explorer, Work Items, and any Work Item fields that exclusively belong to the Team Project. The next phase deletes the project websites. This includes any reports associated to the Team Project as well as project portals on SharePoint.

If you try to access a Team Project that has been deleted, you are likely to get this error message. **TF200016: The following project does not exist**. Verify that the name of the project is correct and that the project exists on the specified Team Foundation Server.

The following data may remain undeleted when using `tfsdeleteproject`:

- **Team Project data in the cube**: The Team Project data in the cube will only be removed with the next rebuild. The default rebuild for the warehouse is set to 2 hours.

- **Build drop files and folders**: Build binaries, build log files, and log files containing test results are published during the build process. The locations for these files are not deleted. These files need to be manually removed from the folder locations.

- **Shared Work Item tracking metadata**: `tfsdeleteproject` does not delete any metadata for Work Item tracking that is shared between Team Projects.

- **Version control shelvesets containing shared code**: Version control shelvesets are not deleted if code in the shelveset is from multiple Team Projects.

2
Setting Up and Managing Code Repositories

"Quality is never an accident; it is always the result of intelligent effort".

–John Ruskin

In this chapter, we will cover:

- Creating a Git repository in an existing TFVC Team Project
- Enabling code analysis check-in policy
- Performing a baseless merge between sibling branches in TFVC
- Reparenting a branch in TFVC
- Unlocking files checked out by someone else
- Unshelving a shelveset created in one branch to another branch
- Ignoring file types from check-in using .tfignore and .gitignore
- Conducting code reviews in TFS
- Setting up policies for branches in Git
- Conducting Pull requests in TFS
- Analyzing code churn with TFS analysis services cube

Introduction

Code repositories enable developers to write code more confidently. More developers are using source control than ever before. The most obvious benefits of a code repository can be seen when multiple developers are collaborating on code. Many hands in the pot means there is a greater need to manage and understand revisions. If you ever have to make an argument to support source control, then the questions to ask would be the following:

▶ Have you ever made a change to code, realized it was a mistake and wanted to revert back?

▶ Have you ever lost code or had a backup that was too old?

▶ Have you ever had to maintain multiple versions of a product?

▶ Have you ever wanted to see the difference between two (or more) versions of your code?

▶ Have you ever wanted to prove that a particular change broke or fixed a piece of code?

▶ Have you ever wanted to review the history of some code?

▶ Have you ever wanted to submit a change to someone else's code?

▶ Have you ever wanted to share your code or let other people work on your code?

▶ Have you ever wanted to see how much work is being done, and where, when, and by whom?

▶ Have you ever wanted to experiment with a new feature without interfering with working code?

Managing code is an essential part of **Application Lifecycle Management**, which spans indiscriminately across programming languages and frameworks. Source control systems can broadly be distinguished as centralized or distributed:

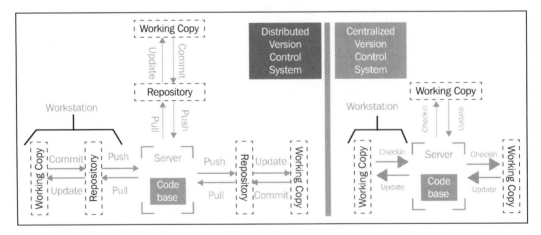

Centralized Version Control Systems (**CVCS**) maintain a single "central" copy of your source code on a server repository. When working with a centralized version control system, developers download the code from the repository to a local workspace. Once changes to the code have been made locally, they are committed to the centralized copy. Additional functions against the repository (branching, merging, shelving, and so on) also take place on the server and require a connection to the server.

TFVC is a Centralized Version Control System. When working with TFVC using Visual Studio or Eclipse, the IDE is in frequent communication with the server. Most common operations cannot be performed in the absence of an active connection to the server.

Distributed Version Control Systems (**DVCS**) does not necessarily rely on a central server to store all the versions of a project's files. Instead, developers "clone" a copy of a repository and have the full history of the project on their own hard drive. This copy (clone) contains all of the data in the repository – all of the branches and the commit history.

Git is a Distributed Version Control System. Most operations (except pushing and pulling) can be performed without an active connection to the server.

TFS is the only platform to support both centralized (TFVC) and distributed (Git) source control systems. The following table should help you decide when centralized is a better option than distributed. More details on the differences between the two can be found at `https://msdn.microsoft.com/en-us/Library/vs/alm/code/overview`.

	Centralized Version Control		Distributed Version Control
	Check-in **Check-out**	**Edit** **Commit**	
Strengths	▸ Scales to very large codebases ▸ Fine level permission control ▸ Allows usage monitoring	▸ Offline editing support ▸ Easy to edit files outside Visual Studio or Eclipse	▸ Full offline experience ▸ Complete repository with portable history ▸ Simplified branching model
Best for	▸ Large Integrated codebase ▸ Control and auditability over source code down to the file level	▸ Medium-sized integrated codebase ▸ A balance of fine-grained control with reduced fiction	▸ Modular codebases ▸ Integrated with open source ▸ Highly distributed Teams

Until TFS 2015, the selection for source control type needed to be made at the time of Team Project creation. In Update 1, a new capability was introduced that allows Teams to create Git repositories within TFVC Team Projects. This is great for Teams that have large investments in TFVC projects but would like to try out Git. This capability and its advantages are discussed at length in the *Creating a Git repository in an existing TFVC Team Project* recipe. The Git for TFVC users is a very useful guide (http://bit.ly/1RgboRk) for anyone coming from a TFVC background interested in learning Git.

Today, the marketplace and business demands are changing more than ever before. Development Teams are constantly under pressure to deliver better quality software faster. This is not sustainable unless the underlying codebase is of good quality and backed by unit tests. A good source control repository can significantly contribute to the quality of the software, but it requires much more than just a good source control repository to drive quality.

Talking of quality, no code reviews, poor DevOps practices, lack of unit tests, too many tactical implementations, and not addressing underlying issues are major contributors to technical debt. Technical debt doesn't hit you overnight, it's a slow and gradual process. Unlike financial debt, technical debt is very hard to recognize. Technical debt will slow your ability to deliver value. Are you seeing any of these signs?

The goal of this chapter is to introduce you to various source control operations in Web Portal and Team Explorer, learn about features that help build quality into the code, and last but not least, understand the code metrics available in the TFS Warehouse. In this chapter, we'll be using the Fabrikam Fiber codebase available on CodePlex (https://fabrikam.codeplex.com). Follow the following instructions to set up the code in the FabrikamTFVC and FabrikamGit Team Project.

Setting up the Fabrikam solution in FabrikamTFVC Team Project

1. Open Visual Studio, and in Team Explorer connect to FabrikamTFVC project. Click on the hyperlink to configure your workspace. Accept the default name and location, and click on **Map & Get**. A success notification is shown when the operation is completed:

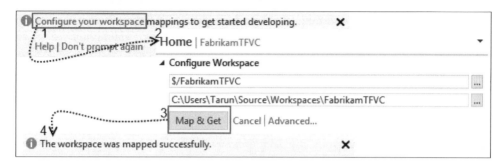

2. Open the workspace location, in this case, `C:\Users\Tarun\Source\Workspaces\FabrikamTFVC`. Create a new folder `Main`; in `Main`, create a folder `Source` and copy the content of Fabrikam codebase downloaded from CodePlex:

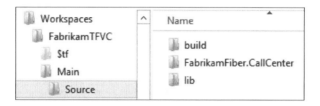

3. Open Source Control Explorer in Visual Studio and from the menu bar, select **Add items to folder** icon. In the **Add to Source Control** window, click on the `Main` folder and then click on **Next**. Following this, click on **Excluded items**, select all the items, and then click on the **include item(s)** icon. There should be no excluded items now. Click on **Finish**, and then click on the **FabrikamTFVC** project and choose **Check in pending changes** from the context menu:

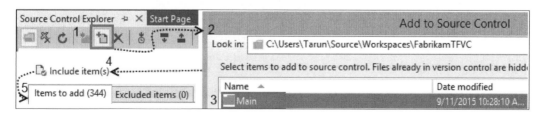

4. In Source Control Explorer, right-click on the `Main` folder and select **Convert to Branch...** from under the branching and merging submenu in the context menu:

5. Open `FabrikamFiber.CallCenter.sln` from `$/FabrikamTFVC/Main/Source/FabrikamFiber.CallCenter`. Right-click on the **Solution** in Solution Explorer and select **Add Solution to Source Control...** from the context menu:

6. Accept warnings and check in the changes from the pending page in Team Explorer. The Fabrikam solution is now successfully set up in the main branch in the FabrikamTFVC Team Project.

Setting up the Fabrikam solution in FabrikamGit Team Project

1. Open Visual Studio and in Team Explorer, connect to the FabrikamTFVC project. Click on the hyperlink to clone this repository. Accept the default name and location and clone. A success notification is shown when the operation is complete:

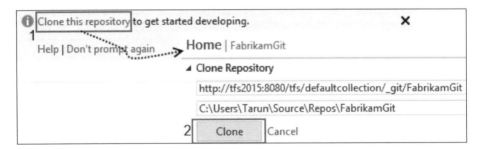

2. Open the local working directory, in this case, `C:\Users\Tarun\Source\Repos\FabrikamGit`. Create a new folder `src` and copy the content of the Fabrikam codebase downloaded from CodePlex:

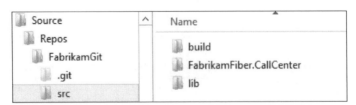

3. In Team Explorer, navigate to the changes page. From the untracked files section, click on the **Add All** hyperlink to include all files recently copied into the working folder. Click on the **Commit** button to commit these changes to the repo:

4. A prompt to sync the changes is raised when the commit operation has been successfully completed. Click on **Sync** and then on **Push** from the **Outgoing Commits (1)** section to push the changes to the remote server:

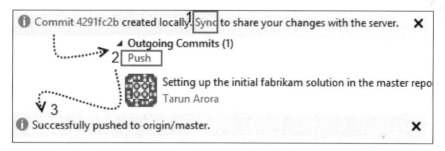

5. Navigate to the branches page in Team Explorer. The **master** branch shows up as well as the **remotes/origin** branch:

The Fabrikam solution is now successfully set up in the **Master** branch in the FabrikamGit Team Project.

Creating a Git repository in an existing TFVC Team Project

Traditionally, it has only been possible to have TFVC as a source control repository. TFS started supporting Git as a source control from TFS 2013 onwards. Git offers many benefits for distributed Teams collaborating across the same codebase; you can read more about the benefits here at `https://git-scm.com/about`. TFVC Teams that are keen to try out Git, but cannot because of the rework involved in migrating their existing investments now have a solution. TFS now supports hybrid Team Projects. In this recipe, you'll learn how to set up a Git repository within an existing TFVC-based Team Project.

Getting ready

In Team Foundation Server 2015 Update 1, you need to be a member of the project administrator group to make an existing TFVC or Git project into a hybrid project, a project that hosts both a TFVC repository and multiple Git repositories. Users will need Visual Studio 2015 Update 1 to work with the hybrid project. Older versions of Visual Studio, including 2015 RTM, will see the project as the type it was originally created as.

If your TFVC project was created prior to TFS 2015 Update 1, a project administrator will need to apply some project-level permissions once the first repository has been created. Go to the version control administration page and select the **Git repositories** node in the tree. To set up the same group permissions as any of the default process templates (Agile, Scrum, and CMMI), add the following TFS groups and grant the following permissions:

- [ProjectName]\Readers
  - **- Allow**: Read
  - **- Not set**: All others

- [ProjectName]\Contributors
  - **- Allow**: Branch creation, Contribute, Note management, Read, and Tag creation
  - **- Not set**: All others

- [ProjectName]\Build Administrators
  - **- Allow**: Branch creation, Contribute, Note management, Read, and Tag creation
  - **- Not set**: All others

Similarly, when creating a TFVC repository with in a Git Team Project that was created before TFS 2015 Update 1, the following folder level permissions need to be amended.

Go to the version control administration page and select the $/_ProjectName_ node in the tree. To set up the same groups as any of the default process templates (Agile, Scrum, and CMMI), add the following TFS groups and grant the following permissions:

- [ProjectName]\Readers
  - ❑ **- Allow**: Read
  - ❑ **- Not set**: All others

- [ProjectName]\Contributors
  - ❑ **- Allow**: Check in, Check out, Label, Lock, Merge, and Read
  - ❑ **- Not set**: All others

- [ProjectName]\Build Administrators
  - ❑ **- Allow**: Check in, Check out, Label, Lock, Merge, and Read
  - ❑ **- Not set**: All others

If your Team Project was created after TFS 2015 Update 1, these permissions will have already been applied for you, and no action is necessary except creating the repository.

How to do it...

1. Navigate to the code hub in FabrikamTFVC Web Portal by browsing to `http://TFS2015:8080/DefaultCollection/FabrikamTFVC/_versionControl`.

2. As illustrated in the following screenshot, click on **FabrikamTFVC** to pull down the **Options** menu. To create a new Git repository, click on **New repository...** from the **Options** menu. Name the repository `FabrikamFeature1` and click on **Create**:

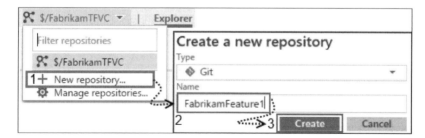

 Note that there is no support for creating multiple TFVC repositories within the same Team Project. There is support for creating multiple Git repositories.

3. The create operation will redirect you to a Git getting started page. The getting started page allows you to generate a clone of the repository and command-line credentials, create a README file to describe your repository and provide commands to set up the Git repository to work with Xcode, Eclipse, and Visual Studio. Click on **Clone in Visual Studio** to start working on the new repository in Visual Studio:

4. As a result of this action, the repository is cloned in Visual Studio:

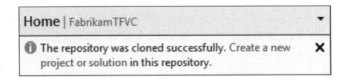

How it works...

Many customers are actively using TFVC repositories and have a rich Work Item history and customization in their Team Project. To make it easy for these Teams to start using Git, the Team Project model in TFS has been modified to support multiple source control repositories. Hybrid projects allow creating as many Git repositories as you need in your TFVC project. This model now also supports creating a TFVC repository in a Git project.

Team Explorer has been enhanced in TFS Update 1 to provide support for operating the hybrid Team Project. As illustrated in the following image, the manage connections page in Team Explorer lists all source control repositories in the Team Project. The workflows in Team Explorer are adjusted based on the repository type you are connected to.

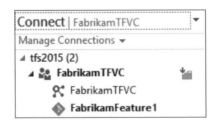

The Web Portal also allows context switching between the TFVC and Git source control in the code hub. The workflows associated to the source control are made available based on the selection. For example, on selecting Git, you can see the option for Pull requests, while in the context of TFVC, you see the option for shelvesets.

There's more...

A recent roadmap of investments in Git experiences for Team Foundation Server and Visual Studio Online talks about support for Pull requests within Team Explorer and support for Git Large File Storage and GitFlow; you can read more about this at `http://bit.ly/1RXQRS1`.

Enabling code analysis check-in policy

Many organizations recommend certain checks be done before committing code into source control. The cost of fixing bad code increases overtime. There is incentive in identifying and fixing issues in code early. We discussed the definition of done in the previous chapter; think of this as the definition of check-in. In TFS, a check-in policy is a rule that is executed during the check-in operation to ensure that the selected change set is okay to commit. The check-in policies are stored on the server and executed on the client machines at the time of check-in. Check-in policies are only supported in TFVC projects. While TFS has some preconfigured check-in policies, several other check-in policies are added by TFS Power Tools. In this recipe, you'll learn how to configure the code analysis check-in policy. The code analysis check-in policy requires that code analysis is run before check-in.

Getting ready

To complete this recipe, you'll need:

- A TFVC Team Project called FabrikamTFVC. Refer to the *Creating a Team Project using the Scrum Template* recipe in *Chapter 1, Team Project Setup,* for instructions on how to create a TFVC Team Project.

- In order to configure check-in policies, you need to have the edit project-level information permission set to **Allow** for your account. Add yourself. If you are part of the Project Administrators or Project Collection Administrators group, you'll already have this permission.

Check-in policies that are defined using Team Explorer everywhere only apply when you check in using the Team Foundation Server plugin for Eclipse or the cross-platform command-line client for Team Foundation Server. If another client such as Team Portal or Team Explorer in Visual Studio is used, these policies do not apply. Similarly, policies that are defined using Team Portal or Team Explorer in Visual Studio are not applied when you check in using the Team Foundation Server plugin for Eclipse or the cross-platform command-line client for Team Foundation Server.

How to do it...

1. In Visual Studio, open Team Explorer and click on **Settings**. Once navigated into the **Settings** view, click on the **Source Control** hyperlink. From the **Source Control Settings** window, select the **Check-in Policy** Tab. Click on the **Add** button and select **Code Analysis**, then click on **OK**.

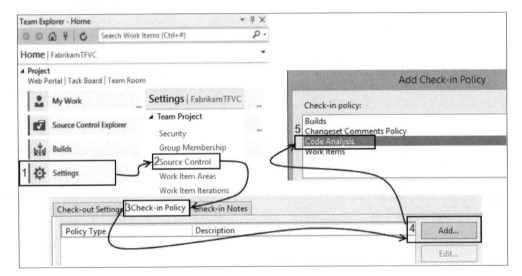

2. In the **Code Analysis Policy Editor** window, from the rule set dropdown, select **Microsoft Managed Recommended Rules** and click on **OK**:

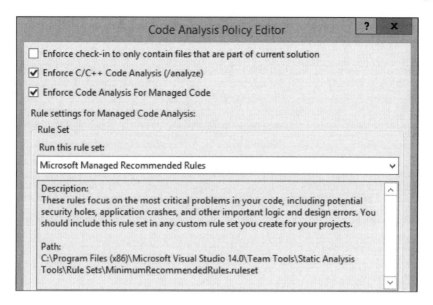

3. Check **Enforce check-in to only contain files that are part of current solution**.
   This option allows you to stop the check-in of any file that is not part of the current
   solution. This is a good option to enable as developers can accidently check in files
   into the source control without linking the file to the solution. This can possibly result
   in build issues.

 The code analysis ruleset definitions are stored in the `C:\Program Files (x86)\Microsoft Visual Studio 14.0\Team Tools\Static Analysis Tools\Rule Sets` folder.

4. From the FarbikamTFVC project, open `FabrikamFiber.CallCenter.sln`:

FabrikamFiber.CallCenter.sln

5. In **FabrikamFiber.Web** from `Controllers`, open `HomeController.cs`:

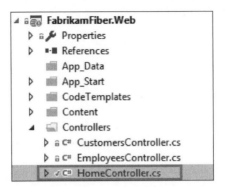

6. Copy the following code in the `Index()` function of `HomeController.cs`:

```
try
{}
catch(Exception ex)
{}
```

7. From Team Explorer, navigate to the pending changes window and check in the code changes into TFS. A policy warning is issued since the static code analysis hasn't been run:

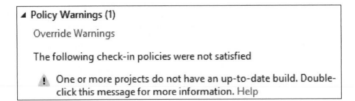

8. Double-click on the warning message to see the details:

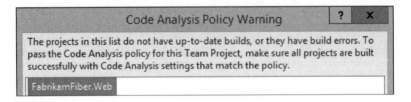

9. Trigger code analysis by selecting **Run Code Analysis on Solution** from the **Analyze** menu in Visual Studio:

10. Code analysis finds the issue with the newly added code. The developer would have missed this if the code analysis wasn't run. The code analysis policy ensures that code analysis is run before the code can be checked in:

11. Since code analysis has now been run, checking in the code will not issue a check-in policy violation warning message.

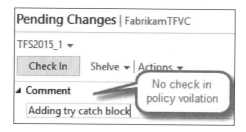

How it works...

Check-in policies are used to enforce mandatory software development practices. Policy is enforced during the check-in process. Since TFVC check-ins are processed on the server, the check-in request is intercepted to force an execution of the check-in policy on the client side. If a user attempts to perform a check-in, in violation of a policy, the check-in is blocked.

There are four Team Project check-in policies that can be specified (in order to use check-in policies, you need to be connected to Team Foundation Server):

► **Builds**: This requires that any build breaking issues that were created during a build must be fixed before a new check-in.

► **Code analysis**: This requires that the code analysis is run before check-in.

► **Testing policy**: This requires that check-in tests are completed before check-in.

► **Work Items**: This requires that one or more Work Items be associated with the check-in.

The check-in policy can be overridden by clicking on the **Override Warnings** hyperlink; you can continue to check in the code after providing a reason for the override:

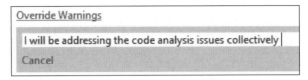

 You can turn off the policy override option in Team Explorer using a no policy override server side plugin. Read the following blog post for more details `http://bit.ly/1jUhZ9y`.

There's more...

So far, we have talked about check-in policies for TFVC projects. Using the TFS API, it is possible to create a custom check-in policy for Git projects. The server-side plugin listens for the `PushNotification` that is raised at the time of Git push event. Refer to `http://bit.ly/1OabagX` on how to create a server-side check-in policy for Git repositories to validate that a commit message has been associated with the push.

Performing a baseless merge between sibling branches in TFVC

Managing source code can get challenging when multiple Teams are contributing to the same repository. Are you already familiar with the branching and merging tools available in TFS? If not, I would encourage you to go through the ALM Rangers Version Control Guidance `http://bit.ly/1He8pmL`. The guidance talks in detail about the various branching strategy and its pros and cons.

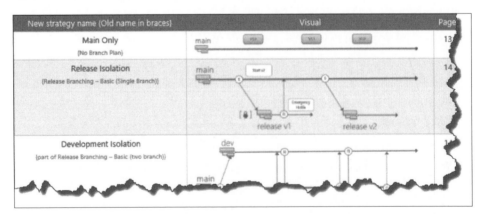

An extract from the ALM Rangers Version Control Guide showing different branching strategies

Branching in TFVC can get complicated over time; branching in Git is lightweight and path independent. In Git, many developers create a branch for each new feature they are coding, sometimes on a daily basis. Git allows you to quickly switch from one branch to another to pivot among different variations of your codebase. When using Git, you can create branches that exist only on your Dev machine and share them if and when you're ready. Consider evaluating your source control requirements against the workflow at `http://bit.ly/1P7UMvO`; you may find Git a better fit.

In this recipe, you will learn how to carry out a merge operation between two unrelated TFVC branches often referred to as sibling branches.

Getting ready

In your TFVC-based Team Project, create a branching structure as illustrated in the following diagram. You can use the TFS Community Branch Tool extension to automate the creation of the branch, as illustrated in the following diagram (`http://bit.ly/1LZR2bx`):

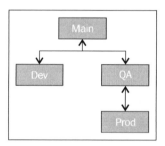

We'll be working through the following scenario in this recipe. The developer working on **Dev** branch has found a critical issue that he has resolved with a code check-in. The QA branch is already being used by another developer to carry out some unrelated work. To get the fix from **Dev** branch into production, the developer decides to perform a baseless merge between the **Dev** and **Prod** branch.

In order to perform a merge operation, your user account needs to have the merge permission. The project administrator group already grants this permission; however, this permission can be set to Allow directly on individual users and groups:

Manage permissions	Allow
Merge	Allow
Read	Allow
Revise other users' changes	Allow

How to do it...

1. In Visual Studio, open Team Explorer, and navigate to the Source Control Explore. Perform a **Get Latest Version** operation on the FabrikamTFVC Team Project:

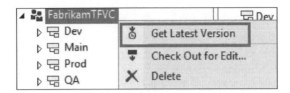

2. To simulate a fix being made in the **Dev** branch, open the `$\Dev\FabrikamFiber.CallCenter\FabrikamFiber.Web\Controllers\HomeController.cs` file and copy the following comment in the `Index` method:

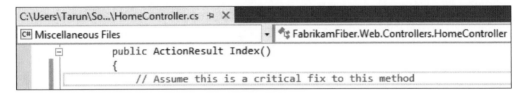

   Check in the code changes to this file from the pending changes view in Team Explorer:

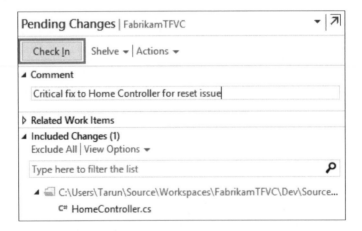

3. Now that the critical change is in the Dev branch, let's look at the steps required to carry out the baseless merge of this change from the Dev branch to the Prod branch. From the source control explorer, right-click on the **Dev** branch and choose **Merge...** from under the **Branching and Merging** submenu:

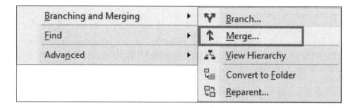

4. The **Merge** wizard will not show the **Prod** branch in the **Target branch** dropdown. Unrelated branches can only be selected using the **Browse...** button. Click on **Browse...** and select **Prod** branch. Then, click on **OK**:

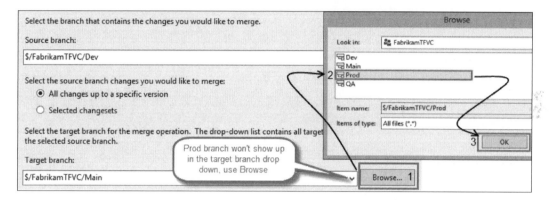

5. A warning sign shows up next to **Target branch** indicating that the chosen branch is unrelated and will cause a baseless merge:

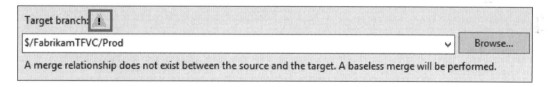

6. Click on **Next** to navigate to the next screen:

> If the selection is changed from **All changes** to **Selected changesets** then a merge relationship between the two branches has not been established. While you would still be able to merge the change, you won't be able to visualize it.

7. Keep the **Latest Version** selected in the dropdown and click on **Next**:

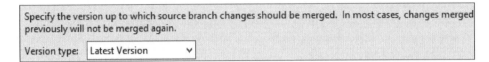

8. Once the merge operation has completed, you'll be navigated to the **Resolve Conflicts** window. Click on **Merge Changes In Merge Tool**, then check and click on **Accept Merge**:

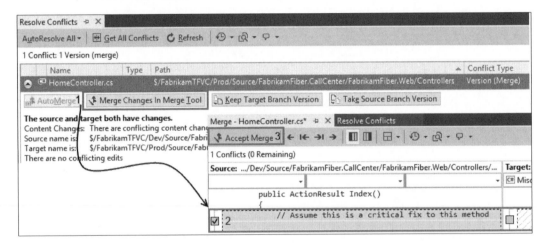

9. The **Resolve Conflicts** window will clear of any conflicts once the merge has completed. From the pending changes viewed in Team Explorer, check in the pending changes:

10. From the Source Control Explorer, right-click on the **Prod** branch and choose **View History**. Check all the branches and click on **Visualize**. The dashed line from Dev to Prod represents the baseless merge.

How it works...

When a baseless merge is carried out, a relationship is established between the two sibling branches. The baseless merge is represented by the dashed line:

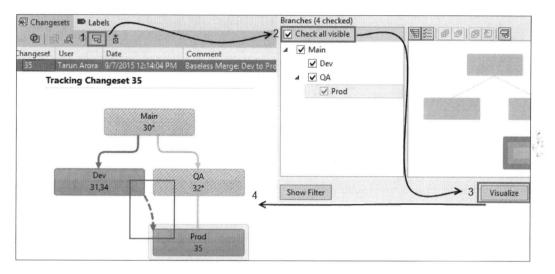

To get a view of the timeline of the change, hit the **Timeline Tracking** view at the top of the screen:

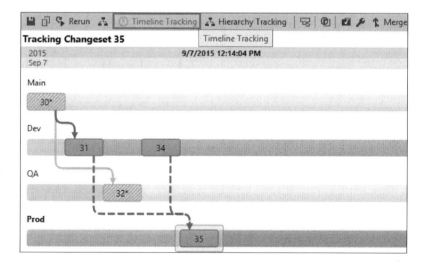

Reparenting a branch in TFVC

Team Foundation Version Control provides you with an option to prune a branch from somewhere in a given hierarchy and graft it on elsewhere in the same hierarchy. Consider using this approach if the branch structure you put in place is incorrectly set up or has stopped working as you have scaled up. In this recipe, you'll learn how to reparent a branch in TFVC.

> The movement of the reparented branch is logical not physical and can be done without stopping developers from working. However, it's a good idea to get developers to shelve changes. You should also endeavor to make the new parent as close in content to the old parent to avoid merge conflicts.

Getting ready

In order to reparent a branch, your user account needs to have the **Manage branch** permission. The project administrator group and project collection administrator group already grant this permission; however, this permission can be set to allow directly on individual users and groups:

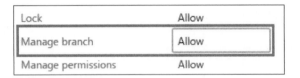

Lock	Allow
Manage branch	Allow
Manage permissions	Allow

The **Manage branch** permission allows you to perform the following:

- ▸ Convert a folder into a branch
- ▸ Execute the following actions
    - ❏ Edit the branch properties
    - ❏ Reparent the branch
    - ❏ Convert the branch into a folder

In your TFVC project, create a branching structure as illustrated in the figure on the left:

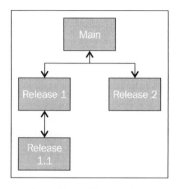

Current branching structure

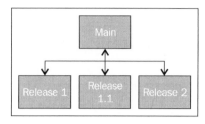

Desired branching structure

The scenario we'll be working through in this recipe, as illustrated in the figure on the left, is the Development Team releases from the **Main** branch; **Release 1.1** was branched from **Release 1**. As illustrated in the figure on the right, the Team wants to move **Release 1.1** directly under the **Main** branch, so changes don't need to go through **Release 1** to be merged to **Release 1.1**.

To reparent the branch **Release 1.1** from **Release 1** to **Main**, a relationship needs to be established between the two branches. This can only be done by performing a baseless merge between the two branches. Refer to the *Performing a baseless merge between sibling branches in TFVC* recipe to learn how to perform a baseless merge.

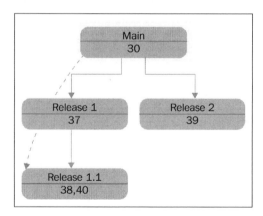

This recipe assumes that a merge relationship has been established between the **Main** and **Release 1.1** branch. In the preceding figure, the dashed line represents a relationship between the two branches.

How to do it...

1. Navigate to Source Control Explorer, right-click on the branch **Release 1.1** and choose **Reparent...** from the **Branching and Merging** submenu:

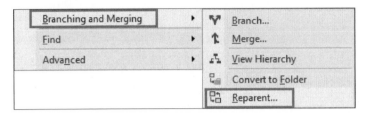

2. In the **Reparent** window, you'll see a list of all branches that have a direct or indirect relationship with **Release 1.1**. Select **Main** and click on **Reparent**. Selecting **No parent** will make **Release 1.1** an independent branch:

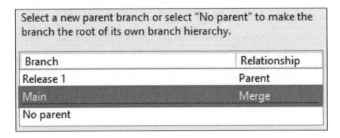

3. The reparent operation takes place on the server. You will not see any pending changes as a result of the reparent operation. The branch hierarchy after the reparent operation is as follows:

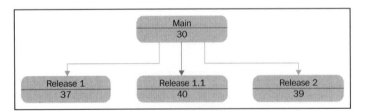

How it works...

Once the reparent operation has been completed, you can view the updated branch hierarchy by right-clicking on the **Release1.1** branch and choosing **Properties** from under the **Advanced** submenu:

Click on the **Relationships** tab from the left menu to see the branch relationships.

Unlocking files checked out by someone else

In distributed Teams, developers often have pending changes that overlap shared code files. Don't you hate it when a developer takes a day off with files exclusively checked out to them or when a developer leaves an organization with files still checked out? When a file is exclusively locked, no check-in can be performed on the file until the lock is removed. In this recipe, you'll learn how to unlock files checked out by other users.

Getting ready

To undo the pending changes in another user's workspace, you must have the **Administer workspaces** permission set to **Allow**:

How to do it...

1. Developer *A* has checked out `$/FabrikamTFVC/Main/Source/FabrikamFiber.CallCenter/FabrikamFiber.Web/Web.config` in the FabrikamTFVC project with a check-in lock type. So while other users can check out the `Web.config` file, no one can check in `Web.config` until developer *A* has lifted this lock:

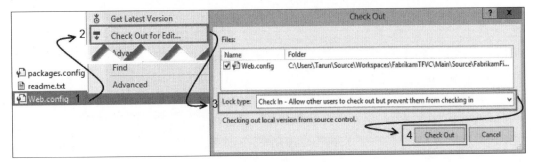

   In the following image, `Web.config` is checked out with the check-in lock. This is represented by **lock** in the **Pending Change** column:

2. Now developer *B* checks out `Web.config` and adds a new section to the config file. To commit changes into version control, developer *B* tries to check in the file. The check-in fails with the following message.

   The following issues were encountered during check-in:

   ```
   Unable to perform operation on $/Fabrikam/Main/.../Web.
   config. The item $/Fabrikam/Main/ .../Web.config is
   locked in workspace TFS2015;DeveloperA.
   ```

3. Developer *B* opens the "Developer Command Prompt for Visual Studio 2015" and runs the following command to undo the changes of developer *A*:

   ```
   tf undo /workspace:TFS2015;"Developer A" /recursive $/
   FabrikamTFVC/Main/Source/FabrikamFiber.CallCenter/FabrikamFiber.
   Web/Web.config" /collection:"http://tfs2015:8080/tfs"
   ```

Key in *Y* when prompted for confirmation of undo. Optionally, use the `/silent` switch in the preceding command for no prompt:

```
C:\Program Files (x86)\Microsoft Visual Studio 14.0>tf undo /workspace:TFS2015;"
Tarun Arora" /recursive "$/FabrikamTFVC/Main/Source/FabrikamFiber.CallCenter/Fab
rikamFiber.Web/Web.config" /collection:"http://tfs2015:8080/tfs"
Undo your changes to C:\Users\Tarun\Source\Workspaces\FabrikamTFVC\Main\Source\F
abrikamFiber.CallCenter\FabrikamFiber.Web\Web.config? (Yes/No) y
The operation completed successfully.  Because you do not have Use permission on
 the workspace TFS2015;Tarun Arora, you must perform a separate get operation in
 that workspace to update it with the changes that have been made on the server.
```

Developer *B* can now successfully check-in the file through the Visual Studio pending changes window.

> While the lock developer *A* had on the `app.config` has been removed, any pending changes that developer *A* might have had in the config file on his machine aren't. So, developer *A* can perform a `get` operation to pull down developer *B*'s changes and merge and continue as appropriate without any information loss.

There's more...

TFS Power Tools provides an option to undo pending changes for other users right from within Visual Studio. If you don't have TFS Power Tools installed, refer to the *Creating a new Team Project through the command line* recipe in *Chapter 1, Team Project Setup*.

Right-click on the file or folder you want to undo. From the context menu, choose **Find by Status...** from under the **Find** in Source Control submenu. You can narrow the search by specifying wildcard and username. The results are presented in **Find** in the Source Control window:

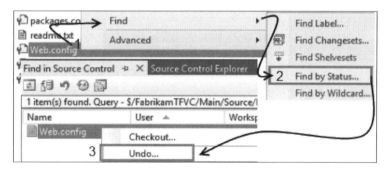

Simply select the file and choose **Undo...** from the context menu to undo the pending changes.

Unshelving a shelveset created in one branch to another branch

When using TFVC, you'll find shelvesets very useful. Shelvesets allow you to effectively back up your local copy of the changes on to the server. Developers are multitasking almost all the time; you may start coding a change in one branch and then realize that the change actually needs to be applied in another branch. In this recipe, you'll learn how to shelve changes in one code branch and then migrate the changes over to another branch without checking in the changes into source control.

Getting ready

The FabrikamTFVC project has three branches, **Dev**, **Main**, and **Prod**, as illustrated in the following diagram. In this recipe, we'll create a shelveset `shelvesetDev1` from the pending changes in the **Dev** branch and unshelve the pending changes over to the **Prod** branch without checking in the pending changes:

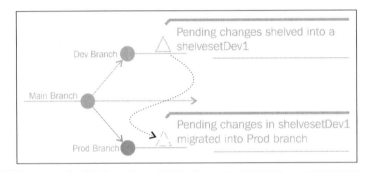

This recipe requires the use of the `tfpt` command-line utility. This utility is installed with TFS Power Tools. If you don't have TFS Power Tools installed, refer to the *Creating a new Team Project through the command line* recipe in *Chapter 1, Team Project Setup*.

Perform a `get latest` operation on both the **Dev** and **Prod** branch to ensure that they are up to date. Ensure that there are no pending changes in the **Prod** branch. If the branches are not up to date, the following error message may be issued during the unshelve operation: `Unable to determine the workspace`.

How to do it...

1. In Team Explorer, open Source Control Explorer and check out the `$\Dev\FabrikamFiber.CallCenter\FabrikamFiber.Web\Controllers\HomeController.cs` file and copy the following comment in the `Index` method:

// Assume this is a critical fix to this method:

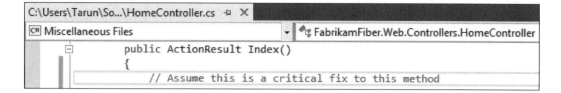

2. Navigate to the **Pending Changes** view in Team Explorer and click on the **Shelve** hyperlink. Enter the shelveset name as `shelvesetDev1` and click on the **Shelve** button:

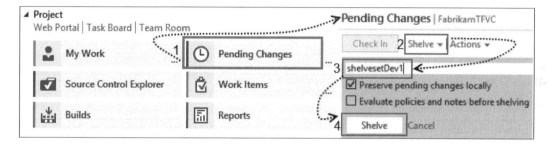

3. Open up the Visual Studio Developer Command Prompt and change the working directory to the target branch workspace directory. The target branch in this case is `Prod`:

```
C:\Program Files (x86)\Microsoft Visual Studio 14.0>cd C:\Users\Tarun\Source\Wor
kspaces\FabrikamTFVC\Prod
C:\Users\Tarun\Source\Workspaces\FabrikamTFVC\Prod>_
```

4. Run the following command to migrate the shelveset from **Dev** to **Prod** branch:

```
tfpt unshelve /migrate /source:"$/FabrikamTFVC/Dev" /target:"$/
FabrikamTFVC/Prod" "shelvesetDev1"
```

5. In the **Shelveset Details** window, click on the **Unshelve** button to continue:

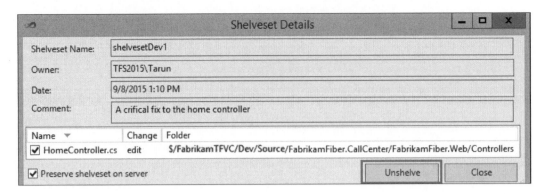

6. The merge button is enabled if TFS recons it can resolve the merge conflict. The **Resolve** button is enabled if TFS requires the conflict to be manually resolved. Click on the **Auto-merge All** button to continue:

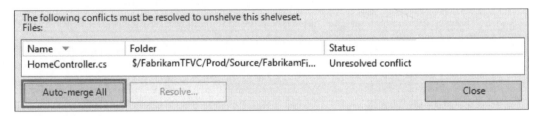

7. Once the auto merge operation has been completed, confirmation message is published in the command prompt:

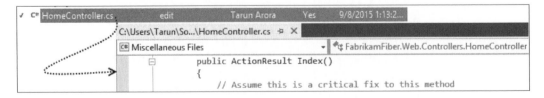

8. In Source Control Explorer, navigate across to the **Prod** branch. Open `HomeController.cs` from `$\Prod\FabrikamFiber.CallCenter\ FabrikamFiber.Web\Controllers`. The changes made in the **Dev** version of the `HomeController.cs` file will reflect in the **Prod** branch version of `HomeController.cs`:

Ignoring file types from check-in using .tfignore and .gitignore

Traditionally, TFS only supported server workspaces. Local workspaces were rolled out in TFS 2012. A local workspace allows you to work disconnected from the server. All core version control operations can be performed without any server connectivity. Local workspaces listen for changes on the filesystem to infer the operations being performed. For example, a new file created in the workspace directly from the filesystem will show up as a pending change. Users who used Subversion source control will be familiar with local workspaces. Read more about the workings of local workspaces at `https://msdn.microsoft.com/en-us/library/bb892960.aspx`.

Many tools and extensions that work in concert with Visual Studio generate temporary files within the local workspace directories. For example, ReSharper, a developer productivity extension for Visual Studio, generates `_Resharper.[SolutionName]` files that are (by default) included in pending changes. These temporary files serve no benefit in version control and should be ignored; `.tfignore` and `.gitignore` allow you to do just that. File types to be ignored can be specified in `.tfignore` and `.gitignore`; these rules are used to automatically exclude specified file types from pending changes. In this recipe, you'll learn how to create `.tfignore` and `.gitignore` files to automatically exclude certain file types.

Getting ready

To work through the recipe, you'll need to create a local workspace. Follow the instructions to create a local workspace in the FabrikamTFVC project:

1. In the local drive, create a folder, `Wks`. This recipe assumes the folder to be `C:\Wks`.

2. Open Team Explorer in Visual Studio and connect to the FabrikamTFVC Team Project.

3. From the Visual Studio menu, navigate to **File | Source Control | Advanced | Workspaces**:

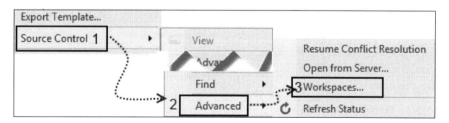

4. In the **Manage workspace** window, click on **Add**. In **Add workspace**, create the workspace TFS2015_99 mapped from $/FabrikamTFVC/Main to C:\Wks. Click on the **Advanced>>** button and confirm if the workspace location is set to **Local**. Then, click on **OK**:

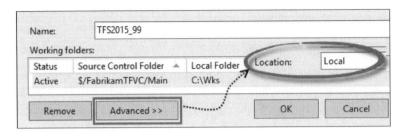

5. After clicking on **OK**, accept the prompt to perform a get latest operation to download the source code into the new local workspace.

How to do it...

Perform the following steps to set up the .tfignore files for TFVC-based source controls:

1. Open C:\Wks and create a new file ThisIsAFakeClass.txt.

2. In Team Explorer, navigate to the **Pending Changes** view for FabrikamTFVC project. In the **Excluded Changes** section, the count of detected shows up as 1.

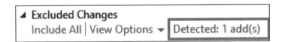

3. Click on the **Detected items** hyperlink. From the **Promote Candidate Changes** window, right-click on ThisIsAFakeFile.txt and choose **Ignore by extension (*.txt)**:

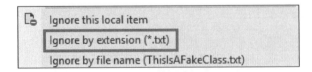

The .tfignore file is automatically created for you and shows up in the **Pending Changes** view. Open .tfignore; the extension *.txt has been added as an item to be ignored. Copy the following text into the .tfignore file to ignore all ReSharper generated files:

```
#####################################
*.txt
```

```
# Ignore Reshaprer files
*_ReSharper.*
*.DotSettings
```

4. Check in the `.tfignore` file into the version control; this ruleset will be evaluated on all developer workstations to ignore all files specified in this `.tfignore` file.

> ▶ TFVC honors multiple `.tfignore` files, where a `.tfignore` file in the scope of the project can override the ignore specification in the `.tfignore` file at the solution level.
> ▶ TFVC accepts exclusion rules, for example, to ignore all TXT files except `help.txt` use `!help.txt`.

Perform the following steps to set up the `.gitignore` files for Git-based source controls:

1. In Team Explorer, open the FabrikamGit project and navigate to the **Settings** view. Click on the **Repository Settings** hyperlink. Then, click on **Add** to create a `.gitIgnore` file:

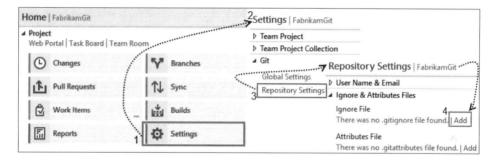

2. Click on the **Edit** hyperlink to edit the `.gitignore` file. Copy the following items in the `.gitIgnore` file:

```
# User-specific files
*.suo
*.user
*.sln.docstates
# Specific files
*.txt
# Build results
[Dd]ebug/
[Rr]elease/
```

3. In Team Explorer, navigate to the **Changes** view and commit the `.gitIgnore` file. Click on the **Sync** hyperlink to push the updated `.gitIgnore` to the repository. All developer workspaces will now ignore the file extensions specified in this `.gitignore` file.

 Git honors multiple `.gitIgnore` files, where a `.gitIgnore` file in the scope of the project can override the ignore specification file at the solution level.

There's more...

The `tfpt` command-line utility installed with TFS Power Tools among other things provides you with two very useful switches: `scortch` and `treeclean`. `scortch` and `treeclean` allow you to mirror the workspace as on the server and remove any unwanted clutter from the workspace. Learn more about `scortch` and `treeclean` at `http://adamprescott.net/2011/09/12/clean-tfs-workspaces-with-scorch-treeclean`.

Conducting code reviews in TFS

In the introduction to this chapter, we briefly talked about technical debt and how it can impact the productivity of a Team. The use of good engineering practices helps tackle issues that are potential contributors to technical debt. There is a consensus across the industry that code review is an effective and practical way to collar code inconsistency and possible defects early in the software development life cycle.

A study on the value and importance of code reviews conducted by Forrester Consulting highlighted the following as perceived benefits of code review:

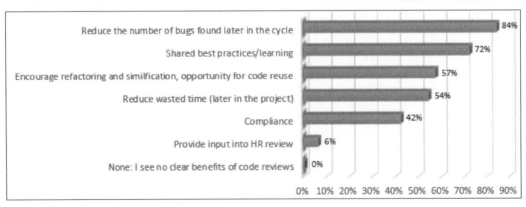

Source - http://www.klocwork.com/getattachment/08c47c41-053c-4fe8-bbf7-91b95734747c/The-Value-and-Importance-of-Code-Review-Forrester?sitename=Klocwork

TFS offers two code review solutions, one through Team Explorer and the other through Team Web Access. The code review solution in Team Explorer, first introduced in TFS 2012, receives criticism for not supporting iterative reviews. On the other hand, the solution in Team Web Access called lightweight code commenting supports iterative reviews, but does not support an integrated Visual Studio IDE experience. You can learn more about the code review solution available in Team Explorer at `https://www.visualstudio.com/en-us/get-started/code/get-code-reviewed-vs`. In this recipe, you'll learn how to use the lightweight code commenting in Team Web Access to conduct code reviews.

Getting ready

In this recipe, we'll be working through the following scenario – Aaron is a developer on the FabrikamTFVC Team. He is working on a new feature in the `FabrikamFiber.CallCenter.sln` Dev codebase to show the `CreatedBy` column on the service ticket dashboard. Aaron has checked in his changes (this has created **Changeset 27**) and he now wants Tarun to perform a code review on the changes. Aaron sends Tarun the changeset by clicking on the share changeset icon in Team Web Access:

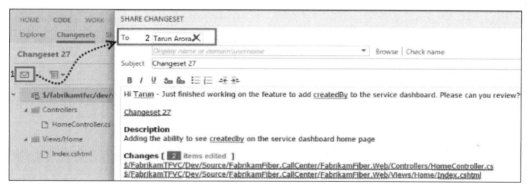

Initiate a code review by clicking the e-mail icon from the Changeset view

Downloading the example code

You can download the example code files from your account at `http://www.packtpub.com` for all the Packt Publishing books you have purchased. If you purchased this book elsewhere, you can visit `http://www.packtpub.com/support` and register to have the files e-mailed directly to you.

How to do it...

1. Tarun receives an e-mail for a feedback request. Clicking on hyperlink **Changeset 27** opens the changeset in review mode, highlighting the code changes in a comparison mode. The changes can also be viewed in side-by-side comparison by clicking on the file name hyperlink:

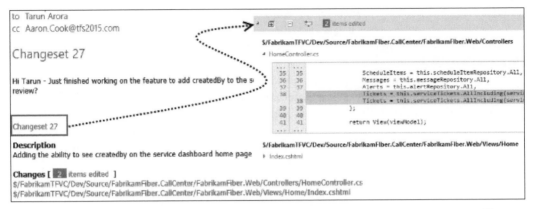

Code comparison window is launched by clicking on the Changeset hyperlink, in this case Changeset 27

2. Looking through the `Index.cshtml`, Tarun find a few issues. He selects the code with the issue and adds an inline comment:

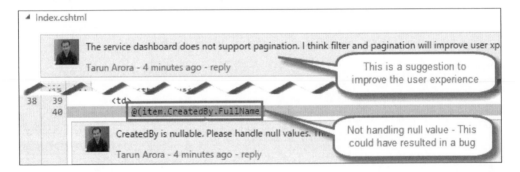

3. Tarun adds an overall comment to the changeset using the **Add Comment** button at the top of the changeset:

4. Tarun submits his feedback by clicking on the **Sharechangeset** button. The e-mail contains a list of all the comments.

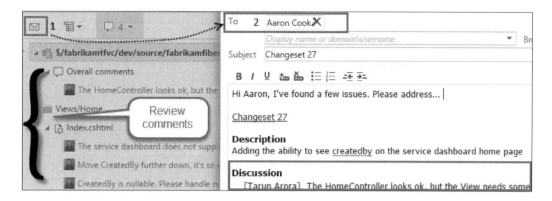

5. Aaron goes through and fixes the issues highlighted by Tarun. Aaron thinks Tarun's comment on pagination and filter should be build out as a common capability. Aaron creates a product backlog item from the code comment and adds it to the Team's backlog:

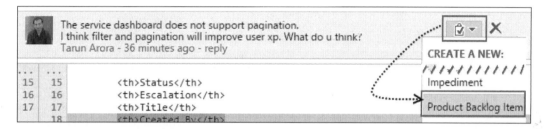

How it works...

Lightweight code commenting is a browser-based code commenting solution in Team Web Access. It provides a nice inline experience for commenting either on whole files or on individual changes. Code commenting enables interactive or time shifted conversations about code. Code commenting is done in a browser so, among other things, it will work wherever you are – including on your mobile phone.

The comments are stored in Team Foundation Server in context to the code. If the code or the underlying code file is removed, the code comment associated to it is automatically removed. Work items created from comments include a reference back to the comment; this helps maintain traceability:

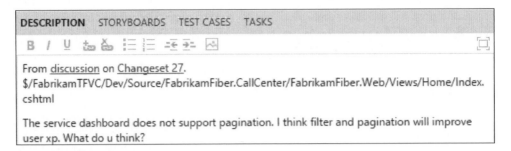

There's more...

While there is a consensus that code reviews are important, the industry is heavily divided whether code reviews should be done before or after check-in. Refer to the following blog post that talks about the pros and cons of both approaches:

```
http://geekswithblogs.net/TarunArora/archive/2012/09/18/vs-2012-code-
review-ndash-before-check-in-or-after.aspx
```

Setting up policies for branches in Git

Building on the theme of code quality and how it helps prevent technical debt, branch policies is a great new feature in TFS that lends itself to improving the quality of the code that goes into the Git repo. In this recipe, you'll learn how to configure code review and Gated check-in policy on the master branch.

Getting ready

To configure branch policies on a branch, the user needs to have administration permission for that branch. To apply branch policy for the entire repo, the user needs admin rights for the repo.

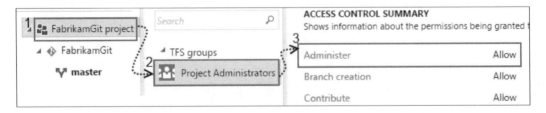

Create a continuous integration build for the FabrikamGit Team; follow the instructions in the Creating a continuous integration build definition in TFBuild recipe in *Chapter 4, Building Your Application*.

Scenario: The FabrikamGit Team wants to protect the master branch by only allowing commits that pass the Fabrikam CI build and have been code reviewed by at least two people in the Team. If the code being changed falls under the `/src/FabrikamFiber.CallCenter/ FabrikamFiber.Web` area, then it must be reviewed by Brian Miller.

How to do it...

1. Open the FabrikamGit Team Administration page at `http://tfs2015:8080/ tfs/DefaultCollection/FabrikamGit/FabrikamGit%20Team/_admin/`. Navigate into the **Version Control** tab and select the **master** branch. To access branch policies, click on the **Branch Policies** tab:

2. The branch policies page allows you to configure policies for gated check-ins and code reviews.

3. In the **Automatically build pull requests** section, check both options and select the **FabrikamGit CI** build definition from the dropdown:

4. In the **Code review requirements** section, check require code reviews and specify the minimum number of reviewers as 2:

5. Click on the **Add a new path** hyperlink. Add the path as `/src/FabrikamFiber.`
    `CallCenter/FabrikamFiber.Web/*` and reviewer as `Brian Miller`:

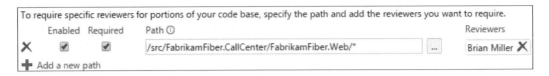

6. Click on the **Save Changes** button to save and apply the gated check-in and code
    review policies.

How it works...

Branch policies are evaluated on the server at the time of commit. With the branch policies
enabled for the master, no code can be committed directly into the master. On directly
committing code into the master, the following error message is issued.

The following errors were reported during push:

```
refs/heads/master, TF402455: Pushes to this branch are not permitted; you
must use pull requests to commit changes.
```

There's more...

There may be justifications at times for bypassing the policies. There is provision for this
in TFS. By setting the **Exempt from policy enforcement** permission to **Allow**, the user or
group is allowed to bypass the policy:

Contribute	Allow
Exempt from policy enforcement	Not set
Note management	Allow

This permission can be scoped to an entire project, a repo, or a single branch. If you are
granted exempt from policy enforcement, you will not be warned nor blocked from pushing
or merging directly to a branch. So, as they rightly say... with great power, comes great
responsibility.

Conducting Pull requests in TFS

Earlier in the chapter, you learned how to restrict unreviewed code from making its way into the master branch. Pull requests are the means to promote code from topic branches (also referred to as feature branch) into the master branch. Pull requests enable developers working in topic branches to get feedback on their changes from other developers prior to submitting the code into the master branch. In this recipe, you'll learn how to conduct a Pull request to accept changes from a topic branch into the master branch.

Getting ready

The scenario we'll be working through in this recipe – Brian is a developer on the FabrikamGit Team. He is working on feature to add a dropdown called `problem type` on the service Dashboard. Brian has created an enum with the list of problem types and he wants to get feedback on this list and merge his changes to the master branch.

1. Open Visual Studio and connect it to the FabrikamGit Team Project. From Team Explorer hub, click on **Branches**. In the **Branches** view, right-click on **master** and select **New local branch From...** in the context menu. Enter the new branch name as `Brian/Feature1` and click on the **Create branch** button:

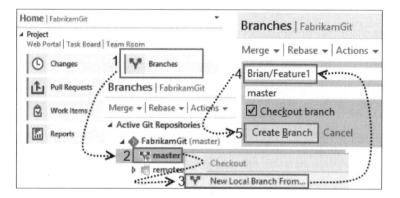

2. From the topic branch, open `FabrikamFiber.CallCenter.sln`. In the **FabrikamFiber.Web** project, add a new folder and call it `Common`. Add a new class and call it `ProblemTypeEnum.cs`. Edit the class and create an enum, as shown in the screenshot:

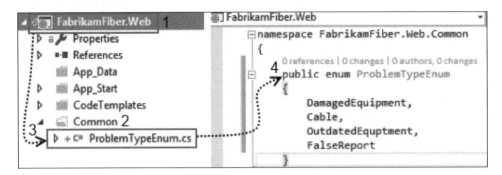

3. From Team Explorer, navigate to the **Changes** view. Commit the pending changes by entering a commit message and clicking on the **Commit** button. Sync and publish the branch:

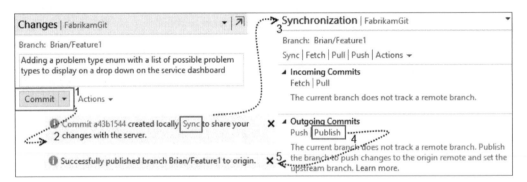

4. Navigate to the branches view page in Team Web Access by browsing to `http://tfs2015:8080/tfs/DefaultCollection/_git/FabrikamGit/branches`. The topic branch shows up here highlighting that it is one change a head of the master branch:

5. Validate that the master branch has gated check in and code review policy setup. If not, follow the steps in the *Setting up policies for branches in Git* recipe.

How to do it...

1. Navigate to the Pull request page in the Web Portal by browsing to `http://tfs2015:8080/tfs/DefaultCollection/_git/FabrikamGit/pullrequests`. You will see a prompt to create a Pull request from the earlier published branch. Alternatively, click on the **New Pull Request** button in the left panel:

2. The **Create Pull Request** page shows the list of changes a long with file-level comparison of the changes. The destination branch is selected as master, since its set up as the default. Optionally, click on the **more options** hyperlink to add a description and an additional group of reviews:

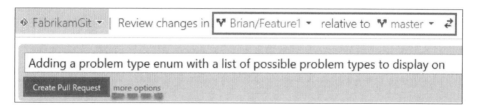

3. The master branch policies are evaluated, the FabrikamGit CI build is automatically kicked off, and code review requests are issued. The engine evaluates the changes and determines that there will be no merge conflicts as part of the merge operation. Since the code changes are under `/src/FabrikamFiber.CallCenter/FabrikamFiber.Web/,'` a code review request is issued to Tom Hacker, too.

4. Now, Tom Hacker logs into Web Portal and, looks up the Pull requests assigned to him. He conducts a code review for this Pull request. Tom suggests a few changes to the enum and marks the Pull request as approved with suggestions:

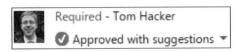

5. Brian makes the suggested changes and commits the changes into the topic branch. Click on **Refresh** to update the changes into the Pull request:

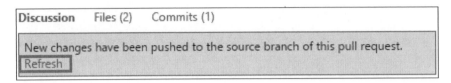

6. The branch policies are reevaluated – the gated check-in build is run and merge is evaluated. Once the required number of reviewers have approved the Pull request, the request is ready to be merged. Clicking on the **Complete Pull Request** button merges the changes into the master and creates a new changeset:

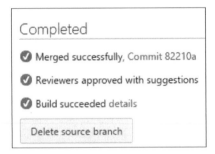

7. Now, click on the **Delete Source Branch** button to delete the `feature1` branch. This is a good practice as leaving unwanted branches causes clutter.

The Pull request has been completed; the updated status reflects in the Team Portal.

How it works...

From the Team Explorer hub, click on **Sync** page, fetch, and pull the incoming changes. From the **Branches** view, click on the **master** branch and choose **View history** from the context menu. The merge into the main branch has completed as part of the Pull request; this now reflects in the branch history:

	82210ac4	Brian Miller	9/10/2015 10:47:48 PM	Updating changes as suggested in the code review during Pull request 2 ◀ master
	a43b1544	Brian Miller	9/10/2015 9:14:20 PM	Adding a problem type enum with a list of possible problem types to display on...
	74d3aa9d	Tarun Arora	9/10/2015 12:29:04 PM	Adding a comment to the master branch

Analyzing code churn with TFS analysis services cube

The TFS analysis services cube computes large datasets that enable users to answer questions about their software project. The TFS data warehouse empowers user to join up various datasets and understand trends in code churn, code coverage, builds, bugs, and so on. In this recipe, you'll learn how to connect Excel with TFS analysis services cube and analyze the code churn in the FabrikamTFVC project.

Getting ready

In order to connect TFS analysis services as a data source using Excel, you need your Windows account permissioned on the TFS data warehouse. Alternatively, use a Windows user name and password that already has access.

How to do it...

1. Open Excel, in the **DATA** tab click on **From Other Sources** and choose **From Analysis Services**. In the data connection wizard, enter the TFS analysis server connection details and click on the **Next** button:

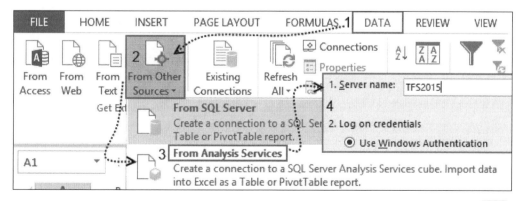

If you are unsure about the warehouse connectivity details, you can check and verify them through the **Reporting** tab in the TFS Administration Console.

2. Select **Tfs_Analysis** in the database dropdown, select **Code Churn**, and click on the **Next** button. The **Modified** column indicates the last processed data time of each cube and perspective. In the next screen, click on **Finish**:

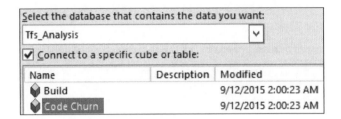

3. Set up the pivot report as indicated in the following screenshot:

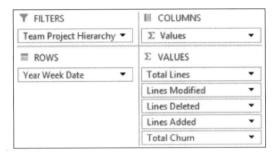

How it works...

The selection of these fields produces the following output. The data is grouped by year, month, and week, showing the total lines in the codebase along with a breakdown of lines modified, lines deleted, lines added, and the total churn:

Team Project Hierarchy	FabrikamTFVC				
Row Labels	**Total Lines**	**Lines Modified**	**Lines Deleted**	**Lines Added**	**Total Churn**
⊟2015	128,858	20	386,811	515,669	902,500
⊕Week ending September 5	129,059	10	0	129,059	129,069
⊟Week ending September 12	128,858	10	386,811	386,610	773,431
9/9/2015	386,626	2	185	257,752	257,939
9/10/2015	386,626				
9/11/2015	128,858	8	386,626	128,858	515,492
9/12/2015	128,858				
Grand Total	128,858	20	386,811	515,669	902,500

In case you are interested in the build quality indicators report, TFS already offers this report out of the box. The report shows test coverage, code churn, and bug counts for a specified build definition. You can refer to `https://msdn.microsoft.com/en-us/library/dd380683(v=vs.120).aspx`, the tutorial, to learn more about this report.

There's more...

Change the fields in the pivot to what is illustrated in the following figure. Now, let's bring the version control hierarchy and build details in to the equation and update the fields in the pivot as in the screenshot here:

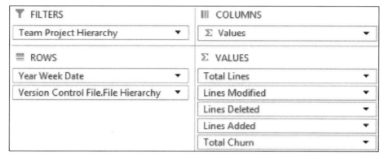

In the values section add Total Lines, Lines Modified, Lined Added, and Total Churn.

This will result in the results pivoted by year, week, and date and the version control hierarchy. As you can see in the screenshot here, the output shows the changes to the branch. You can drill down further to the specific project and class:

Row Labels	Lines Modified	Lines Deleted	Lines Added	Total Churn
⊟ Dev\	2	128,878	128,878	257,758
⊟ Source\	2	128,878	128,878	257,758
⊞ build\	0	0	0	
⊟ FabrikamFiber.CallCenter\	2	128,878	128,878	257,758
FabrikamFiber.CallCenter.sln	0	75	75	150
FabrikamFiber.CallCenter.vssscc	0	10	10	20
⊞ FabrikamFiber.DAL\	0	1,008	1,008	2,016
⊞ FabrikamFiber.Extranet.Web.Tests\	0	300	300	600

Now, change the file hierarchy to be the filter and add the file extension to be presented as a row. In the file extension filter on `.asax`, `.config`, and `.cshtml`, the output will show you the code churn in these file types overtime.

Team Project Hierarchy	FabrikamTFVC				
Version Control File.File Hierarchy	All				
Row Labels	**Total Lines**	**Lines Modified**	**Lines Deleted**	**Lines Added**	**Total Churn**
⊟ 2015	2,214	1	6,652	8,866	15,519
⊟ **Week ending September 5**	2,220	0	0	2,220	2,220
.asax	2	0	0	2	2
.config	518	0	0	518	518
.cshtml	1,700	0	0	1,700	1,700

The possibilities are limitless. Once you have the basics of analysis reports nailed down, you can begin spelunking into the other dimensions available to you in the data warehouse to correlate the data to drive more interesting trends about your software project.

3

Planning and Tracking Work

"A goal without a plan is just a wish."

–Antoine de Saint-Exupéry

In this chapter, we will cover the following:

- ▶ Selecting the backlog levels displayed on the Team Portal
- ▶ Mapping, assigning, and tracking Work Items shared by multiple Teams
- ▶ Adding additional columns to the Kanban board
- ▶ Customizing cards displayed on the boards
- ▶ Setting up Team's capacity and activity for a sprint
- ▶ Querying Work Items by Tags
- ▶ Creating charts using Work Item Queries
- ▶ Using Service Hooks to integrate with Trello boards
- ▶ Deleting Work Items in TFS permanently
- ▶ Using Microsoft Feedback Client to provide feedback

Introduction

Traditionally, businesses looked at technology as a cost of doing business; businesses now look at technology as an opportunity to do more business. The use of sophisticated software systems for critical decision making is increasing more than ever before. Pioneering companies have already realized the benefits of tapping into a digital ecosystem and are leveraging technology as a differentiator. To keep pace with the changes in the marketplace, software systems need to change too.

Requirements that are implemented but never used, or those that are used just long enough to identify, do not satisfy the needs of the users and cause waste, rework, and dissatisfaction. Whether you are following Scrum, Waterfall, or any other delivery approach, good requirement management is the cornerstone to the success of a software project.

In TFS, Work Items are the means to record and track work. Process (formally known as the Process Template) is used to orchestrate the delivery framework terminology and workflow. While TFS comes preloaded with the Scrum, Agile, and CMMI Process Templates, TFS supports customizing existing process and creating new process to best meet the needs of your Team. The planning and tracking tools in TFS are web based, which means that you can access them from any platform and any device.

Let's start off by covering a few key concepts to better understand the planning and tracking tools in TFS. All recipes in this chapter are based on the Scrum Process Template.

- ► **Work Item**: This is used to record work. TFS provides different types of Work Items for different types of work. Tasks, Product Backlog Items, Features, Bugs, Test Cases, and Feedback Response are some of the different Work Item types available in TFS. Refer to `http://bit.ly/1WWDPuB` to learn more about Work Items.

- ► **Backlog**: This is a list of Work Items ordered by priority. TFS offers different backlogs for different levels of planning. You'll be learning about the Epics, Features, and Backlog Items backlog in this chapter. The backlogs in TFS allow you to add new items, prioritize items, visualize the relationship between different Backlog Items, and see the state of the existing Backlog Items. It is now possible to configure whether bugs show up on the backlog. The backlog views in TFS also include charts for Team velocity and cumulative flow. Refer to `http://bit.ly/1RZT9Qw` to learn more about backlogs.

- ► **Area Path**: This allows you to add a dimension of grouping to Work Items. Area Path can be used to group Work Items by Team, Product, or Feature Area. When using a multiple Team setup in a Team Project, the Area Path is used to map the Work Items to a Team. Area Path supports access restriction to Work Items by permission. Refer to `http://bit.ly/1j4baRr` to learn more about Area Path configuration.

- ► **Iteration Path**: This allows you to add a dimension of time to Work Items. An Iteration Path can be used to group Work Items into sprints, releases, or other event-specific milestones. Refer to `http://bit.ly/1NAbyQh` to learn more about Iteration Path configuration.

- ► **Kanban board**: This is a way to visualize the backlog with respect to the delivery workflow. Every backlog in TFS comes with a board. The boards are useful in planning and tracking Work Items in a backlog.

- ► **Sprint board**: This is a way to visualize the Work Items assigned to an iteration. The work on the sprint board can be visualized by Backlog Items or people. The sprint board can now be configured to show or hide bugs.

▸ **Process**: This defines the delivery framework followed in a Team Project. Work Item types, states, workflows, queries, and reports reflect the process and its terminology. Refer to `http://bit.ly/1Sy1v1D` to learn more about the different processes available in TFS.

In this recipe, we will be using the FabrikamTFVC Team Project. If you do not already have the FabrikamTFVC Team Project, create one by following the *Creating a Team Project using the Scrum Template* recipe in *Chapter 1, Team Project Setup.*

Selecting the backlog levels displayed on the Team Portal

The default configuration in the Team Project only provides two backlog levels for every Team. These two levels in the Scrum Template are referred to as Features and Backlog Items.

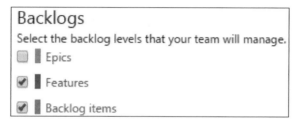

 Epics are very high-level requirements that represent a significant amount of work. They are broken down into Features and worked on in multiple sprints. They are also needed for safe implementations as per `http://bit.ly/1H5j1Kt`.

In this recipe, you'll learn how to activate the Epics backlog from the Team's Administration console.

Getting ready

To create a new Team, you need to be a member of the Project Administrator Group. To change the Team settings, you need to be a Team administrator. If you don't already have these permissions, then follow the instructions at `http://bit.ly/1MS1Xn9`.

Scenario: The `FabrikamTFVC` Team Project has two Teams, namely, FabrikamFeature1 Team and the default FabrikamTFVC Team.

▸ **FabrikamTFVC Team**: The product owner, stakeholders, and end users are heavily collaborating on the Epics and Features Backlog.

► **FabrikamFeature1 Team**: The Development Teams are developing the features prioritized by the FabrikamTFVC Team.

The FabrikamTFVC Team manages the Epics and Features Work Item for Fabrikam. The FabrikamFeature1 Team work on the Feature Work Items assigned to them by the FabrikamTFVC Team. The FabrikamTFVC Team only wants to see two levels of backlogs in its portal, namely, Epics and Features. The FabrikamFeature1 Team want to see only one level of backlogs in its portal, namely, Backlog Items.

To create the FabrikamFeature1 Team, navigate to the FabarikamTFVC Project Control Panel by browsing to `http://tfs2015:8080/tfs/DefaultCollection/FabrikamTFVC/_admin`. Click on the **New team** button, enter the Team name as `FabrikamFeature1 Team` and click on the **Create team** button:

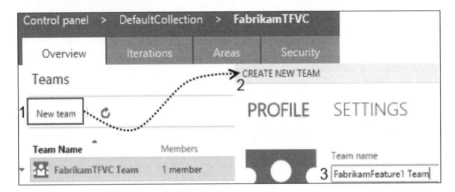

As part of the Team creation process, a new area (**FabrikamFeature1 Team**) is created and mapped to the Team. All Work Items assigned to the Area Path FabrikamFeature1 Team will show up on the FabrikamFeature1 Teams backlog.

How to do it...

1. Navigate to the FabrikamTFVC Team Control Panel by browsing `http://tfs2015:8080/tfs/DefaultCollection/FabrikamTFVC/FabrikamTFVC%20Team/_admin`. Click on **Settings** to navigate to the Team settings page:

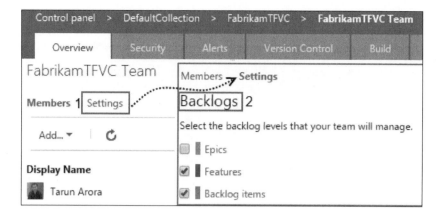

2. Under the **Backlogs** section in the Team settings page, check **Epics** and uncheck **Backlog items**:

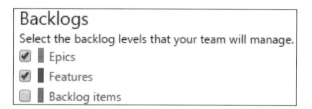

3. Navigate to the FabrikamFeature1 Team Control Panel. From under the **Backlogs** section in the Team settings page, uncheck **Features**:

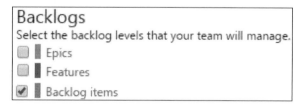

4. The backlog views for the Teams are updated as per the settings shown in the following screenshot. The **FabrikamTFVC** Team on the left only has **Epics** and **Features** backlog; the **FabrikamFeature1 Team** has only **Backlog items** backlog:

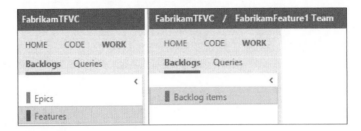

How it works...

Every Team can configure which backlogs show up on the Team Portal. This allows Teams to focus on backlogs they manage and not be distracted by backlog levels not used by them.

There's more...

The Team settings page also allows configuration of working days. If a Team only works for 4 days of a week or is off weekly on a Monday instead of Sunday, then this can be configured by changing the working days setting. The working days are used in the calculation of the Team's total capacity and are shown in the burndown chart. The intent of not showing a Team's days off on the burndown is to avoid the false perception of no work completed on the day.

The behavior of Bug Work Item type on the backlogs and board can also be customized from the Team settings page:

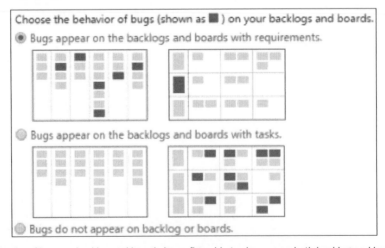

The behavior of bugs on backlog and boards is configurable to show up on both backlog and board with requirements, to show up on both backlog and board with tasks, or to not appear on backlog or boards.

There is strong argument for all of these settings; some pros and cons can be found at
`http://bit.ly/1PL7SzD`.

Mapping, assigning, and tracking Work Items shared by multiple Teams

Hosting multiple Teams in a Team Project helps you share Work Items, backlogs, and other artifacts such as code, builds, tests, and releases. In the *Selecting the backlog levels displayed on the Team Portal* recipe, you learned how to activate backlog levels displayed in the Team Portal. In this recipe, you will learn how to map, assign, and track Work Items assigned across multiple Teams.

Getting ready

Scenario: FabrikamTFVC Team Project has three Teams. The FabrikamTFVC Team focuses on managing Epics and Features; the other two Teams manage the Product Backlog Items for the Features they own:

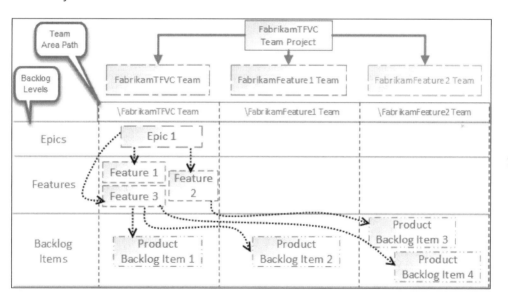

The **Epic 1** Work Item is broken down into several Features and Product Backlog Items. FabrikamTFVC Team wants to map these Work Items before assigning them out to different Teams. FabrikamTFVC Team wants to track the progress the Teams have made on **Epic 1**.

To set up this scenario, create a new Team `FabrikamFeature2 Team` in the FabrikamTFVC Team Project:

Next, navigate to the FabrikamTFVC Team Portal and create the following Work Items:

Work Item type	Title	Area Path
Epic	Epic 1	FabrikamTFVC Team
Feature	Feature 1	FabrikamTFVC Team
Feature	Feature 2	FabrikamTFVC Team
Feature	Feature 3	FabrikamTFVC Team
Product Backlog Item	Product Backlog Item 1	FabrikamTFVC Team
Product Backlog Item	Product Backlog Item 2	FabrikamTFVC Team
Product Backlog Item	Product Backlog Item 3	FabrikamTFVC Team

How to do it...

1. Open the Team Web Portal for the FabrikamTFVC Team and navigate to Features backlog. Click on the **Column options** icon and add **Area Path** as a selected column:

2. Toggle the **Parents** switch to **Show**. All orphaned Features (Features that aren't associated to an Epic-type Work Item) will show up under a header named **Unparented Features**:

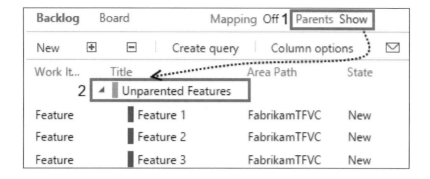

3. Toggle the **Mapping** switch to **On**:

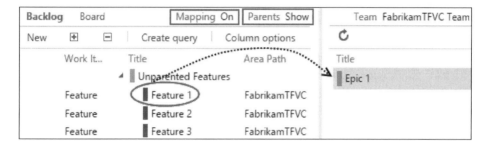

Drag **Feature 1** to **Epic 1**. This will map **Epic 1** as the parent of **Feature 1**. The Feature backlog board is updated to reflect this change:

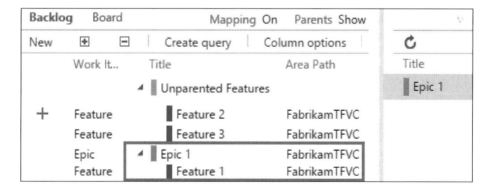

Reparenting can also be done by drag and drop. Drag **Feature 3** into **Epic 1** to reparent it to **Epic 1**:

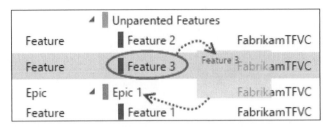

Drag Feature 3 from Unparented Feature section to under Epic 1 Epic Work Item

Drag and drop can also be used on a hierarchical list to reorder the priority of the items. In the following screenshot, **Feature 1** is being dragged at the top to reflect that its higher priority than **Feature 2**:

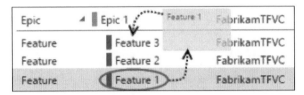

Feature 1 can be prioritized over Feature 3 by simply dragging and dropping it in place of Feature 3

Now, map the other Features and Product Backlog Items as indicated in the *Getting ready* section. Multiselect drag and drop is also supported:

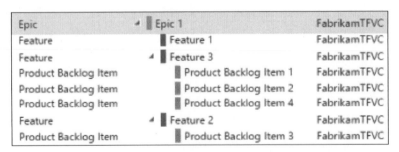

Map the other features and product backlog items as indicated in the Getting ready section

4. Assign the Product Backlog Items to the **FabrikamFeature1** and **FabrikamFeature2 Team** as illustrated in the *Getting ready* section. Team allocation can be changed by changing the Area Path to the respective Area Path of the Team.

5. Once the allocation of the Backlog Items has been changed. Work Items that are not assigned to the FabrikamTFVC Team are shown with a hollow rectangle before them. This simplifies tracking which items the Team owns and which it doesn't:

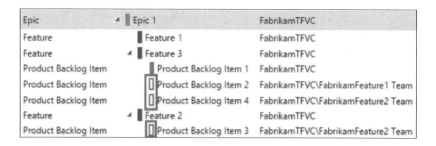

How it works...

Show parent allows Teams to track the full hierarchy of Work Items independent of the Team the Work Item is assigned to. Work Items on the backlog that the Teams do not own are reflected with a hollow rectangle before them.

In summary, you learned how to map Work Items using the story-mapping feature; this also helps identify Unparented Work Items. You also learned how to drag and drop Work Items in the backlog to reorder the priority of the Work Items on the backlog. You learned how to view the Work Item hierarchy by enabling the **Show** parent switch. Last but not least, you also learned how to identify work assigned to different Teams.

There's more...

Let's look at a few useful options available in the toolbar window in the backlog view:

- ▶ **New**: Launches the **Add New Work Item** widget. This is extremely useful when you want to capture an idea into the backlog.

- ▶ **Expand all**: This expands all collapsed nested Backlog Items.

- ▶ **Collapse all**: This collapses all expanded nested Backlog Items.

- ▶ **Create query**: A new Work Item Query is created by replicating the query used to generate the backlog view this action is triggered from.

- ▶ **Column options**: This is used to add or remove columns in the backlog view. This setting is per user, and the changes you make won't impact other users view.

- ▶ **Email**: This e-mails the view visible to you in the backlog. If you filter the items and then click on **Email**, it will only show e-mails in the filtered view.

- ▶ **Filter**: This textbox does a text search on the backlog view. This is really useful for narrowing down to a subset of Backlog Items by searching for a keyword.

TFS 2015 Update 1 provides support for multiselect drag-and-drop assignment, reordering, reparenting, multiedit, move to iteration, and move to position.

Adding additional columns to the Kanban board

The Kanban board in TFS provides a visual representation of the backlog. The board can be modeled to match the delivery workflow used in your organization. In this recipe, you'll learn how to add additional columns and configure a workflow in the Kanban board.

The name 'Kanban' originates from Japanese and translates roughly as "signboard" or "billboard". Kanban in the context of software development can mean a visual process management system that tells you what to produce, when to produce it, and how much to produce (`http://bit.ly/1j4bT57`).

Getting ready

You need to be a Team Administrator or a member of the Team Project Administrator group to customize the Kanban board.

Scenario: The FabrikamFeature1 Team use a **Dev**, **Test**, and **Release** workflow for every Backlog Item before marking it as **Done**. The Team has an exit criteria for each stage in the cycle. FabrikamFeature1 Team has limited testing capacity. To limit the items in **Test**, a limit has been set for items in **Dev**:

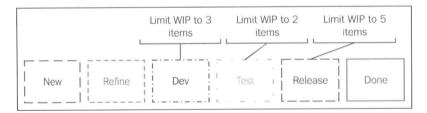

How to do it...

1. Navigate to the Kanban board for the FabrikamFeature1 Team by browsing to the **FabrikamFeature1 Team** Portal and clicking on board from the **Backlog items** backlog:

2. Click on the gear icon from the top-right side of the page. This is used to launch the **Settings** window. The icon to the left of the gear icon is the search icon. This can be used to perform a text search on the backlog. The icon to the right of the gear icon is used to maximize the Kanban board view into fullscreen:

3. In the **Settings** window, select the column from the **Board** section. This will display the configuration for the existing columns. The settings can be configured for both **Bug** and **Product Backlog Item** (these are the default Work Item types in the requirements category):

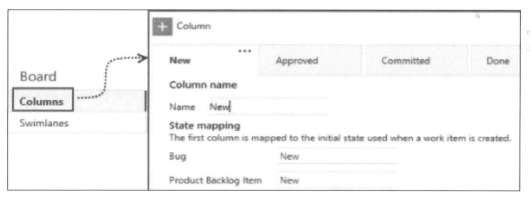

Configure the Kanban board by adding new columns using the Settings window

4. Click on the green plus icon to add a new column. Name the column `Refine`, set the WIP limit to `20` and split the column into doing and done. Map this column to the Work Item state **Approved**. Add a definition of done as illustrated in the screenshot (the text written in the definition of the **Done** textbox can be formatted using markdown):

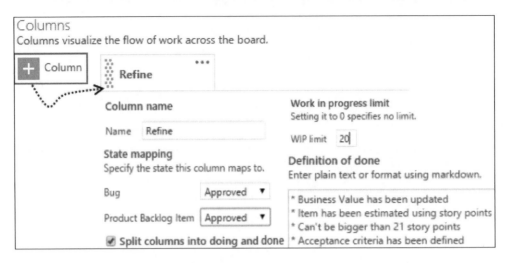

5. Rename the **Approved** column to `Dev`, change the state mapping to **Committed**, set the WIP limit to `3`, check the **Split columns into doing and done** checkbox, and add a definition of done as illustrated in the following screenshot:

6. Rename the **Approved** column to `Test`, set the WIP limit to `2`, keep the Work Item state as **Committed**, check to split columns into doing/done, and add a definition of done.

7. Click on the green plus icon to add a new column. Name the column `Release`, set the WIP limit to `5`, don't split the column into doing and done. Map this column to the Work Item state **Committed**. Add a definition of done. Click on **Save and close** to navigate back to the Backlog Items Kanban board.

8. The Kanban board is now configured with the delivery workflow FabrikamFeature1 Team use to deliver their Product Backlog Items:

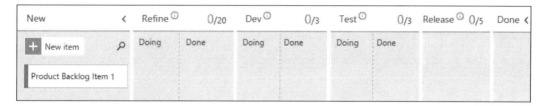

How it works...

The Kanban board can be configured at the Team level, and this empowers a Team to define and follow a process that best works for them. One Kanban board can be configured per backlog. Therefore, if the Team has Epics, Features, and Backlog Items backlog, then the Team has three Kanban boards that can customize and be used to manage work.

Traditionally, the process needed to be customized to add additional states in the Work Item. A new extensibility model called **WIT Extension** was introduced in the product in 2013. WIT extension allows new Work Item fields to be created and associated to a Work Item state without the need for any Work Item customization. More information on how the WIT extensibility dynamically updates the Work Item definition at runtime can be found at `http://bit.ly/1N7FAAt`.

In the scenario we have been working through in this recipe, the **Dev**, **Test**, and **Release** fields are all associated to the committed state. When a Work Item transitions from **Approved** to **Committed**, it shows up in the **Dev / Doing** column. The individual responsible for the Work Item can promote the Work Item into the **Dev / Done** column once the changes have been completed and the definition of done has been met. The state on the Work Item will continue to show as **Committed**. When the individual accountable for testing is ready to test the change, the Work Item can be pulled into the **Test / Doing** column. The state on the Work Item will continue to show as **Committed**. The work can be promoted to the **Test / Done** column once the changes have been tested and the definition of done has been met. The state on the Work Item will continue to show as **Committed**. The Work Item can be pulled into the **Release** column once the Team is ready to schedule a release. The Work Item state will continue to show as **Committed**.

Once the changes have been successfully released, the Work Item can be moved into the **Done** column. This will update the Work Item state from **Committed** to **Done**:

Work Item state transition history

▲	Tarun Arora *made field changes* *(less than a minute ago)*		

▲ Fields

Field	New value	Old value
Rev	6	5
Board Column	Test	Dev
Board Column Done	false	true
[FabrikamTFVC\FabrikamFeature1 Team] Backlog items Column	Test	Dev
[FabrikamTFVC\FabrikamFeature1 Team] Backlog items Column Done	0	1

Work Item field transition history showing the transition from Dev\Done column to Test\Doing column

Splitting the column into **Doing** and **Done** provides better visibility into the progress of the work. The Work Item fields from the Kanban board are used to generate a cumulative flowchart. The chart gives a visual representation of the time spend per column. This is useful in identifying the flow of value and possible bottlenecks in the delivery process:

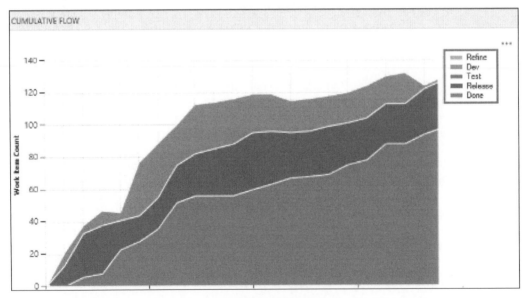

Cumulative flow chart

The eclipse on the cumulative flowchart can be used to customize the start date of the chart.

The Kanban board also lets you keep a check on the number of WIP items. For example, if the number of WIP items in the **Test** column goes above the limit of 3, the WIP is changed to red indicating the violation.

Clicking on the information icon next to the column name shows the definition of done as illustrated in the following screenshot:

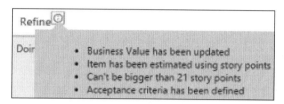

Clicking the information icon shows the definition of done

The board also supports collapsing the **New** and **Done** column. The board can also be maximized to a fullscreen view.

There's more...

Tasks can directly be added to the Product Backlog Item from within the Kanban board. The board also shows a count of completed versus total tasks on the Work Item cards:

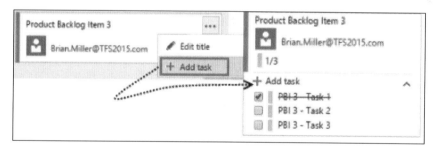

Add tasks directly from the Product Backlog Item Card in the Kanban board.

The Kanban board also supports horizontal swimlanes. The most common use is the creation of an "expedite lane" for emergency work that can skip queues and preempt the other work. Swimlanes can be configured from the **Settings** window; the **Settings** window can be launched by clicking on the gear icon on the Kanban board:

The configuration window allows the configuration of the order of the swimlanes. In this case, the expedite lane will show up above the default lane. Swimlanes can be collapsed. Work Items can be moved between lanes; the lane movement is also tracked in Work Item history.

In TFS 2015 Update 1, three new fields, namely, **Board Column**, **Board Column Done**, and **Board Lane** have been added to Work Item Queries to query Work Items on the Kanban board. The following screenshot illustrates a query to retrieve all Work Items in the default swimlane assigned to the **Test / Doing** column in the FabrikamFeature 1 Team Kanban board:

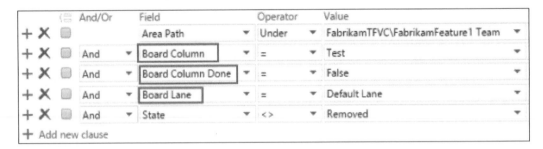

The Kanban columns can now be queried, charted, and alerted upon. For a use case and setup walkthrough, refer to `http://bit.ly/1MS3QA8`.

Customizing cards displayed on the boards

The Kanban board helps visualize, track, and share progress of the Backlog Items. The sprint board, on the other hand, helps visualize, track, and share the Team's progress in the sprint. Both the boards in the Web Portal are useful information radiators that are beneficial for the planning and tracking of work. Work Items are displayed as cards on the boards. Several new features have been added to the boards in TFS 2015 and Update 1 to make the cards even more actionable. In this recipe, you'll learn how to customize the cards to show additional Work Item fields and style the cards based on rules.

Getting ready

You need to be a Team Administrator or a member of the Team Project Administrator group to customize the Team settings.

The scenario we'll be working through in this recipe: the FabrikamFeature1 Team wants to display the **Work Item ID**, **Tags**, **Created By**, **Effort**, **Priority**, and **Value Area** fields on all Backlog Item cards. The Team only wants to see the **Created By**, **Assigned To**, and **Identified In** fields on the Bug cards. The Team wants all priority 1 items to be styled with a bold title and gray background.

How to do it...

1. In the FabrikamFeature1 Team Portal, navigate to the backlog view by browsing `https://tfs2015:8080/tfs/FabrikamTFVC/FabrikamFeature1%20Team/_backlogs/board/Backlog%20items`.

2. Navigate to the board view and click on the gear icon to launch the **Settings** window. In the **Settings** window, select fields from the cards section.

3. In the **Product Backlog Item** tab, check all core fields:

4. Add the **Value Area**, **Created By**, and **Priority** fields from the additional fields:

5. By default, a field is hidden from the Work Item cards if it does not have value. You can optionally choose to change this behavior by checking the **Show empty fields** checkbox:

☐ Show empty fields
  Check if you want to display fields, even when they are empty.

6. Flip to the **Bug** tab and select all the core fields. In the additional fields, add the **Identified In** field.

7. In the **Settings** window, select **Styles** from under the cards section. Add a new styling rule and name the rule `Priority 1`. Change the card color to gray and card header to bold. In the rule criteria, set the rule criteria as *priority = 1*. Multiple fields can be added in one rule criteria:

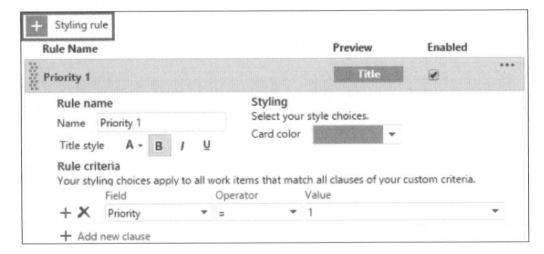

Note that the styling rules for each Kanban board and sprint board can be configured separately.

8. Click on **Save** and close. The Work Items in the board will refresh and will now be rendered to show the additional Work Item fields and styled according to the rules. Styling rules make the cards with important information stand out. When a Work Item matches more than one rule, the first rule is used.

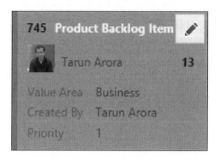

All Work Item fields on the cards can directly be updated from within the card. This allows the cards to be a lot more actionable.

Setting up the Team's capacity and activity for a sprint

In the previous recipes in this chapter, you learned about the Product backlogs. If Product Backlog Items are requirements for work, the sprint backlog is the plan to complete that work. In order to plan the work for a sprint, the Team needs a view of the total available capacity. Up until TFS 2015, the Team capacity functionality was limited to one activity per individual per sprint. In this recipe, you'll learn how to enter multiple activities and capacity per Team member in a sprint.

Getting ready

Scenario: The FabrikamFeature1 Team has the next sprint starting from tomorrow for 2 weeks. The Team is comprised of eight members, and a few individuals have planned vacations during this period. The Team wants to know the total capacity available in this sprint.

To add a new sprint and configure the start and end dates for the sprint, navigate to the FabrikamFeature1 Team control panel by browsing `http://tfs2015:8080/DefaultCollection/FabrikamTFVC/FabrikamFeature1%20Team/_admin` and switch to the **Iterations** tab. Click on the **New child** button to add a new iteration under FabrikamTFVC; double-click on the iteration to set the dates:

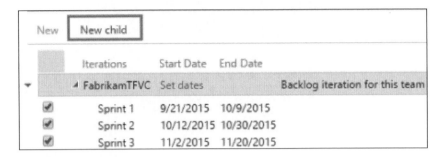

How to do it...

1. Navigate to the FabrikamFeature1 Team work hub by browsing `http://tfs2015:8080/DefaultCollection/FabrikamTFVC/FabrikamFeature1%20Team/_backlogs`. The newly added sprint will show up on the left in this page. Click on **Sprint 1** and navigate to the **Capacity** tab:

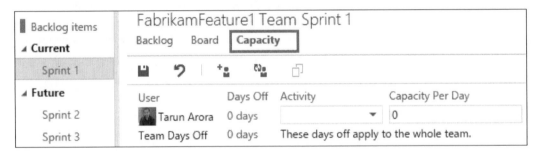

2. Click on the **Add missing team members** icon (as highlighted here) to add all the missing Team members:

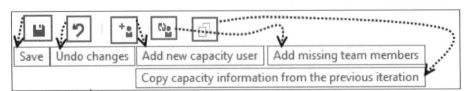

3. Set the activity and number of hours per day as indicated in the following screenshot. Use the eclipse at the end of the row to add multiple activities for the individual:

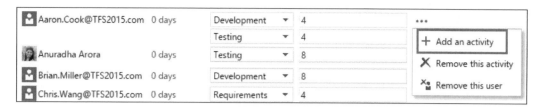

4. John isn't available to the Team for this sprint. Delete John from the list by clicking on the eclipse from the end of the row and choosing **Remove this user** from the context menu:

5. Click on the day's hyperlink next to **Team Days Off** to update the Team off days as indicated in the following screenshot:

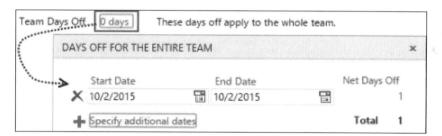

The days off for individuals can be updated by clicking the day's hyperlink in the days off column. This helps make the Team capacity even more accurate.

6. Click on the **Save** icon to save the Team's capacity. The total Team capacity, Team capacity by activity, and individual Team capacity is updated in the work details pane.

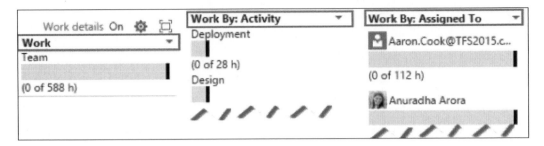

How it works...

In the *Selecting the backlog levels displayed on the Team Portal* recipe, you learned that the Team working days are configured in the Team settings window. The Team working days are used to extrapolate the total working hours in a sprint. Any Team or individual days off are subtracted from the total working hours; this helps us arrive at the Team's available capacity for a sprint. In the work details section, the activity and the individual pivot the Team capacity.

The Team capacity is useful in planning the activities for the sprint; it is equally useful in tracking progress and balancing work between Team members. To see the work details pane in action, drag **Product Backlog Item 1** into **Sprint 1**. Use the **+** sign next to the Product Backlog Item to create a few tasks as illustrated in the following screenshot:

	Title	State	Assigned To	Effort	Remaining Work
+	◢ **Product Backlog Item 1**	**Approved**	**Tarun Arora**	**34**	**34**
	PBI 1 - Task 1	To Do			15
	PBI 1 - Task 2	To Do			12
	PBI 1 - Task 3	To Do			7

Now, flip to the sprint board and assign these tasks to the Team members by changing the **Assigned To** field on the cards. You can optionally change the **Group By** field on the sprint board from Backlog Items to people. This helps you visualize the task distribution by an individual. Now, flip back to the backlog view; the work details section is updated to reflect the work allocation overall, by activity, and individual:

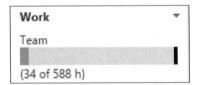

The tasks can be directly assigned to the individuals in the work allocation pane. As you can see in the following screenshot, **PBI 1 – Task 2** is being assigned to Chris by dragging the task over Chris in the work allocation pane:

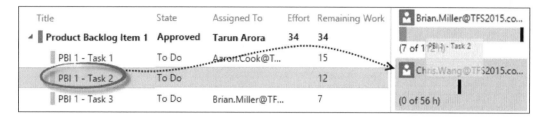

The capacity bar in the work allocation pane goes red when the Team, activity, or individual has more work allocated than the available capacity.

There's more...

A sprint burndown chart helps you identify the work completion trend in a sprint and gives you a view of the remaining work in a sprint. The sprint burndown chart in Web Portal also shows the available capacity and ideal burndown measure in the chart. More information on how the sprint burndown chart works can be found at `http://bit.ly/1MiMTlm`.

The velocity represents the total work completed by the Team in a sprint. Once the Team has completed a few sprints, you can start to see the completed work trend. This data can be useful in forecasting work for future sprints. More information on how the velocity is calculated can be found at `http://bit.ly/1H5nkoU`.

Querying Work Items by Tags

Work Item Tags are a great way to associate keywords to Work Items. These keywords act as metadata helping you group, search, and filter Work Items. In this recipe, you'll learn how to query Work Items by Tags.

Getting ready

All project valid user group members have permissions to create Tags. The stakeholder Access Level does not allow creation of Tags. Stakeholders can tag Work Items using pre-existing Tags only.

Scenario: The FabrikamTFVC Team has a backlog of Features that they want to tag by releasing a Feature that is forecasted to ship in. Features that are yet to be reviewed need to be tagged as **Pending Review**. The product owner wants to create a Work Item query for Work Items tagged for release 1 (exclude any Work Items that are marked as blocked) and share the query with the stakeholders.

A Work Item can be tagged by opening up the Work Item form and clicking on the **Add** icon. Select an existing Tag from the list or add a new Tag:

In the FabrikamTFVC Feature backlog, tag the features that need to be shipped in release 1 as **R1**, release 2 as **R2**, and the ones that are yet to be reviewed as **Pending Review**:

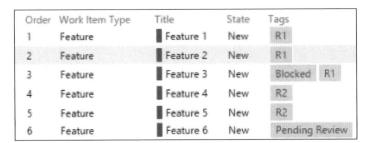

Order	Work Item Type	Title	State	Tags
1	Feature	Feature 1	New	R1
2	Feature	Feature 2	New	R1
3	Feature	Feature 3	New	Blocked R1
4	Feature	Feature 4	New	R2
5	Feature	Feature 5	New	R2
6	Feature	Feature 6	New	Pending Review

tagging the features that need to be shipped in release 1 as R1, release 2 as R2, and the ones that are yet to be reviewed as Pending Review

How to do it...

1. To review the Work Items that are being forecasted to ship in **R1**, navigate to the Features backlog in the FabrikamTFVC Team Portal. Click on the funnel to load the Tags toolbar; the Tags toolbar displays a list of Tags ordered by count:

    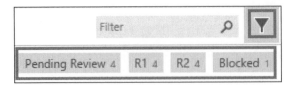

2. Click on **R1** to filter the backlog for Features tagged as R1. One of the items tagged as **R1** is also tagged as **Blocked**. Click on **All** to remove the Tag filter criteria:

3. Navigate to the queries page from the work hub. Click on the **New** icon and from the dropdown select new query. In the query editor window, add a filter criteria for Tags, as illustrated in the following screenshot:

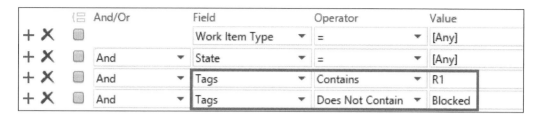

4. To copy the URL to this query without saving the query, click on the **Copy query URL** button:

5. Click on *Ctrl + C* from the pop-up window. E-mail this URL to stakeholders. This URL will directly display the Work Item results. The temporary URL self expires after 90 days:

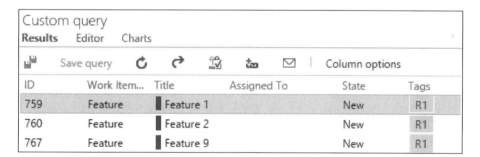

There's more...

The Kanban boards allow styling by Tags. This customization can be applied from the Team settings window in the backlog view. If multiple styling rules have been specified for a Tag, the first match takes precedence. In the following screenshot, Tag **R1** has been styled to render as yellow:

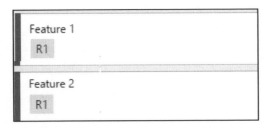

Creating charts using Work Item Queries

Work Item Query (**WIQ**) gives you the means to narrow down the Work Items you need based on your specific requirements. WIQs uses a custom language known as **Work Item Query Language** (**WIQL**); the complexity of this language is abstracted away behind the Work Item Query editor. The WIQs return a list of Work Items and, at times, you may feel the need for a visualization tool to analyze the results. Data visualization tools help spot trends that may otherwise go unnoticed. The lightweight charting feature in Team Portal allows you to use WIQs to create charts. In this recipe, you'll learn how to create and share charts using WIQs.

Getting ready

The Stakeholder Access Level does not allow authoring of charts. The Basic or Advanced Access Level is required to author charts.

Scenario: The FabrikamFeature1 Team wants to track the trend of open bugs in the application over the past 12 weeks.

Create a new WIQ using the filter criteria is illustrated in the following screenshot. Click on the **Column options** icon to include the **State** column in the query result:

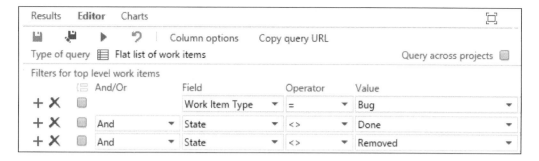

Save the query as `FabrikamFeature1 Bugs - Open` into the `My Queries` folder:

How to do it...

1. On the query page, open the **FabrikamFeature1 Bugs - Open** query and click on the **Charts** tab:

2. Click on the **+** icon to launch the new chart window, select **Area** from the **Trend** section, and name the chart `Feature1 Bugs 12 Weeks - Trend`. Change the range to 12 weeks:

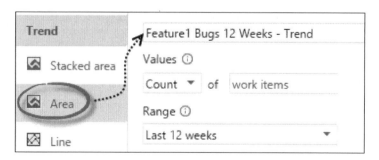

3. The color of the chart can be edited by clicking on the chart and picking the color from the picker. Click on the chart and choose the color red. Click on **OK** to close:

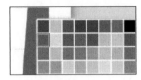

4. The new chart is loaded in the **Charts** tab:

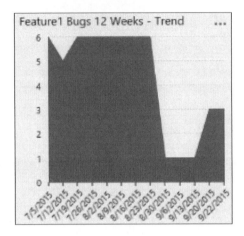

5. If you click on the eclipse on the top right of the chart you will see the option to edit or delete the chart. In order to share the chart with the Team, the underlying Work Item Query needs to be shared first. Drag the Work Item Query from the My Queries to the Shared Queries folder:

Dragging the Work Item query from My Queries to Shared Queries

6. The eclipse in the chart now gives you the option to share the chart on one of your dashboards. Select the **Technical Debt** dashboard (dashboards can be designed; review the *Configuring Dashboards in Team Project* recipe in *Chapter 1, Team Project Setup*):

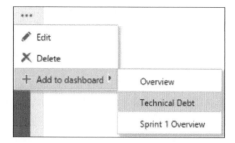

7. The chart is added to the **Technical Debt** dashboard:

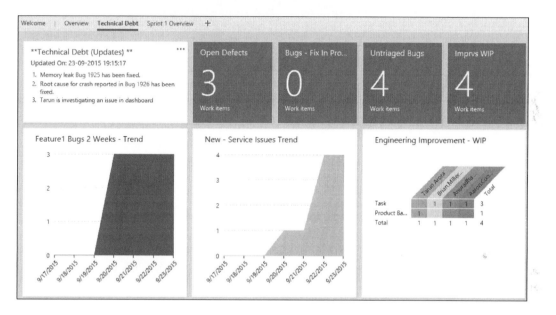

How it works...

Two kinds of charts can be authored in the Web Portal: snapshot and trend. The snapshot charts simply represent the WIQ result on the chart. The trend charts use the data in TFS to calculate the query result over the chosen period. The trend charts can show trends from up to the past year.

The charts are calculated using the Work Item data in the transactional database. When Work Items are updated, the charts reflect the updates immediately. Only Flat Work Item Queries can be used to author charts. The following warning message is shown if you try to create charts using other query types:

> You can create a chart for a flat list query, but not for a tree query or a direct links query.

Using Service Hooks to integrate with Trello boards

Traditionally, applications depending on data from TFS would continuously poll TFS to check for updates. Service Hooks, a new introduction in TFS 2015, provides the means to cascade an event in TFS to another application. When an application registers in TFS for an event notification, a secure queue is created between TFS and the application. When the event the application has registered for happens in TFS, it is published across to the application. This removes the need for applications to poll TFS for updates.

If you aren't familiar with Trello, it is a fantastic web-based tool that helps you set up a Kanban board for pretty much anything. Many organizations use Trello boards for product planning purposes. You can learn more about Trello at `https://trello.com`.

In this recipe, you'll learn how to create a Service Hook to securely publish a new feature Work Item from Team Portal in TFS to a board in Trello.

Getting ready

Permissions: To configure Service Hooks, you need to be a member of the Team Project Administrator group.

In the next few steps, we'll configure a Trello board that we'll later use to publish data to:

1. Navigate to the Trello signup page by browsing `https://trello.com/signup`. Enter your details and click on the **Create New Account** button.

2. Login to Trello with your account and create a new Team. Name the Team `Fabrikam`:

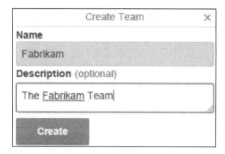

3. Create a new board and name the board `Feature Tracker`:

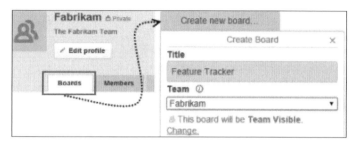

Click on Boards to create a new board for the Fabrikam Team, name the board Feature Tracker

4. Navigate to the **Feature Tracker** board and add the **To-Do**, **In Progress**, and, **Done** lists:

How to do it...

1. Navigate to the FabrikamTFVC Service Hooks in Team Administration console by browsing `http://tfs2015:8080/tfs/DefaultCollection/FabrikamTFVC/_admin/_servicehooks`:

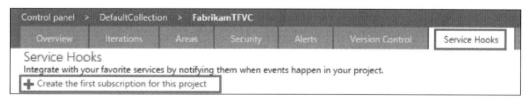

Creating the first subscription for the project

2. Click on the **Create the first subscription for this project** hyperlink and choose **Trello** from the new subscription window. Click on **Next** to navigate to the **Trigger** window.

3. In the **Trigger** window, change the selection to the **Work item created** event, set the Area Path to **FabrikamTFVC**, and the Work Item type to **Feature**. Click on **Next**:

4. In the **Settings** window, select the **Get it now** hyperlink to get an authorization token. It is issued by Trello and allows TFS to access your Trello board:

5. Click on **Log in** and authenticate with your Trello login details:

6. Copy the authorization token issued by Trello:

7. In the **Service Hooks Trigger Configuration** window, enter the details as illustrated in the following screenshot:

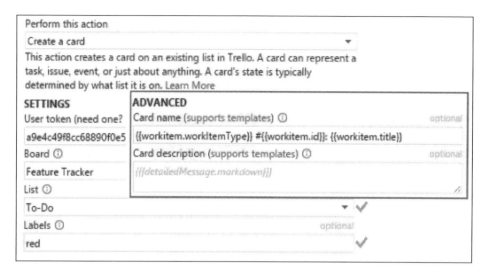

8. Click on **Test** to trigger a test using the configuration:

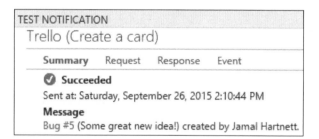

9. Click on **Finish** to complete the configuration.

10. To try out the integration between TFS and Trello, navigate to the TFVC feature backlog by browsing `http://tfs2015:8080/tfs/DefaultCollection/FabrikamTFVC/_backlogs#level=Features`. Add a new feature to the backlog, as illustrated in the following screenshot:

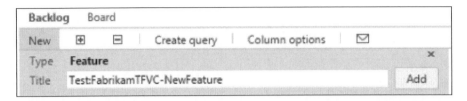

11. Now, navigate to the Trello board. The feature has also been created in the **Feature Tracker** board in Trello:

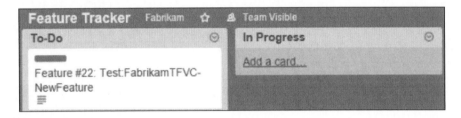

How it works...

When an event happens in TFS, all enabled subscriptions in the project are evaluated. The consumer action is performed for all matching subscriptions. In this case, the subscription to Trello is executed and results in a new card in the to-do list in the Feature Tracker board.

The Service Hook configuration screen in the Team Administration Console shows the traffic against each subscription for a period of 14 days:

The Service Hook Configuration window allows you to configure the format for the card title and description. The wizard supports placeholder expressions. In the following screenshot, the card title is configured to be in the `Work Item Type #Work Item Number: Work Item Title` format:

An important thing to remember when using Service Hooks to publish data from TFS to other systems is that TFS permissions do not cascade in to other systems. For example, the FabrikamTFVC Team has four members; however, if the Trello board is public, then the Work Item card will be visible to anyone.

There is more...

TFS also offers other Service Hooks. A full list of supported Service Hooks can be found at `http://bit.ly/1lOOZgi`.

Deleting Work Items in TFS permanently

Work Items are used for capturing, planning, and tracking work in TFS. The **History** tab in a Work Item provides a full audit trail of the changes done to that Work Item. It is not uncommon to create a Work Item that you later decide is not needed. A Work Item can be excluded from the backlog by changing the Work Item state to **Removed**; however, the Work Item isn't deleted. As it stands today, there is no provision to permanently delete a Work Item from the user interface. In this recipe, you'll learn how to use the `witadmin` command line utility to permanently delete a Work Item and all history associated to it from TFS.

 Removing Work Items using the `witadmin` command permanently removes the Work Items from the TFS database and cannot be restored nor reactivated.

Getting ready

To delete a Work Item using the `witadmin` command, you need to be a member of the Project Administrators Group or the Team Foundation Administrators Group for that collection.

How to do it...

1. Open the Visual Studio Developer Command Prompt in elevated mode and run the following command. Navigate to the `Common7\IDE` folder:

```
Administrator: Developer Command Prompt for VS2015
C:\Program Files (x86)\Microsoft Visual Studio 14.0>cd Common7\IDE_
```

2. Run the following command to permanently delete Work Item IDs: `15`, `16`, and `17`:

```
witadmin destroywi /collection:http://tfs2015:8080/tfs/
DefaultCollection /id:15,16,17
```

3.   When prompted, press *Y* to acknowledge that this action is not recoverable:

```
C:\Program Files (x86)\Microsoft Visual Studio 14.0\Common7\IDE>witadmin destroy
wi /collection:http://tfs2015:8080/tfs/DefaultCollection /id:15,16,17
Are you sure you want to destroy work item(s) 15,16,17? This action is not recov
erable. (Yes/No) y
The work item(s) were destroyed.
```

How it works...

The `witadmin` command line utility has a collection of commands and switches that allow you to import, export, and manage Work Items in a Team Project. In this recipe, we used the `detroywi` command, which permanently deletes the Work Items specified in the command.

Since a Work Item ID is unique across a collection, a Team Project name does not need to be provided; the `/collection` switch is used to specify the Team Foundation Collection the Work Item belongs to. The `/id` switch is used to specify one or more Work Item IDs. The `/noprompt` switch can be optionally used to disable the prompt for confirmation.

Using Microsoft Feedback Client to provide feedback

A constant feedback loop with stakeholders helps software development teams produce better software. At times, feedback from stakeholders gets lost because it is verbal or just isn't tracked. The feedback loop between development teams and stakeholders can be improved using tools that simplify capturing and tracking feedback. In this recipe, you'll learn how to use the Microsoft Feedback Client to provide feedback.

Getting ready

This recipe requires that you have Microsoft Feedback Client installed. The standalone installer can be downloaded at `http://bit.ly/1H5osc8`.

No license is required to submit feedback. Since there is no notion of anonymous users in TFS, the feedback can only be requested from user setup in TFS. All stakeholders with relevant permissions can submit feedback by either responding to feedback request or by optionally submitting feedback from the Microsoft Feedback Client. However, requesting feedback and viewing submitted feedback requires an advanced license.

In the next few steps, you will learn how to raise a feedback request from the Team's Web Portal:

1. Navigate to the FabrikamFeature1 Team's Web Portal. From the other links section, click on **Request feedback**:

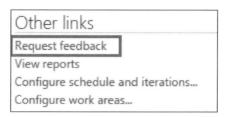

 If you don't see the **Request feedback** hyperlink, your access type isn't set up correctly. Add yourself to the **Advanced** access type.

2. This will launch the **Feedback Request** window. The feedback request form includes a section to provide information on how to launch the application, a section to specify what the feedback should focus on, and last but not least, a section to specify the list of users you want to solicit feedback from. Fill out the feedback request form as illustrated in the following screenshot.

3. Enter the names of people you would like to request feedback from:

 You cannot request feedback from a user who does not have TFS access.

4. Specify how the users need to access the application. The available choices are **Web Application**, **Remote Machine**, and **Client Application**. This generates an actionable link that the user can click on to launch the application directly from the feedback request:

5. Provide direction by specifying the area you would like feedback on. Multiple feedback items can be added by clicking on the **Add feedback item** hyperlink:

6. Click on the preview icon to preview the feedback request:

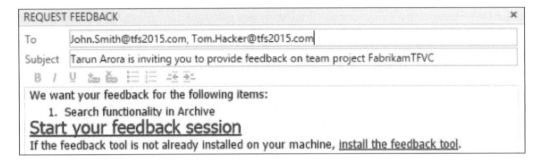

7. On clicking **Send**, the feedback request is sent to John and Tom.

How to do it...

1. The stakeholder receives the feedback request e-mail. The feedback click can be started by clicking on the **Start your feedback session** hyperlink from within the e-mail. As the session starts, you'll notice that instructions filled out in the feedback request form are loaded in the feedback session:

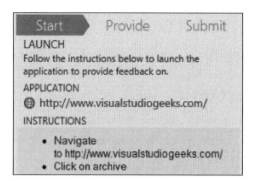

2. The Microsoft feedback client allows screen and voice recording as well as the inclusion of screenshots and attachments, along with comments, during the feedback capture process:

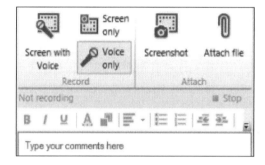

3. An overall rating can also be added to the feedback response:

4. Once the feedback response has been completed, the feedback response tile on Team Portal reflects this:

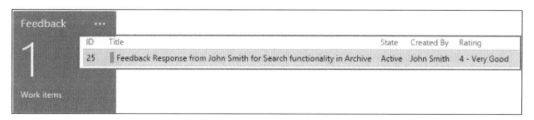

The feedback response

How it works...

The feedback response is recorded in a Work Item. As illustrated in the following screenshot, the Work Item has all the details captured via the Microsoft Feedback Client. The feedback response, being a Work Item, gives you all the benefits of a Work Item. We have already covered a few in this chapter, such as tracking, tagging, pinning, dash boarding, and reporting:

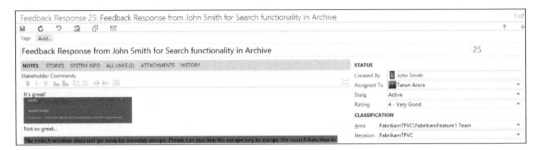

The feedback response is recorded in a Work Item. The Status section of the Work Item shows who the feedback item was created by, who it is assigned to, status, and over all rating

4

Building Your Application

"Measuring programming progress by lines of code is like measuring aircraft building progress by weight."

–Bill Gates

TFS has introduced a new build system in TFS 2015 called TFBuild. In this chapter, you'll learn the following:

- ► Configuring TFBuild Agent, Pool, and Queues
- ► Setting up a TFBuild Agent using an unattended installation
- ► Creating a continuous integration build definition in TFBuild
- ► Pinning a build badge to the welcome page in Team Portal
- ► Managing build resources using role-based access
- ► Using the build retention policy to automate build deletion
- ► Using user capabilities to identify a build agent in a pool
- ► Version DLLs in build output with build number
- ► Creating a new build task using the TFBuild Extensibility framework
- ► Integrating SonarQube with TFBuild to manage technical debt
- ► Building GitHub code repositories with TFBuild

Introduction

As a developer, compiling code and running unit tests gives you an assurance that your code changes haven't had an impact on the existing codebase. Integrating your code changes into the source control repository enables other users to validate their changes with yours. As a best practice, Teams integrate changes into the shared repository several times a day to reduce the risk of introducing breaking changes or worse, overwriting each other's.

Continuous integration (**CI**) is a development practice that requires developers to integrate code into a shared repository several times a day. Each check-in is verified by an automated build, allowing Teams to detect problems early.

The automated build that runs as part of the CI process is often referred to as the CI build. There isn't a clear definition of what the CI build should do, but at the very minimum, it is expected to compile code and run unit tests. Running the CI build on a non-developer remote workspace helps identify the dependencies that may otherwise go unnoticed into the release process. We can talk endlessly about the benefits of CI; the key here is that it enables you to have potentially deployable software at all times.

Deployable software is the most tangible asset to customers.

Moving from concept to application, in this chapter, you'll learn how to leverage the build tooling in TFS to set up a quality-focused CI process. But first, let's have a little introduction to the build system in TFS. The following image illustrates the three generations of build systems in TFS:

Generation	Name	Configuration	Introduced In
Generation 1	MS Build	XML	TFS 2005
Generation 2	XAML Build	WWF	TFS 2010
Generation 3	TFBuild	JSON	TFS 2015

TFS has gone through three generations of build systems. The very first was MSBuild using XML for configuration; the next one was XAML using Windows Workflow Foundation for configuration, and now, there's TFBuild using JSON for configuration. The XAML-based build system will continue to be supported in TFS 2015. No automated migration path is available from XAML build to TFBuild. This is generally because of the difference in the architecture between the two build systems.

The new build system in TFS is called **Team Foundation Build** (**TFBuild**). It is an extensible task-based execution system with a rich web interface that allows authoring, queuing, and monitoring builds. TFBuild is fully cross platform with the underlying build agents that are capable of running natively on both Windows and non-Windows platforms. TFBuild provides out-of-the-box integration with Centralized Version Control such as TFVC and Distributed Version Controls such as Git and GitHub. TFBuild supports building .NET, Java, Android, and iOS applications. All the recipes in this chapter are based on TFBuild.

TFBuild is a task orchestrator that allows you to run any build engine, such as Ant, CMake, Gradle, Gulp, Grunt, Maven, MSBuild, Visual Studio, Xamarin, XCode, and so on. TFBuild supports Work Item integration, publishing drops, and publishing test execution results into the TFS that is independent of the build engine that you choose. The build agents are xCopyable and do not require any installation. The agents are auto-updating in nature; there's no need to update every agent in your infrastructure:

TFBuild offers a rich web-based interface. It does not require Visual Studio to author or modify a build definition. From simple to complex, all build definitions can easily be created in the web portal. The web interface is accessible from any device and any platform:

The build definition can be authored from the web portal directly

A build definition is a collection of tasks. A task is simply a build step. Build definition can be composed by dragging and dropping tasks. Each task supports **Enabled**, **Continue on error**, and **Always run** flags making it easier to manage build definitions as the task list grows:

The build system supports invoking PowerShell, batch, command line, and shell scripts. All out-of-the-box tasks are open source. If a task does not satisfy your requirements, you can download the task from GitHub at `https://github.com/Microsoft/vso-agent-tasks` and customize it. If you can't find a task, you can easily create one. You'll learn more about custom tasks in this chapter.

Changes to build definitions can be saved as drafts. Build definitions maintain a history of all changes in the **History** tab. A side-by-side comparison of the changes is also possible. Comments entered when changing the build definition show up in the change history:

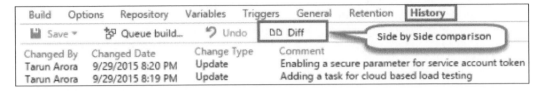

Build definitions can be saved as templates. This helps standardize the use of certain tasks across new build definitions:

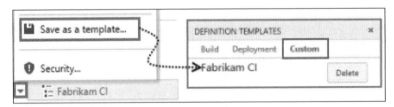

An existing build definition can be saved as a template

Multiple triggers can be set for the same build, including CI triggers and multiple scheduled triggers:

Rule-based retention policies support the setting up of multiple rules. Retention can be specified by "days" or "number" of the builds:

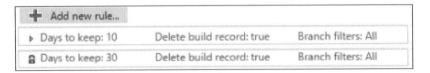

The build output logs are displayed in web portal in real time. The build log can be accessed from the console even after the build gets completed:

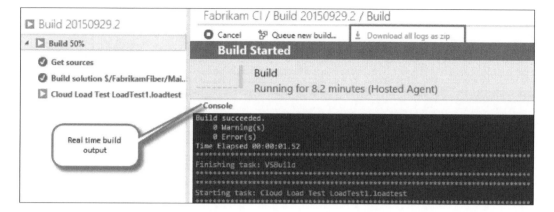

The build reports have been revamped to offer more visibility into the build execution, and among other things, the test results can now directly be accessed from the web interface. The .trx file does not need to be downloaded into Visual Studio to view the test results. We'll be covering this in detail in *Chapter 5, Testing Your Application*:

Outcome	Test Case Title	Duration	Error Message
✕ Failed	LoadFromFileTest	0:00:02.422	Test method Infrastructure.Data.Tests.
✓ Passed	ShouldAllowPlantsToBeAdded	0:00:00.002	
✓ Passed	ShouldImplementRepositoryInterface	0:00:00.000	

Run 66 - VSTest Test Run release any cpu
Run summary   Test results   Filter

Create bug   Update analysis

The old build system had restrictions on one Team Project Collection per build controller and one controller per build machine. TFBuild removes this restriction and supports the reuse of queues across multiple Team Project Collections. The following image illustrates the architecture of the new build system:

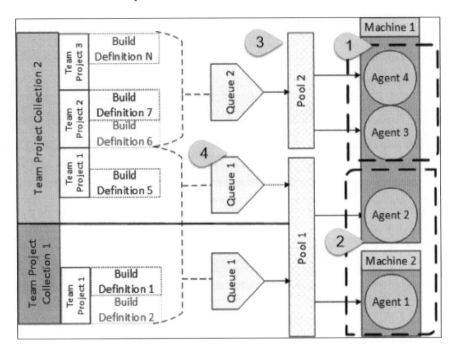

In the preceding diagram, we observe the following:

▶ Multiple agents can be configured on one machine

▶ Agents from across different machines can be grouped into a pool

▶ Each pool can have only one queue

▶ One queue can be used across multiple Team Project Collections

To demonstrate the capabilities of TFBuild, we'll use the FabrikamTFVC and FabrikamGit Team Projects. If you don't already have these Team Projects, follow the *Creating a Team Project using the Scrum Template* recipe, in *Chapter 1, Team Project Setup*.

Configuring TFBuild Agent, Pool, and Queues

In this recipe, you'll learn how to configure agents and create pools and queues. You'll also learn how a queue can be used across multiple Team Project Collections.

Getting ready

Scenario: At Fabrikam, the FabrikamTFVC and FabrikamGit Team Projects need their own build queues. The FabrikamTFVC Teams build process can be executed on a Windows Server. The FabrikamGit Team build process needs both Windows and OS X. The Teams want to set up three build agents on a Windows Server; one build agent on an OS X machine. The Teams want to group two Windows Agents into a Windows Pool for FabrikamTFVC Team and group one Windows and one Mac Agent into another pool for the FabrikamGit Team:

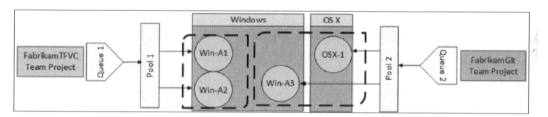

Permission: To configure a build agent, you should be in the Build Administrators Group.

The prerequisites for setting up the build agent on a Windows-based machine are as follows:

▶   The build agent should have a supporting version of Windows. The list of supported versions is listed at `https://msdn.microsoft.com/en-us/Library/vs/alm/TFS/administer/requirements#Operatingsystems`.

▶   The build agent should have Visual Studio 2013 or 2015.

▶   The build agent should have PowerShell 3 or a newer version.

A build agent is configured for your TFS as part of the server installation process if you leave the **Configure the build service to start automatically** option selected:

For the purposes of this recipe, we'll configure the agents from scratch. Delete the default pool or any other pool you have by navigating to the **Agent pools** option in the TFS Administration Console `http://tfs2015:8080/tfs/_admin/_AgentPool`:

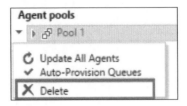

How to do it

1. Log into the Windows machine that you desire to set the agents upon. Navigate to the **Agent pools** in the TFS Administration Console by browsing to `http://tfs2015:8080/tfs/_admin/_AgentPool`. Click on **New Pool**, enter the pool name as `Pool 1`, and uncheck **Auto-Provision Queue in Project Collections**:

2. Click on the **Download agent** icon. Copy the downloaded folder into `E:\` and unzip it into `E:\Win-A1`. You can use any drive; however, it is recommended to use the non-operating system drive:

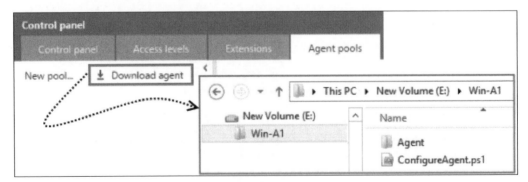

3. Run the PowerShell console as an administrator and change the current path in PowerShell to the location of the agent in this case `E:\Win-A1`. Call the `ConfigureAgent.ps1` script in the PowerShell console and click on *Enter*. This will launch the Build Agent Configuration utility:

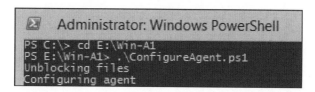

4. Enter the configuration details as illustrated in the following screenshot:

```
Enter the name for this agent (default is Agent-TFS2015) Win-A1
Enter the URL for the Team Foundation Server (default is ) http://tfs2015:8080/t
fs
Configure this agent against which agent pool? (default pool name is 'default')
Pool 1
Enter the path of the work folder for this agent (default is 'E:\Win-A1\_work')

Would you like to install the agent as a Windows Service (Y/N) (default is N) y
Enter the name of the user account to use for the service (default is NT AUTHORI
TY\LOCAL SERVICE)
Installing service vsoagent.tfs2015.Win-A1...
Service vsoagent.tfs2015.Win-A1 has been successfully installed.
Creating EventLog source vsoagent.tfs2015.Win-A1 in log Application...
```

 It is recommended to install the build agent as a service; however, you have an option to run the agent as an interactive process. This is great when you want to debug a build or want to temporarily use a machine as a build agent.

The configuration process creates a JSON settings file; it creates the working and diagnostics folders:

_diag	10/1/2015 6:45 PM	File folder	
_work	10/1/2015 6:45 PM	File folder	
Agent	10/1/2015 6:25 PM	File folder	
ConfigureAgent.ps1	10/1/2015 6:15 PM	Windows PowerS...	14 KB
settings.json	10/1/2015 6:45 PM	JSON File	1 KB

5. Refresh the **Agent pools** page in the TFS Administration Console. The newly configured agent shows up under **Pool 1**:

6. Repeat steps 2 to 5 to configure **Win-A2** in **Pool 1**. Repeat steps 1 to 5 to configure **Win-A3** in **Pool 2**. It is worth highlighting that each agent runs from its individual folder:

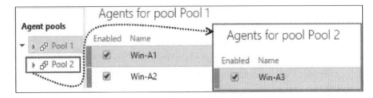

7. Now, log into the Mac machine and launch terminal:

```
                   tarunarora — bash — 80×24
Last login: Fri Oct  2 13:10:28 on ttys000
tarun-Air:~ tarunarora$
```

8. Install the agent installer globally by running the commands illustrated here. You will be required to enter the machine password to authorize the install:

```
tarun-Air:~ tarunarora$ sudo npm install vsoagent-installer -g
Password:
```

This will download the agent in the user profile, shown as follows:

The summary of actions performed when the agent is downloaded

9. Run the following command to install the agent installer globally for the user profile:

```
:~ tarunarora$ sudo chown -R $USER ~/.npm
```

10. Running the following command will create a new directory called `osx-A1` for the agent; create the agent in the directory:

```
:~ tarunarora$ mkdir osx-A1
:~ tarunarora$ cd osx-a1
:osx-a1 tarunarora$ vsoagent-installer
```

11. The agent installer has been copied from the user profile into the agent directory, shown as follows:

```
Installing agent to /Users/tarunarora/osx-A1
Copying:  /usr/local/lib/node_modules/vsoagent-installer/agent /Users/tarunarora/osx-A1
Copying:  /usr/local/lib/node_modules/vsoagent-installer/node_modules /Users/tarunarora/osx-A1
making scripts executable
Done.
```

12. Pass the following illustrated parameters to configure the agent:

```
tarun-Air:osx-a1 tarunarora$ node agent/vsoagent
Enter alternate username > tarunarora
Enter alternate password >
Enter server url > https://geeks.visualstudio.com
Enter agent name (enter sets Anuradhas-Air)  > OSX-1
Enter agent pool name (enter sets default)  > Pool 2
successful connect as Tarun Arora
Retrieved agent pool: Pool 2 (12)
```

13. This completes the configuration of the xPlatform agent on the Mac. Refresh the **Agent pools** page in the TFS Administration Console to see the agent appear in **Pool 2**:

14. The build agent has been configured at the Team Foundation Server level. In order to use the build agent for a Team Project Collection, a mapping between the build agent and Team Project Collection needs to be established. This is done by creating queues. To configure queues, navigate to the Collection Administration Console by browsing to `http://tfs2015:8080/tfs/DefaultCollection/_admin/_BuildQueue`. From the **Build** tab, click on **New queue**; this dialog allows you to reference the pool as a queue:

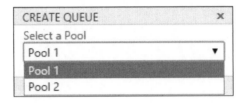

15. Map **Pool 1** as **Queue 1** and **Pool 2** as **Queue 2** as shown here:

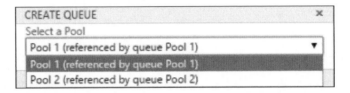

16. The TFBuild Agent, Pools, and Queues are now ready to use. The green bar before the agent name and queue in the administration console indicates that the agent and queues are online.

How it works...

To test the setup, create a new build definition by navigating to the FabrikamTFVC Team Project Build hub by browsing to `http://tfs2015:8080/tfs/DefaultCollection/FabrikamTFVC/_build`. Click on the **Add a new build definition** icon. In the **General** tab, you'll see that the queues show up under the **Queue** dropdown menu. This confirms that the queues have been correctly configured and are available for selection in the build definition:

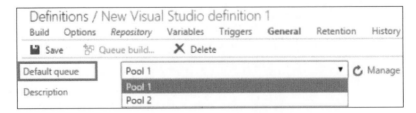

Pools can be used across multiple Team Project Collections. As illustrated in the following screenshot, in Team Project Collection 2, clicking on the **New queue...** shows that the existing pools are already mapped in the default collection:

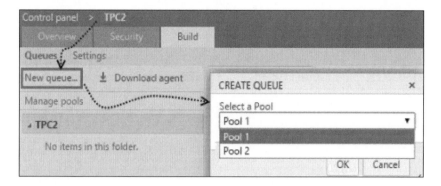

Setting up a TFBuild Agent using an unattended installation

The new build framework allows the unattended setup of build agents by injecting a set of parameter values via script. This technique can be used to spin up new agents to be attached into an existing agent pool. In this recipe, you'll learn how to configure and unconfigure a build agent via script.

Getting ready

Scenario: The FabrikamTFVC Team wants the ability to install, configure, and unconfigure a build agent directly via script without having to perform this operation using the Team Portal.

Permission: To configure a build agent, you should be in the Build Administrators Group.

Download the build agent as discussed in the earlier recipe *Configuring TFBuild Agent, Pool, and Queues*. Copy the folder to `E:\Agent`. The script refers to this `Agent` folder.

How to do it...

1. Launch PowerShell in the elevated mode and execute the following command:

```
.\Agent\VsoAgent.exe /Configure /RunningAsService /
ServerUrl:"http://tfs2015:8080/tfs" /
WindowsServiceLogonAccount:svc_build /WindowsServiceLogonPasswor
d:xxxxx /Name:WinA-10 /PoolName:"Pool 1" /WorkFolder:"E:\Agent\_
work" /StartMode:Automatic
```

Replace the value of the username and password accordingly.

Executing the script will result in the following output:

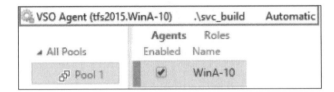

2. The script installs an agent by the name **WinA-10** as Windows Service running as `svc_build`. The agent is added to **Pool 1**:

3. To unconfigure **WinA-10**, run the following command in an elevated PowerShell prompt:

```
.\Agent\VsoAgent.exe /Unconfigure "vsoagent.tfs2015.WinA-10"
```

> To unconfigure, script needs to be executed from outside the scope of the `Agent` folder. Running the script from within the `Agent` folder scope will result in an error message.

```
PS E:\Agent> .\Agent\VsoAgent.exe /Unconfigure "vsoagent.tfs2015.WinA-10"
Removing EventLog source vsoagent.tfs2015.WinA-10.
Service vsoagent.tfs2015.WinA-10 is being removed from the system...
Service vsoagent.tfs2015.WinA-10 was successfully removed from the system.
Attempt to stop service vsoagent.tfs2015.WinA-10.
```

How it works...

The new build agent natively allows configuration via script. A new capability called **Personal Access Token** (**PAT**) is due for release in the future updates of TFS 2015. PAT allows you to generate a personal OAuth token for a specific scope; it replaces the need to key in passwords into configuration files.

Creating a continuous integration build definition in TFBuild

In this recipe, you'll learn how to author a continuous integration build definition.

Getting ready

Scenario: The FabrikamTFVC Team wants to set up a build definition that is executed on every code check-in. The Team wants to run this build definition using **Pool 1**, which has the required frameworks installed to compile the code and execute unit tests.

To create a new build definition, you need to have the build definition author or builder's permissions. This permission can be granted by adding yourself to the Build Administrators Security Group.

How to do it...

1. Navigate to the **Build** hub in FabrikamTFVC Team Portal by browsing to `http://tfs2015:8080/tfs/DefaultCollection/FabrikamTFVC/_build`. Click on the **+** icon to create a new build definition. Select **Visual Studio** from the **DEFINITION TEMPLATES** window:

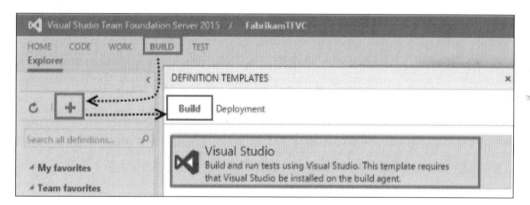

This loads an empty build definition called **New Visual Studio definition 1**:

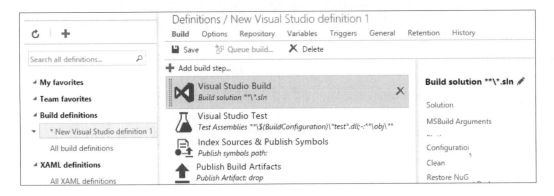

2. Navigate to the **General** tab, set the fields as illustrated in the following screenshot:

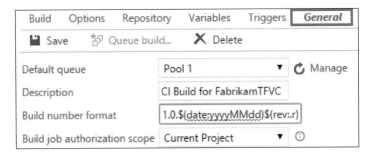

A build job timeout allows you to enter the minimum time a build job requires to execute, before it is cancelled by the server. An empty or 0 value in this field signifies an infinite timeout.

The default value of **Build job authorization scope** is **Project Collection**. You should only use Project Collection if the build definition needs to access resources outside the scope of the Team Project.

The default value of **Build number format** is $(date:yyyyMMdd)$(rev:.r). As a development best practice, it is always advisable to stamp the DLLs of the build output with the build number. This approach won't work with the default build number format. Change the build number format to an assembly version format such as 1.0.$(date:yyyyMMdd)$(rev:.r). A complete list of build number macros can be found at https://msdn.microsoft.com/en-us/library/hh190719.aspx.

3. Navigate to the **Repository** tab. It allows you to specify source control settings for the build. Set the fields as illustrated in the following screenshot. The **Clean** field forces the server workspace to be recreated for each build. In general, cleaning the workspace prior to building will take more time to build a solution. To only pull incremental changes into the build workspace, set the value to **false**. Label sources labels the version of the code build by the build definition. The **Label format** field specified here will create the label names as `BuildDefinitionName_BuildNumber`:

4. Navigate to the **Triggers** tab and check CI. Configure the filters as illustrated in the screenshot here. The batch changes setting allows multiple check-ins queued for the same build to be bundled together into a single CI build:

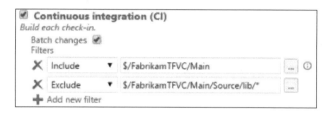

At least one filter needs to be applied when configuring CI. Any check-ins done under the path set as included will trigger the build definition. The **Exclude** filter is used to exclude check-ins from under the specified path to trigger the build definition. In this case, any check-ins under the `$/FabrikamTFVC/Main/Source/lib` folder will not trigger this build definition. Navigate to the **Options** tab and set the fields as illustrated in the following screenshot. **MultiConfiguration** allows you to build more than one configuration as a part of the same pass. It is recommended to build multiple configurations as a part of the same build definition specifically if the code being built has platform dependencies. Checking **Parallel** allows the build for multiple configurations to be executed in parallel:

5. Now, navigate to the **Build** tab. The new build engine manifests itself as an orchestrator. The steps orchestrated need to be specified in the **Build** tab. As you can see in the **Build** tab, four build steps namely **Visual Studio Build**, **Visual Studio Test**, **Index Sources And Publish Symbols**, and **Publish Build Artifacts** are pre-added for you through the chosen template. Click on **Visual Studio Build** and update the fields as illustrated in the following screenshot:

The Build tab includes the Visual Studio Build, Visual Studio Test, Index Sources And Publish Symbols, and Publish Build Artifact tasks. These tasks are pre added on creating a new build definition using the Visual Studio Build Template.

6. Select the path to the solution that you wish to compile. Leaving it to the default value of `**/*.sln` will build all solutions under the path specified in the **Repositories** tab.

7. The **MSBuild Arguments** textbox allows you to pass additional MS Build Arguments. A complete list of MS Build Arguments can be found at `https://msdn.microsoft.com/en-us/library/ms164311.aspx`.

8. You'll notice that the platform and configuration are preconfigured with a variable. Variables provide you with the ability to centrally manage values rather than hard coding them into the build definition. Variables also provide you with the ability to overwrite the values at run time. The values for these variables are specified in the **Variables** tab; you can optionally navigate to the **Variables** tab to overwrite the default values injected by the template.

9. Selecting the **Restore NuGet Packages** checkbox allows the build system to download any dependant NuGet packages during the build execution time.

 The auto restore of NuGet packages is quite a useful feature; this allows you to avoid having to check-in dependency packages into TFS.

10. The **Advanced** settings allow you to specify a specific version of MSBuild or Visual Studio to compile against your code. The default is x86.

11. The **Control Options** textarea allows you to disable a specific build definition; this option also allows you to specify the behavior on build errors. You can choose to stop the build process on encountering the first build error.

12. Next, click on the **Visual Studio Test** step; you will see the list of configurable variables on the left panel. Similar to the build step, this step also offers you the ability to choose the version of VS Test Runner to use for executing the tests. The **Advanced** section also allows you to specify the path to custom test adapters. This is extremely useful if you are planning to use a non-VS Test Runner to execute the tests. Check the **Code Coverage Enabled** checkbox, and leave the defaults in the other fields:

Check the code coverage enabled checkbox, and leave the defaults in other fields

- ❑ **Test Assembly**: The **Test Assembly** field should be used to specify the path to the test projects that you want the VS Test Runner to execute. The field accepts wildcards; as per the default, all the projects that have `*test*.dll` as an output will be picked up by the test runner for execution.

- ❑ **Test Filter criteria**: This field allows you to run selective tests using a specific filter. A run settings file can be passed in the **Run Settings File** field. This is useful if the Development Team wants to execute the tests using the same test settings on developer machines and build servers. Test run parameters specified in the test settings file can be overwritten using the **Override TestRun Parameters** field.

13. Next, click on **Index Sources And Publish Symbols**. During the source code compilation process, the build engine generated symbol files. The symbol files are the `.PDB` files that match a particular assembly and contain information used by debugging tools. The symbol files for the .NET assemblies contain source file names, line numbers, and local variable names. The build definition is capable of publishing the symbols to the symbol server. The developers can point to this symbol server in Visual Studio; this automatically downloads the correct symbols during debugging. Follow the instructions here to set up a file share-based symbol server if you don't already have one: `https://msdn.microsoft.com/en-us/library/windows/hardware/mt146873(v=vs.85).aspx`.

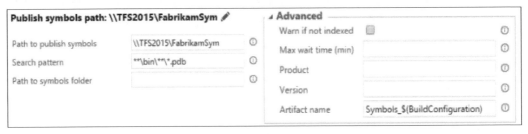

Set the artifact name as Symbols_$(BuildConfiguration)

Last but not least, navigate to the **Publish Build Artifacts** task. This task allows you to specify the settings where the build artifacts are published. Choose the server to store the artifact on your TFS. This is the best and simplest option in most cases:

In the Publish Artifact, set the Artifact Type as Server

14. Click on **Save** and give the build definition a name; add a comment as illustrated in the following screenshot:

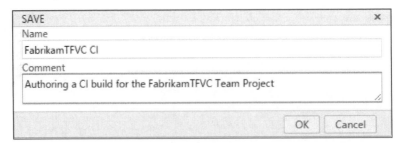

15. Click on **Queue Build** to manually trigger a new build for this build definition. The Build Output Console starts to show the build agent activity in real time:

```
 Console    Logs

 *********************************************************************
 Starting: Build (any cpu,debug)
 *********************************************************************
 Executing the following commandline:
 E:\Agent\agent\worker\vsoWorker.exe   /name:Worker-33d0513c-6bcd-4a1f-802d-08b06a
 tFolder:"E:\Agent" /logger:Forwarding,1.0.0;Verbosity=Verbose,Name=Agent11-819d1
 -802d-08b06ae368fd
 *********************************************************************
 Starting: Get sources
 *********************************************************************
 Syncing repository: FabrikamTFVC (TFVC)
```

How it works...

As you would have noticed, the out-of-the-box experience after selecting the Visual Studio Template preconfigures most of the settings for you giving you the ability to set up your CI process in next to no time.

There's more...

The build output has also been revamped in the new build framework. As illustrated in the following screenshot, the build output includes the test results and code coverage results. The output also includes a separate view for timeline and artifacts for easier access:

Summary	Timeline	Artifacts

Build details

Definition	FabrikamTFVC CI (edit)
Source branch	$/FabrikamTFVC
Source version	30
Requested by	Tarun Arora
Queued	Thursday, October 15, 2015 1:45:45 PM
Started	Thursday, October 15, 2015 1:45:46 PM
Finished	Thursday, October 15, 2015 1:47:30 PM

Test results ↻

No test runs available for this build.
Enable automation in your build definition by adding one of the CI or CD tasks available Test, Visual Studio Test using Test Agent

Code coverage ↻

No build code coverage data available.
Enable code coverage via a test task in your build definition eg. Visual Studio Test

Pinning a build badge to the welcome page in Team Portal

Build badge is a dynamically generated image showing the status of the last build for a build definition. In this recipe, you'll learn how to pin a build badge to a Dashboard in Team Portal.

Getting ready

To modify a build definition, you need to have the build definition author or builder's permissions. This permission can be granted by adding yourself to the Build Administrators Security Group.

How to do it...

1. Navigate to the **Build** hub for FabrikamTFVC Team Project; browse to `http://tfs2015:8080/tfs/DefaultCollection/FabrikamTFVC/_build`.

2. Locate the build definition **FabrikamTFVC CI** from under the build definitions menu in the left panel and choose to edit the build definition.

3. Navigate to the **General** tab of the build definition and check the option **Badge enabled**:

4. Click on **Save** to update the changes in order to enable the badge build definition. Upon saving the changes, a new hyperlink **Show url...** appears next to the **Badge enabled** field. Click on the **Show url...** hyperlink and copy the hyperlink:

5. Navigate to the **Welcome** page of the FabrikamTFVC Team in Team Portal by browsing to `http://tfs2015:8080/tfs/DefaultCollection/FabrikamTFVC/_welcome`.

6. Edit `README.md` and paste the build badge URL. Save the changes. In the following screenshot, the current status of the FabrikamTFVC build is represented in red as **Failed**. A passing build is represented in green. A partially successful build is in orange:

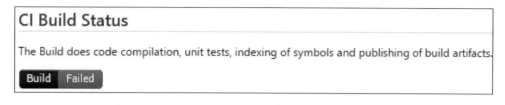

How it works...

The Team Foundation Server Build API exposes a public endpoint for the status of the last build. The URL calls into this endpoint by passing the build definition ID requesting for the build definition status to be rendered as a badge `_apis/public/build/definitions/94fb1544-b441-45f5-a54d-466fc5d66817/4/badge`.

There is more

The build definitions now support saving changes as drafts. This can be done by choosing the **Save as a draft** option, as illustrated in the screenshot here:

The build definitions, which are also saved as a draft, support the queue build function. Builds generated by draft build definitions contain the `DRAFT` keyword in the build name:

This gives you a great way to validate build definition changes before sharing them broadly.

Managing build resources using role-based access

The old build permissions model for build resources was flat, meaning you could grant someone permission to manage all or no build resources. In the new build system, the security is a proper hierarchy, so you can control permissions on a queue-by-queue or pool-by-pool basis. The build system provides a "role-based access control" instead of exposing the underlying permissions directly. In this recipe, you'll learn how to permission build resources at the pool and queue levels.

Getting ready

Scenario: To manage the all pools membership, you need to be a member of the Team Foundation Administrators Group. Membership to Team Project Collection Administrator Group is required to manage permissions for individual pools. In order to manage the permissions for the queues, you need to be a member of the Project Collection Build Administrators Group. Build Definition Administration requires membership to the Build Administrators Group.

How to do it...

1. Navigate to the **Agent** tab in the Account Administration Console by browsing to `http://tfs2015:8080/tfs/_admin/_AgentPool`. Click on **All Pools** and add build agent service accounts that you intend to use globally across TFS into the **Agent Pool Service Accounts** role:

To scope a service account only to **Pool 1**, click on **Pool 1**, select the **Agent Pool Service Accounts** option, and click on **Add...** to add the account:

2. Navigate to the **Agent queues** tab in the Default Project Collection scope in Administration Console by browsing to `http://tfs2015:8080/tfs/DefaultCollection/_admin/_AgentQueue`. Click on **All Queues**. The role membership for all queues administrators, creators, and users can be set from here:

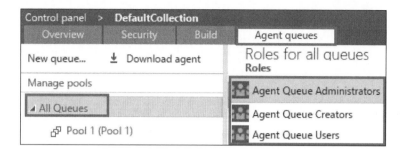

Administration, creation, and user roles at the Pool 1 level scope these permissions at the Pool 1 level only. These can be set by clicking on **Pool 1** and adding the users and groups to the relevant roles.

How it works...

As illustrated in the following figure, the new build system contains a hierarchical role-based access control model. In the next section, we'll go through each of the roles and accesses that they offer:

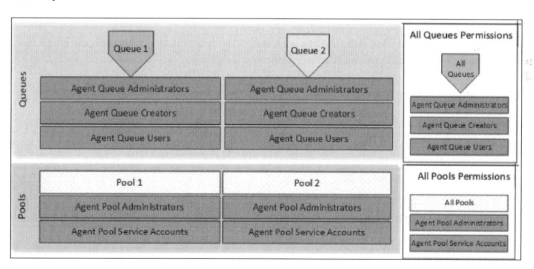

- ► **All Queues**:
  - ❑ **Agent Queue Administrators**: Users in this role have the ability to manage all the queues within the Project Collection.

- **Agent Queue Creators**: Users in this role have the ability to create new queues. If there is no pool with the same name as the queue, one will be provisioned at the queue creation time, and the caller will be added as an administrator of both the queue and the corresponding pool. If a pool with the same name already exists, the caller must have the **Manage** permission (must be a pool administrator) on the pool to create a new queue that uses the pool.

- **Agent Queue Users**: Users in this role have the ability to use all the queues for the entire collection. Use means they can assign the queues to be used by definitions in the build space.

▶ **Individual Queues**:

- **Agent Queue Administrators**: This is same as the previous role, but the permissions are restricted to a specific queue.

- **Agent Queue Users**: This is same as the previous role, but the permissions are restricted to a specific queue.

▶ **All Pools**:

- **Agent Pool Administrators**: Users in this role have the ability to manage all the pools within the entire account.

- **Agent Pool Service Accounts**: Users in this role have the ability to connect to the pool and receive messages regarding build jobs, including control messages such as "update yourself" and "cancel this job".

▶ **Individual Pools**:

- **Agent Pool Administrators**: This is same as the previous role, but the permissions are restricted to the specific pool.

- **Agent Pool Service Accounts**: This is same as the previous role, but the permissions are restricted to the specific pool.

Using the build retention policy to automate build deletion

The build retention policy allows you to delete older builds including its output and related artifacts using a set of rules. The build retention policy in the old build system had two drawbacks:

▶ The retention policy could only be applied per build definition

▶ The retention was based on the number of builds only

The new build system allows a global retention policy; this makes it easier to administer build retention. The new system allows retention by the age of build, making it easier to create meaningful retention rules. In this recipe, you'll learn how to apply the build retention policy both globally at the Team Project Collection level and locally at the build definition level.

Getting ready

To administer build resources for the collection, you need to be a member of the Project Collection Build Administrators Group.

Scenario: The Fabrikam Team would like to enforce a default retention policy of 20 days across all build definitions in the Default Team Project Collection. The FabrikamTFVC Team only wants to keep builds from FabrikamTFVC CI build definition for 5 days. At Fabrikam, all the builds older than 45 days that haven't been marked to be retained indefinitely should be deleted.

The retention policy applies to all builds in a Team Project Collection. There may be a few builds that you would like to retain longer than the maximum retention enforced by the global policy. This can be achieved by marking a build for indefinite retention. Browse to the specific build that you would like to exclude from the retention policy. Then, right-click on the build and set the **Retain indefinitely** flag on the build:

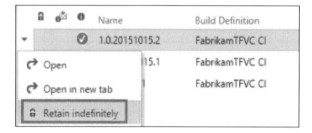

How to do it...

Navigate to the **Build** tab in the Administration Console for the Default Project Collection by browsing to `http://tfs2015:8080/tfs/DefaultCollection/_admin/_buildQueue`.

In the **Maximum Retention Policy** section, update the **Days to keep** textbox to `45`. This will enforce a maximum retention of 45 days for all builds excluding those marked as retain indefinitely. Click on **Save changes** to apply the changes:

Maximum Retention Policy	
Days to keep:	45
Delete build record:	true
Delete test results:	true
Branch filters:	All

In the **Default Retention Policy** section, update the **Days to keep** textbox to 20 days. This setting is cascaded to all the newly created build definitions. Click on **Save changes** to apply the changes:

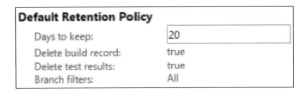

Navigate to the FabrikamTFVC CI build definition, and then to the **Retention** tab. Update the value of **Days to keep** to 5 days. A retention rule can be deleted by clicking the delete icon; a new retention rule can be added by clicking on the **Add new rule...** icon:

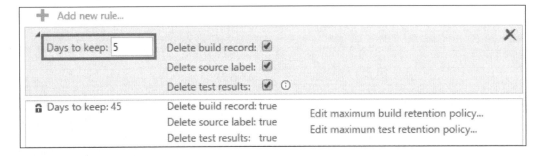

How it works...

TFS has a set of background jobs that are scheduled to run to manage various operations in TFS. The build retention policy is orchestrated by the TFS Agent; only those builds that have been marked as retain indefinitely will be excluded from the deletion process. At the moment, it is not possible to change the global settings for deleting build records and test records, and applying branch filters.

At the build definition level, it is possible to change the settings for what is deleted as a part of the retention policy. The **Delete test results** setting only deletes test runs, results, and attachments, manual test results are not deleted:

There's more...

The new build system also has a provision for associating tags within individual builds and filtering builds using tags. Let's start off by tagging a build. Open a build and add a few tags under the **Tags** section as illustrated in the following screenshot:

In the build list page, enter the tags you would like to filter the build list by. As illustrated in the following screenshot, the build list is filtered by the **Bug#1291** and **Investigate** tags:

Using user capabilities to identify a build agent in a pool

It is not uncommon to have specialized build agents for specific builds. For example, an application may have dependency on SharePoint SDK. A build agent can be stood up to cater for builds that have such dependencies. The new build system introduces the concept of **capabilities**. Capabilities, in their most basic form, are a collection of key value pairs used to recognize the abilities of a build server. A build that requires a specific ability for its execution can be routed to a relevant build agent by referring to these key/value pairs. A build agent supports both system and user capabilities. System capabilities are a list of software frameworks already available on the build agent. They are generated by the build agent. User capabilities can be manually added to a build agent; this is a useful way to tag on a key value pair to recognize a build agent. In this recipe, you'll learn how to add a user capability to a build agent to recognize it in a pool of build agents.

Getting ready

Scenario: The FabrikamTFVC Team has a solution that has dependency on SharePoint 2016 SDK. It has supplemented Pool 1 with an additional agent that has SharePoint 2016 SDK installed. While other build definitions can use both **Win-A1** and **Win-A2**, all build requests from FabrikamTFVC CI build need to be routed to **Win-A2** only:

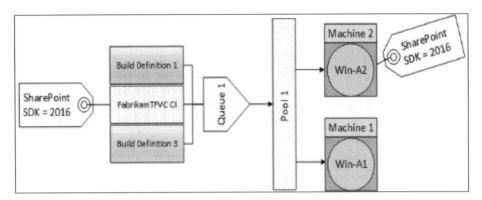

For example, to amend the build agent capabilities, you need to be a member of the Build Administrators Group.

How to do it...

1. Navigate to the **Agent pools** tab in the Administration Console by browsing to `http://tfs2015:8080/tfs/_admin/_AgentPool`.

2. Click on **Pool 1** and select **Win-A2**. From the **USER CAPABILITIES** section, click on the **Add capability** hyperlink. Add `SharePoint.SDK` as the key and `2016` as the value:

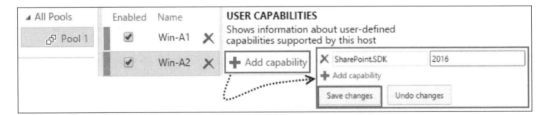

3. Navigate to the FabrikamTFVC CI build, edit the build definition, and browse to the **General** tab. In the **Demands** section, click on the **Add demand** hyperlink. Add `SharePoint.SDK` and set the comparator to **equals** and the **Value** field to `2016`. Click on **Save** to apply the changes to the build definition:

4. Click on the **Queue build** icon. In the launched window, click on the **Demands** tab. You'll see the newly added `SharePoint.SDK` demand shows up in this view. Demands can be added, removed, or edited directly from this window. Click on **OK** to trigger a build from this build definition:

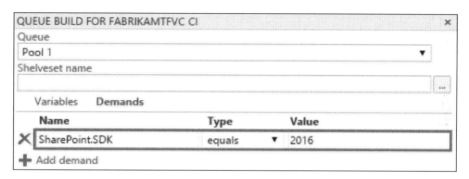

How it works...

The build framework scans **Pool 1** for agents that match the list of demands specified in the build definition. In case no agent fulfils the demands raised by the build definition, a warning message is generated by the queued build indicating that there are no available build agents to process the build request.

The following screenshot illustrates that the build has successfully been routed to **Win-A2** by matching the build demand and the agent capability:

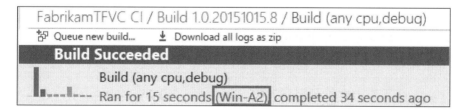

The prior versions of TFS have allowed build routing via build agent and build definition tagging. The new build system enriches the experience by providing an auto-generated list of system capabilities as well as the use of comparators for authoring demands in the build definition.

Version DLLs in build output with build number

Traceability is very important in the software develop lifecycle. Teams strive for traceability between requirements and test cases, code check-ins and builds, and code changes and test runs. Talking of traceability, it would be useful to map the binaries in the build output back to the build. In this recipe, you'll learn how to stamp the DLLs in the build output with the build number they are being generated from.

Getting ready

Scenario: The FabrikamTFVC Team wants to label the source code used in the build and tag the label and build output using the build number:

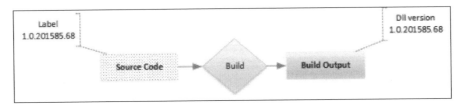

Download the `StampBuildNumber.ps1` script provided in the course material. Check-in the `StampBuildNumber.ps1` script into the `script` folder as illustrated in this screenshot:

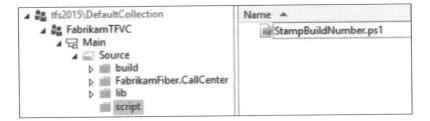

Permissions: You'll need to edit build definition permissions to execute this recipe; you can get these permissions by being added to the Build Administrators Group.

How to do it...

1. Navigate to the **Build** hub in the FabrikamTFVC Team Project by browsing to `http://tfs2015:8080/tfs/DefaultCollection/FabrikamTFVC/_build`. Select the **FabrikamTFVC CI** Build for editing.

2. Navigate to the **General** tab and change the **Build number format** field to `1.0.$(Year:yy).$(DayOfYear).$(BuildID)`.

3. Navigate to the **Repository** tab in the build definition, select the **Labeling Of Source** option on successful build, and change the **Label format** field to `$(build.buildNumber)`.

4. Navigate to the **Build** tab, click on **Add build step...**, and select the **PowerShell** task:

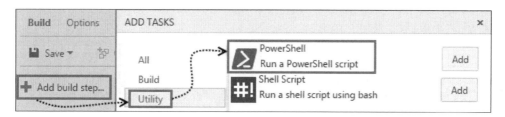

5. Update the script file path in the **PowerShell** task to point to the location of the `StampBuildNumber.ps1` script, which in this case is `$/FabrikamTFVC/Main/Source/script/StampBuildNumber.ps1`. The script expects build number and agent workspace as input parameters. These values can be injected using the predefined variable `$(Build.BuildNumber) $(Agent.BuildDirectory)\$(Build.Repository.Name)`. A complete list of predefined variables can be found at `https://msdn.microsoft.com/Library/vs/alm/Build/scripts/variables`.

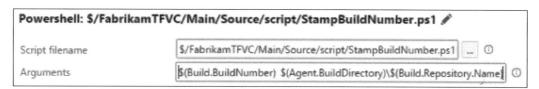

6. Click on **Save** and enter a comment to apply the changes made to the FabrikamTFVC CI build definition. Queue a build to validate the build number stamping on the DLLs in the build output:

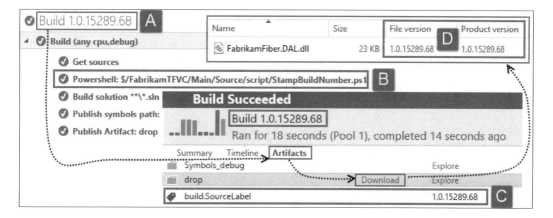

Build 1.0.15289.68 successfully executes the `StampBuildNumber.ps1` script; a build source label matching the build number is generated as a result of a successful build. The build output can be downloaded from the **Artifacts** view. The **File version** and **Product version** fields have the same values as the build number. This provides an end-to-end mapping of the build number across the different artifacts.

How it works...

In order to successfully stamp the build number on to the DLLs, the build number needs to use the assembly version format. There are some interesting recommendations on Semantic Versioning that you can read more about at `http://semver.org/`.

Each C# project contains a file `AssemblyInfo.cs`; as illustrated in the following screenshot. This class contains properties for `AssemblyVersion` and `AssemblyFileVersion`. The `StampBuildNumber.ps1` script overwrites the `AssemblyVersion` and `AssemblyFileVersion` fields with the injected build number:

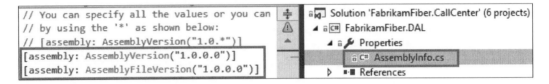

The PowerShell task executing `StampBuildNumber` script needs to be run before the Visual Studio Build task to ensure the updated values for `AssemblyVersion` and `AssemblyFileVersion` properties are used during the compilation process.

The `StampBuildNumber` script accepts two parameters as illustrated here. These parameters are injected through predefined variables via the build definition:

```
Param(
    # TFBuild Number
    [string]$buildNumber,
    # Agent Workspace
    [string]$stagingFolder
)
```

The `Set-AssemblyVersion` function validates that the build number value abides to the assembly version format. A scan is then performed in the build workspace to locate the `AssemblyInfo.cs` class. The `AssemblyVersion` and the `AssemblyFileVersion` properties in the `AssemblyInfo.cs` file are then replaced with the value of the build number:

```
# Stamp Build Number Function
function Set-AssemblyVersion()
{   try
    {   # Supported Assembly Pattern
        [regex]$pattern = "\d+\.\d+\.\d+\.\d+"
        if ($buildNumber -match $pattern -ne $true) {
            throw "Could not extract a version from [$buildNumber] using pattern [$pattern]"}
        [string]$searchFilter = "AssemblyInfo.*"
        [regex]$assemblyVersion = "(AssemblyVersion\("")(\d+\.\d+\.\d+\.\d+)(""\))"
        $newAssemblyVersion = "`${1}$($buildNumber)`$3"
        [regex]$assemblyFileVersion = "(AssemblyFileVersion\("")(\d+\.\d+\.\d+\.\d+)(""\))"
        $newAssemblyFileVersion = "`${1}$($buildNumber)`$3"
        gci -Path $pathToSearch -Filter $searchFilter -Recurse | %{
            Write-Host "  -> Updating $($_.FullName)"
            # Remove the read-only flag on the file
            sp $_.FullName IsReadOnly $false
            # Replace using regex
            (gc $_.FullName) | % { $_ -replace $assemblyVersion, $newAssemblyVersion } | sc $_.FullName
            (gc $_.FullName) | % { $_ -replace $assemblyFileVersion, $newAssemblyFileVersion } | sc $_.FullName
        } }
    finally
    {
        Write-Host "The script execution is now complete.'}
}
```

The following screenshot illustrates the processed `AssemblyInfo.cs` file from the agent work directory:

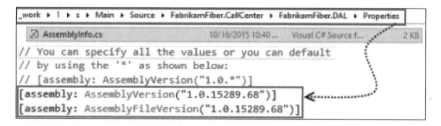

Creating a new build task using the TFBuild Extensibility framework

The new build system comes with a wide range of prepackaged build tasks. Out-of-the-box tasks are complimented with the presence of popular scripting engines. This helps address scenarios that aren't directly covered with the out-of box-tasks. The new build system has been architected from the ground up with a special focus on extensibility. In this recipe, you'll learn how to create a new build task using the extensibility framework available in the new build system.

Getting ready

The TFS Extensions command-line utility (`tfx-cli`) needs to be used for building task management. The utility is based on Node.js. As a prerequisite to using `tfx-cli`, download and install Node.js from `https://nodejs.org/en/download`. The extensibility command-line utility can directly be installed by launching command prompt and running the following command:

`npm install -g tfx-cli`

```
C:\Users\Tarun>npm install -g tfx-cli
C:\Users\Tarun\AppData\Roaming\npm\tfx -> C:\Users\Tarun\AppData\Roaming\npm\nod
e_modules\tfx-cli\tfx-cli.js
tfx-cli@0.1.11 C:\Users\Tarun\AppData\Roaming\npm\node_modules\tfx-cli
├── os-homedir@1.0.1
├── async@1.4.2
├── colors@1.1.2
├── minimist@1.2.0
├── node-uuid@1.4.3
├── read@1.0.7 (mute-stream@0.0.5)
├── q@1.4.1
├── validator@3.43.0
├── shelljs@0.5.3
├── vso-node-api@0.3.4
└── archiver@0.14.4 (buffer-crc32@0.2.5, lazystream@0.1.0, async@0.9.2, readable
-stream@1.0.33, tar-stream@1.1.5, glob@4.3.5, zip-stream@0.5.2, lodash@3.2.0)
```

To authenticate with TFS, the `tfx-cli` utility only accepts **Personal Access Tokens** (**PAT**) or alternate credentials. Since support for PATs is yet to be released in TFS, alternate credentials need to be used for authentication. Guidance on how to set up alternate credentials can be found at `https://github.com/Microsoft/tfs-cli/blob/master/docs/configureBasicAuth.md`.

The following screenshot illustrates how to authenticate with `tfx-cli` by passing the connection details of the Team Project Collection along with alternate credentials:

```
C:\Users\Tarun>tfx login --authType basic
Copyright Microsoft Corporation

Enter collection url > http://tfs2015:8080/tfs/defaultcollection
Enter username > Tarun
Enter password >
logged in successfully
```

To validate that you have performed the setup correctly, try retrieving a list of build tasks by running the command `tfx build tasks list`:

```
id    : 730d8de1-7a4f-424c-9542-fe7cc02604eb
name : SonarQubePostTest
friendly name : SonarQube for MSBuild - End Analysis
visibility: Build
description: Finish the analysis and upload the results to SonarQube
version: 1.0.28
```

How to do it...

1. To create a new task, run the command `tfx build tasks create`, shown as follows:

```
C:\Users\Tarun>tfx build tasks create
Copyright Microsoft Corporation

Enter short task name > MyTask
Enter friendly name > Sample
Enter description > Testing
Enter author > Tarun

created task @ C:\Users\Tarun\MyTask
id   : 55dd4b40-74ef-11e5-a128-5760e4927d7e
name: MyTask

A temporary task icon was created.  Replace with a 32x32 png with transparencies
```

A template task is downloaded to the working folder that is ready for you to start editing:

Name	Date modified	Type	Size
icon.png	10/17/2015 5:51 PM	PNG image	3 KB
sample.js	10/17/2015 5:51 PM	JavaScript File	1 KB
sample.ps1	10/17/2015 5:51 PM	Windows PowerS...	1 KB
task.json	10/17/2015 5:51 PM	JSON File	2 KB

2. To upload this task to the library, run `tfx build tasks upload.\MyTask`:

```
C:\Users\Tarun>tfx build tasks upload .\MyTask
Copyright Microsoft Corporation

task at: .\MyTask uploaded successfully!
```

3. Navigate to the FabrikamTFVC CI build definition and click on **Edit** to edit the build definition. Select the newly added **MyTask** which shows up in the task list under the **Utility** section. Include this task in the definition by clicking **Add**:

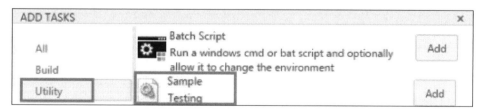

4. Update the message in the **Message** textbox and save the changes. Queue a new build:

MyTask 🖉		
Working Directory		... ⓘ
Message	Hurray! My First Build Task...	ⓘ

The build successfully runs **MyTask** and prints the message `Hurray! My First Build Task...` in the console output:

How it works...

On running the `create new task` command, a set of template files are downloaded. The `task.json` file contains metadata about the task. As illustrated in the following screenshot, the file contains task metadata, agent dependencies, task specific properties, and output behavior. For example, if the default category is `utility`, the category that the build task gets uploaded to can be amended by changing the value of the category:

```
"id": "55dd4b40-74ef-11e5-a128-5760e4927d7e",
"name": "MyTask",
"friendlyName": "Sample",
"description": "Testing",
"author": "Tarun",
"helpMarkDown": "Replace with markdown to show in help",
"minimumAgentVersion": "1.83.0",
"instanceNameFormat": "MyTask $(message)",
"inputs": [
```

The other files also have their significance:

► The `sample.ps1` file contains the PowerShell build task logic that is executed when running on a Windows agent

► The `sample.js` file contains the JavaScript build task logic that is executed when running on a cross-platform agent (e.g. OS X or Linux)

▸ The `icon.png` file is a default icon and should be replaced with a custom 32×32 PNG file with transparencies set appropriately

If you are looking for inspiration, all existing out-of-the-box tasks are open source and can directly be enhanced with contributions on GitHub at `https://github.com/Microsoft/vso-agent-tasks`.

Integrating SonarQube with TFBuild to manage technical debt

Technical debt can be classified as the measure between the current state and an optimal state of codebases. Technical debt saps productivity by making code hard to understand, easy to break, difficult to validate, and in turn, creating unplanned work ultimately blocking the progress. Technical debt is inevitable! It starts small and grows overtime through rushed changes and lack of context and discipline. Organizations often find that more than 50% of their capacity is sapped by technical debt. As discussed in *Chapter 2, Setting Up and Managing Code Repositories*, the biggest challenge is in identifying and managing Technical Debt. SonarQube is an open source platform that is the de facto solution for understanding and managing technical debt. In this recipe, you'll learn how to integrate with SonarQube using TFBuild to analyze .NET-based applications.

Getting ready

SonarQube is an open platform for managing code quality. As such, it covers the seven axes of code quality as illustrated in the following image. Originally famous in the Java community, SonarQube now supports over 20 programming languages. The joint investments made by Microsoft and SonarSource make SonarQube easier to integrate with TFBuild and better at analyzing .NET-based applications. You can read more about the capabilities offered by SonarQube at `http://www.sonarqube.org/resources/`.

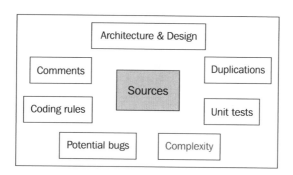

In this recipe, we'll analyze the technical debt in the FabrikamTFVC codebase using SonarQube. If you don't already have an instance of SonarQube, then set one up by following the instructions at `https://github.com/SonarSource/sonar-.net-documentation/blob/master/doc/installation-and-configuration.md`.

To work through this recipe, you'll need the Sonar database connection string and user account details to connect to SonarQube from TFBuild. This recipe uses the single server setup described in the installation and configuration link shared earlier:

```
Database Connection String -
jdbc:jtds:sqlserver://TFS2015:1433/Sonar;instance=SQLEXPRESS;SelectMe
thod=Cursor
UserName - SonarUser
Password - SonarUser
```

How to do it...

1. Navigate to the FabrikamTFVC CI build definition by browsing to the **Build** hub in FabrikamTFVC Team Portal. Click on the **Edit** hyperlink to start editing the FabrikamTFVC CI build definition.

2. Add a new task by clicking on **Add Build** step. From the **Build** category, choose **SonarQube for MSBuild - Begin Analysis** and **SonarQube for MSBuild - End Analysis**:

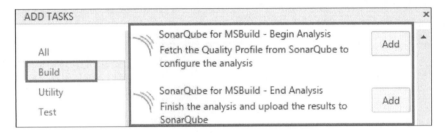

3. Organize the begin analysis task before the Visual Studio Build task and the end analysis task after all the code build and test tasks have been executed:

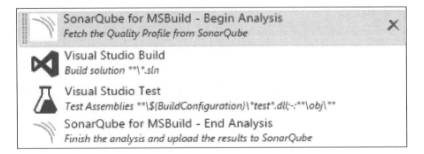

4. In the **SonarQube Begin Analysis** task, specify the connection details of your SonarQube instance. The SonarQube endpoint needs to be mapped and added through the endpoint manager as illustrated here:

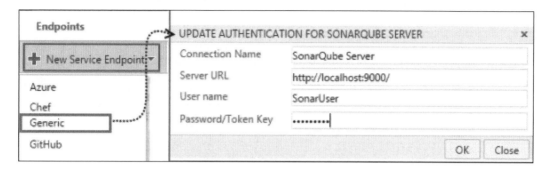

5. Endpoints provide a role-based access control model similar to the build permission model. Users and groups can directly be set up for endpoint administration and consumption through this access control model:

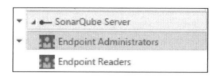

6. Select the SonarQube service endpoint and update the database settings:

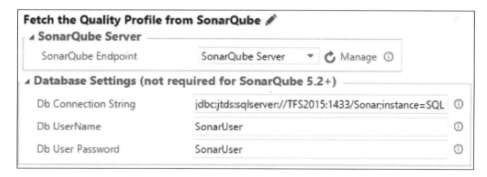

7. Update the project settings as illustrated here:

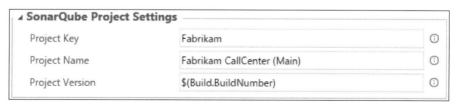

8. Save the changes to the build definition and queue a new build. Using the information in the **SonarQube Start Analysis** task, the build agent will connect to the SonarQube instance. It will process the code using the Sonar MSBuild runner performing .NET and JavaScript code analysis, code clone analysis, code coverage analysis, and calculating the metrics for .NET and JavaScript. These results will be published by the **SonarQube End Analysis** task:

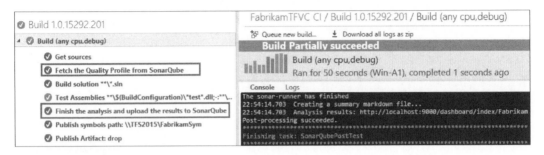

How it works...

The SonarQubeMSBuild runner is used to invoke the SonarQube analysis from TFBuild. Let's see the results of the code analysis performed by the runner. Navigate to the SonarQube Dashboard by browsing to `http://localhost:9000/`. The home page shows the **Fabrikam CallCenter (Main)** project as follows:

QG	NAME ▲	VERSION	LOC	TECHNICAL DEBT	LAST ANALYSIS
★	Fabrikam CallCenter (Main)	1.0.15292.201	1,877	1h 7min	22:54

By drilling into the Dashboard for the **Fabrikam CallCenter (Main)** project, you can see high-level metrics around various analyses:

The dashboard gives you a high-level summary of analysis of code, complexity, duplications, unit test coverage, and debt analysis

The issues section displays a complete list of issues found across the codebase using the .NET code analysis ruleset. The issues can be tracked, suppressed, assigned, and planned for releases right from within this view:

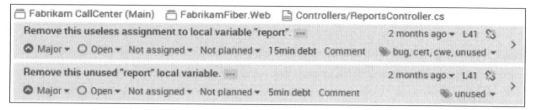

The issues section shows a list of issues identified in the codebase during the analysis

There's more...

The new build framework provides the ability to create custom variables. Variables provide the means to share common values across multiple fields in a build definition. Unlike values, variables can be dynamically updated during runtime. The framework also allows flagging a variable as secure, in which case its value is not displayed in the build definition not logged during the build execution. In this recipe, the SonarQube connection string and account details were passed directly in the build task. These values can instead be passed through using build variables as illustrated in the following screenshot:

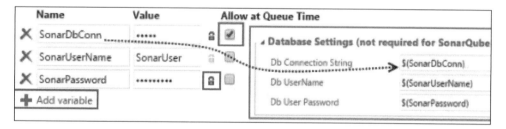

Building GitHub code repositories with TFBuild

The new build system offers seamless integration with GitHub. In this recipe, you'll learn how to use TFBuild to build a repository in GitHub.

Getting ready

If you don't already have a GitHub repository, create one from `https://help.github.com/articles/create-a-repo`.

For the walkthrough in this recipe, we'll be using the `VisualStudioGeeks` repository available at `https://github.com/visualstudiogeeks/`.

How to do it...

1. Log into the GitHub repository from your profile menu, navigate to **Settings**, and select **Personal access tokens**. Click on the **Generate new token** button to create a new personal access token:

2. Specify a name and select the access scope for the token. In order to trigger builds, the `admin:repo_hook` access level needs to be selected:

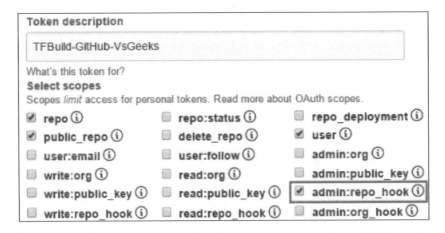

3. Click on the **Generate token** button. Copy the access token and store it in a safe location. Note that you'll not be able to see this token again; should you lose it, you'll have to generate a new token:

4. Navigate to the FabrikamTFVC Team Project and browse to the **Build** hub. Click on the **+** icon to create a new build definition. Select the Visual Studio Template, and click on **OK**. Save the build definition as `VisualStudioGeeks` CI.

5. Navigate to the **Repository** tab, and select **Repository type** to **External Git**. Enter the repository name, the URL of the repository, the username, and the personal access token to access this repository:

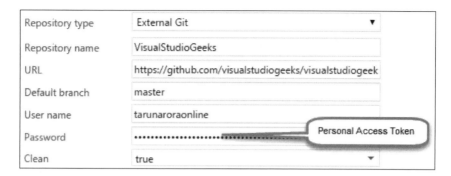

6. From the **Triggers** tab, select the **Scheduled** option and specify the schedule for triggering the builds from this build definition. Save changes to this build definition and trigger a new build:

As illustrated in the previous screenshot, the `Build 20151020.5` successfully synchronizes the code from the repository `VisualStudioGeeks`.

How it works...

The personal token generated for the Visual Studio Geeks repository with scope `admin:repo_hook` provides full control over the repository hooks. This access permits the listener to subscribe to the commit event generated when the code changes are committed to the repository. While TFBuild provides the capability to build GitHub repositories in TFS 2015, it does not allow the continuous integration flow yet. As indicated in the TFS feature timeline, continuous integration build workflow is expected to be introduced in a future update of TFS 2015: `https://www.visualstudio.com/en-us/news/release-archive-vso.aspx`.

5

Testing Your Application

"Walking on water and developing software from a specification are easy...If both are frozen!"

– Edward Berard

In this chapter, we will cover the following:

- ▶ Running NUnit tests in the CI Pipeline using TFBuild
- ▶ Creating and setting up a Machine Group
- ▶ Deploying a test agent through the TFBuild task
- ▶ Distributing test execution on a Lab Machine Group
- ▶ Triggering Selenium Web Tests on a Selenium Test Grid using TFBuild
- ▶ Integrating the Cloud Load Testing Service in TFBuild
- ▶ Analyzing test execution results from the Runs view
- ▶ Exporting and importing test cases in Excel from TFS
- ▶ Copying and cloning test suites and test cases
- ▶ Exporting test artifacts and test results from the test hub
- ▶ Charting testing status on Dashboards in Team Portal

Introduction

Software teams are constantly under pressure to deliver more... faster. End users expect software to simply work. Low quality software just isn't acceptable. But, you may ask what the right level of quality is? Quality is a very subjective term; it is therefore important for Teams to agree to a definition of quality for their software. Teams that are unable to define quality usually end up testing for coverage rather than testing for quality.

The toolkit in Team Foundation Server provides tooling for both manual and automation testing. **Microsoft Test Manager** (**MTM**), first introduced with TFS 2010, enables testers to plan, track, and run manual, exploratory, and automated tests. While Test Manager fully integrates with TFS, it does not offer any integration with other testing platforms. The Test Manager architecture does not lend itself to extensibility. Microsoft has ambitions to support every developer and every app; however, it isn't possible with tooling that can't be run on non-window platforms. The test tooling is gradually moving out from the Test Manager client into the web-based Team Web Portal to enable extensibility, cross-platform availability, and integration with other testing platforms. The following screenshot provides a comparison of testing features already in test hub, those that will gradually move, and those that will remain in MTM. For a full comparison of all the features, download `Microsoft Test Manager Vs Test Hub Feature Comparison.png` from the course material:

Test Plan Management	TH	MTM		Test Suite Management	TH	MTM
Create/Edit Test Plans	✓	✓		Create/Edit Test Suites	✓	✓
Assign Build	!	✓		Add/Remove Tests	✓	✓
Create/Edit/Assign Config	!	✓		Assign Individual Testers	✓	✓
Assign Environments	!	✓		Assign configurations	!	✓
Assign Test Settings	!	✓		Add tests from other suites	!	✓
Clone Test Plan	!	✓		Clone Suites	!	✓
Explore Test Plan	✓	✗		Export Test Suites	✓	✗

TH - Test Hub MTM - Test Manager	✓	Exists Today	!	Planned for future	✗	No plans

To speed up the software delivery loop, software testing needs to be incorporated into the **Continuous Integration** (**CI**) Pipeline. In order to do this, software testing needs to shift left in the development processes. **Test-driven development** (**TDD**) enables developers to write code that's maintainable, flexible, and easily extensible. Code backed by unit tests helps identify change impact and empowers developers to make changes confidently. In addition to this, functional testing needs to be automated. This enables software testers to focus on high-value exploratory testing rather than just coverage of test matrix.

The DevOps movement at large supports bringing testing into the CI Pipeline. The tooling in TFS has evolved to enable this. The pre 2015 version of TFS shipped with a separate test controller and test agent, with the introduction of the new build framework in TFS 2015 test runner has been distilled down to a task in the build definition. TFS now provides a task based open and extensible build framework that allows you to pick not only a build framework of your choice, but also provides you full autonomy to pick and assemble the test frameworks of your choice too. The new build system enables the agent to be a generic task orchestrator. The agent is capable of executing the entire CI Pipeline. This new approach removes the need for managing multiple single purpose agents. This takes away the friction from the setup process and enables a scale up option without the need for tedious configuration. This also enables integrating other testing frameworks and platforms into the same pipeline:

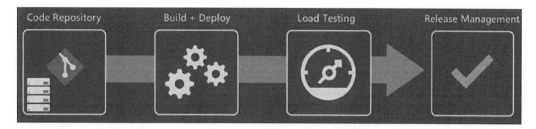

Through the recipes in this chapter, you'll learn how to leverage tasks in the build definition to provision test agents on demand, perform a distributed test execution that includes a large number of diverse automated tests such as unit, functional UI, Selenium and, coded UI on remote Machine Groups. We'll also look at integrating with Visual Studio Team Systems to run cloud load tests. Last but not least, we will look at the rich test reports and test result analysis from the test executions.

Look at the richness of testing features within the bigger DevOps capabilities available in TFS; should you decide to move from your existing Test Case Management Solutions to the Microsoft Test Manager, you may wonder what the possibilities for migration are. We'll briefly cover a few tools that are available today to help you with the migration. In the end, we'll look at how to export and visualize test execution results with the help of light weight charts.

Along with providing world-class tooling for manual and automation testers, TFS also provides rich, integrated test tooling to stakeholders. The web-based testing extension allows you to perform exploratory testing of your web or mobile application right from the browser on any platform (Windows, Mac, or Linux). Your stakeholders now do not need to follow predefined test cases or test steps. Stakeholders can capture and annotate screenshots, log bugs, and share notes. The testing session records and logs every step providing developers rich action logs for diagnosing application and user experience issues. Read more on this at http:// bit.ly/1I82pfK.

These investments are taking the testing tooling from good to great. It is a very exciting time to be in the testing space!

Running NUnit tests in the CI Pipeline using TFBuild

Traditionally, developers using the NUnit framework had to install the NUnit Test Adapter on the build machines. While this approach worked if you were dealing with a small number of build servers, it quickly became tedious when dealing with large number of build servers. An alternative to installing the NUnit adapter was to inject the NUnit adapter DLLs to the build machines using the custom assembly field available in the build controller properties. While this worked with TFVC-based repositories, there were challenges using this approach for Git-based repositories. This is a classic example of configuration hell when using non-Microsoft testing frameworks.

The new build framework makes running non-Microsoft unit test frameworks completely configuration free. In this recipe, you'll learn how to use the Visual Studio Test task in the build definition to run NUnit tests or generally any non-Microsoft unit testing frameworks.

Getting ready

In order to create a build definition, you'll need to be a member of the Project Build Administrator Group.

How to do it...

1. Launch Team Explorer and connect to the FarbikamTFVC Team Project. From the Source Control Explorer, open the `FabrikamFiber.CallCenter.sln` in Visual Studio:

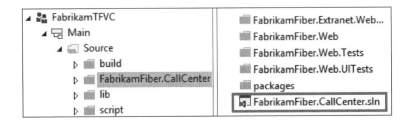

2. Follow the instructions at `http://bit.ly/1XgG0UG` to create a new NUnit test project. Call the project `FabrikamFiber.Web.NUnit.Tests.csproj`.

3. Right-click on the `FabrikamFiber.Web.NUnit.Tests.csproj` project and select **Manage NuGet Packages...** from the context menu:

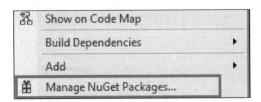

4. From the NuGet package manager, search and install the NUnit test adapter.

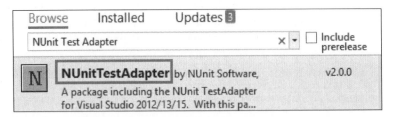

5. Open the folder location of the solution and you'll notice that the `NUnitTestAdapter` `NuGet` package has been added under the packages folder:

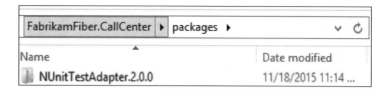

6. Check in the code changes from the **Pending Changes** view in Team Explorer:

7. In the FabrikamTFVC Team Web Portal, navigate to the **BUILD** hub and click on the **+** icon to add a new build definition. Create it using Visual Studio Build Template:

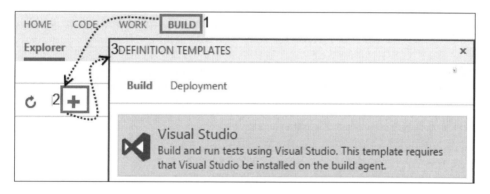

8. In the Visual Studio Build Task, ensure that the **Restore NuGet Packages** flag is checked. You don't need to make any other changes in the build or test task. Ensure that the code repository is mapped as FabrikamTFVC in the repository tab. Save the build definition as `FabrikamTFVC NUnit CI`. You can learn more about setting up a build definition in the *Creating a continuous integration build definition in TFBuild* recipe in *Chapter 4, Building Your Application*.

9. Queue a build. Once the build completes, you will see a summary of the test results in the build summary section. The build successfully executes all NUnit tests without any manual configuration specific to NUnit:

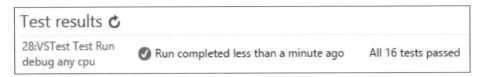

Test results ↻

| 28:VSTest Test Run debug any cpu | ✓ Run completed less than a minute ago | All 16 tests passed |

How it works

Let's now understand how TFBuild manages to identify the test runner for NUnit tests. Open the FabrikamTFVC NUnit CI build definition. In the **Advanced** section of the Visual Studio Test task, you'll see a field for specifying the path to custom adapters:

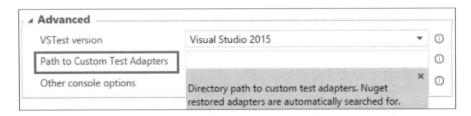

With the restore NuGet packages flag checked in the Visual Studio Build task, all NuGet packages that the solution has dependency on are downloaded into the agent's working directory. The Visual Studio Test task scans the agent working directory for all test adapter packages. In this instance, the NUnit Test Adapter NuGet package was checked into source control. The package would have been restored into the agent working directory during the package restore process; as a result the Visual Studio Test task loaded up the NUnit Test Adapter during the scan.

 TFBuild publishes the test and coverage results into TFS independent of the testing framework used. This is automatically handled by the TFBuild framework.

This approach scales really well, as you add more machines to carry out testing, you do not need to worry about manually adding the NUnit Test Adapter on the test machines. This also simplifies upgrading test adapters. The test task can load multiple versions of one test adapter and use the adapter referenced by the unit tests.

The **Path to Custom Test Adapters** field wasn't really put to use in this case. However, this field is useful for specifying the test adapter path if your solution uses a unit test framework that does not have a NuGet package associated with it. The path to the test adapter needs to be constructed using the build agent's source directory variable. The `Build.SourceDirectory` variable points to the directory in the build agent where the source code has been synced. If your custom test adapter was in the `$\FabrikamTFVC\myAdapters` folder, you would need to specify the path: `$(Build.SourcesDirectory)\src\myAdapters\TestAdapter.1.2`.

Creating and setting up a Machine Group

Simply put, Machine Group is a logical grouping of machines. The Machine Group holds metadata, connectivity, and login details of the machines in the group. Machine Group can directly be referenced from build and release definitions. In this recipe, you'll learn how to create and set up a Machine Group.

Getting ready

Scenario: The FabrikamTFVC Team has a lab environment in the `Fabrikam.lab` domain. `Fabrikam.lab` comprises of five servers that serve different roles. The FabrikamTFVC Team wants the ability to directly reference these machines from the build definition and release definition to deploy test agents on all the machines and trigger a distributed test run. `Fabrikam.Lab` is managed by the Fabrikam Environments Team who cannot share environment credentials with the FabrikamTFVC Team. In this recipe, we'll walk through the process followed by the Fabrikam Environments Team to set up and configure the Machine Group `Fabrikam-QA` for the FabrikamTFVC Team:

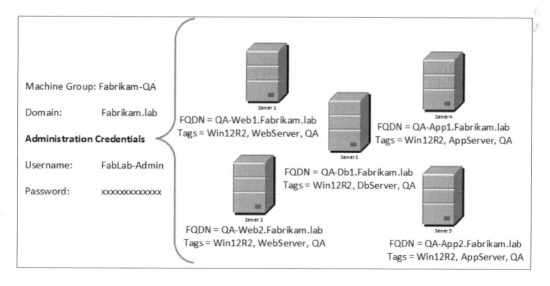

The Machine Group will be accessed by a remote host; the remote host will likely be playing the role of a build agent or release agent. As illustrated in the following figure, the remote host is in the same network as the Machine Group and has a trust relationship with the Machine Group:

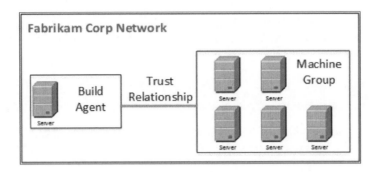

The build agent uses Windows PowerShell remoting that requires the **Windows Remote Management** (**WinRM**) protocol to connect to the machines in the Machine Groups. WinRM needs to be enabled on a machine as a prerequisite before it can be added into the Machine Group. In this case, Kerberos will be used as the mode of authentication since the agent and Machine Group are in the same corp network.

Target Machine state	Target Machine trust with automation agent	Machine Identity	Auth Account	Auth Mode	Auth Account permission on target machine	Conn Type
Domain-joined machine in the corp network	Trusted	DNS name	Domain account	Kerberos	Machine admin	WinRM HTTP

In the next few steps, we'll walk through how to configure WinRM on a machine, and you'll learn how to test connectivity through WinRM:

1. PowerShell 2.0 and Windows Management Framework 4.0 (http://bit.ly/1kNlxuW) are required to be installed on both the agent and machines in the Machine Group.

2. Log into the QA-Web1.Farbikam.lab machine, start Windows PowerShell as an administrator by right-clicking on the Windows PowerShell shortcut and selecting **Run as Administrator**.

3. By default, the WinRM service is configured for manual startup and stopped. Executing the `winrmquickconfig -q` command performs a series of actions:

    1. Starts the WinRM service.
    2. Sets the startup type on the WinRM service to **Automatic**.
    3. Creates a listener to accept requests on any IP address.
    4. Enables a firewall exception for WS-Management communications.
    5. Registers the `Microsoft.PowerShell` and `Microsoft.PowerShell.Workflow` session configurations, if they are not already registered.
    6. Registers the `Microsoft.PowerShell32` session configuration on 64-bit computers, if it is not already registered.
    7. Enables all session configurations.
    8. Changes the security descriptor of all session configurations to allow remote access.
    9. Restarts the WinRM service to make the preceding changes effective.

4. The next few commands will prepare WinRM for Kerberos authentication.

5. Increase the maximum memory allocation per session:

    ```
    winrm set winrm/config/winrs '@{MaxMemoryPerShellMB="300"}'
    ```

6. Next, increase the session timeout period:

    ```
    winrm set winrm/config '@{MaxTimeoutms="1800000"}'
    ```

7. Allow the traffic between agent and Machine Group to be unencrypted:

    ```
    winrm set winrm/config/service '@{AllowUnencrypted="true"}'
    ```

8. Disable basic authentication:

    ```
    winrm set winrm/config/service/auth '@{Basic="false"}'
    ```

9. Setup a firewall exception to allow inbound traffic on port 5985; this is the default port used by WinRM when using HTTP:

    ```
    netshadvfirewall firewall set rule name="Windows Remote Management
    (HTTP-In)" profile=public
    protocol=tcplocalport=5985 remoteip=localsubnet new remoteip=any
    ```

10. Disable digest for client authentication:

    ```
    winrm set winrm/config/client/auth '@{Digest="false"}'
    ```

11. Set service authentication to use Kerberos:

    ```
    winrm set winrm/config/service/auth '@{Kerberos="true"}'
    ```

12. Trust all connections between agent and Machine Group:

    ```
    winrm set winrm/config/client '@{TrustedHosts="*"}'
    Set-Item WSMan:\localhost\Client\TrustedHosts *
    ```

13. Restart the `win-rm` service:

```
Restart-Service winrm-Force
```

14. To ensure Kerberos authentication is enabled on WinRM, run the following command:

```
winrm get winrm/config/service/auth
```

```
PS C:\Users\tarun> winrm get winrm/config/service/auth
Auth
    Basic = false
    Kerberos = true
    Negotiate = true
    Certificate = false
    CredSSP = false
    CbtHardeningLevel = Relaxed
```

15. Now, let's validate whether WinRM has correctly been set up on QA-Web1. Fabrikam.lab. Log into another VM in the lab, in this case QA-Web2.Fabrikam. lab. Launch PowerShell as an administrator by right-clicking on the Windows PowerShell shortcut and selecting **Run as administrator**. Execute the following command:

```
Test-Wsman -computerName QA-Web1.Fabrikam.lab
```

```
wsmid             : http://schemas.dmtf.org/wbem/wsman/identity/1/wsmanidentity.xsd
ProtocolVersion : http://schemas.dmtf.org/wbem/wsman/1/wsman.xsd
ProductVendor   : Microsoft Corporation
ProductVersion  : OS: 0.0.0 SP: 0.0 Stack: 2.0
```

16. Execute the following command to check the port WinRM is listing on:

```
winrm e winrm/config/listener
```

```
PS C:\Users\tarun.b.arora> winrm e winrm/config/listener
Listener
    Address = *
    Transport = HTTP
    Port = 5985
    Hostname
    Enabled = true
    URLPrefix = wsman
    CertificateThumbprint
    ListeningOn = 127.0.0.1, 192.168.110.54, ::1, fe80::5efe:192.168.110.54%11, fe80::98eb:6e43:8554:bb35%10
```

 Execute the following command should you want to change the port WinRM is currently configured to listen on:

```
Set-Item WSMan:\localhost\listener\*\Port 8888
```

17. Most importantly, validate that you are able to invoke the Pssession on QA-Web1. Fabrikam.lab by manually running the following command from QA-Web2. Fabrikam.lab. Once you execute the first statement, you'll receive a prompt to enter your credentials. Enter your domain account that has admin permissions:

```
$cred = get-credential
```

18. Executing the next command will use your domain account to connect to the destination server; DNS will be used to resolve the destination name:

```
Enter-Pssession -ComputerNameQA-Web1.Fabrikam.lab-Credential $cred
```

```
PS C:\Users\tarun> $cred = Get-Credential

cmdlet Get-Credential at command pipeline position 1
Supply values for the following parameters:
Credential
PS C:\Users\tarun> Enter-Pssession -ComputerName QA-Web1.Fabrikam.lab -Credential $cred
[QA-Web1.Fabrikam.lab]: PS C:\Users\tarun\Documents>_
```

19. Follow steps 1 to 5 to configure WinRM on other machines in the lab. Follow step 6 to validate WinRM connectivity before moving forward.

How to do it...

1. Navigating to the test hub in the FabrikamTFVC Team Web Portal, on the **Machines** page, click on the **+** icon to create a new Machine Group:

2. Enter the details as illustrated in the following screenshot:

CREATE MACHINE GROUP

Machine group name	Fabrikam-QA
Description	The Fabrikam QA Machine Group

Administrator credentials for all machines

Username	Fabrikam.lab\FabLab-Admin
Password	••••••••

☐ Use custom credentials for each machine along with global credentials

WinRM Protocol	◉ HTTP ○ HTTPS

Machines

Machine FQDN/IP Address	WinRM Port	Tags
✕ QA-Web1.Fabrikam.lab	5985	OS:Win12R2; Role:WebServer; Environment:QA
✕ QA-Web2.Fabrikam.lab	5985	OS:Win12R2; Role:WebServer; Environment:QA

3. The WinRM protocol in `Fabrikam.lab` will use HTTP since the remote machine has a trust relationship with `Fabrikam.lab.Add` and the details for all the machines. Now, click on **Done** to complete the setup:

Group Name	Provider	Created By	Date Created ▾
▾ Fabrikam-QA	Pre-existing machines	Tarun Arora	less than a minute ago

How it works...

The Fabrikam-QA Machine Group setup uses a common administrator credentials for all machines in the Machine Group. It is alternatively possible to specify different credentials for the individual machines added in the Machine Group:

1. To enter credentials per machine, check the option **Use custom credentials for each machine along with global credentials**.

Machine FQDN/IP Address	WinRM Port	Username	Password	Tags
✕ QA-Web1.Fabrikam.lab	5985	Fabrikam.lab\FabLab-i	*Using global password*	Environment: QA ; OS: Win12R2 ; Ro

2. The password field is masked in the user interface. In addition to this, the value of this field is not printed in any of the log files either.

3. The tags provide a great way to query for machines with in the Machine Group. For example, when using the test agent deployment task in build definition, you can specify a Machine Group and use Tags to filter the execution of the action on machines that include the Tag.

4. Machine Groups, at the moment, support limited scenarios mainly domain joined on premise machine and standalone machines in Azure. Refer to `http://bit.ly/1NFqYma` for a full list of supported scenarios.

Deploying a test agent through the TFBuild task

In previous versions of TFS, the test controller and agent used to ship as separate installers. While the installers supported unattended installation, the configuration needed manual intervention. This limited the ability to scale out the test agents on demand. In TFS 2015, the test controller and agent do not ship as separate installers; instead, the capability offered by the test agent has been distilled into one build task. In this recipe, you'll learn how to deploy a test agent on multiple machines in a Machine Group.

Getting ready

Scenario: The FabrikamTFVC Team has a dependency on the cucumber framework, since cucumber conflicts with the existing framework on the build agent, it cannot be installed on the build agent. The FabrikamTFVC Team instead wants the test agent to be deployed on the `QA-App1.Fabrikam.lab` server. This server is already part of the Fabrikam-QA Machine Group:

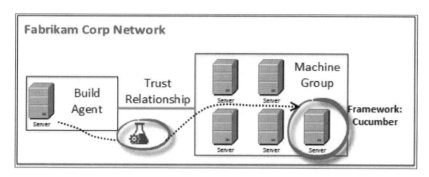

In this recipe, we'll be using the Fabrikam-QA Machine Group. If you don't already have Machine Group set up, follow the instructions in the recipe *Creating and setting up a Machine Group*.

How to do it...

1. Navigating to the test hub in the FabrikamTFVC Team Web Portal, in the **Machine** page, edit the Fabrikam-QA Machine Group. Append the Tag `Framework: Cucumber` for the machine `QA-App1.Fabrikam.lab` and save.

2. Navigate to the build hub and create a new build definition using the empty build template. Ensure that the code repository is mapped as FabrikamTFVC in the repository tab. Add the **Visual Studio Test Agent Deployment** task from the test section. The task comprises of three sections; configure the Fabrikam-QA Machine Group, select the machine by machine names or tags, and filter the machine using the Tag `Framework:Cucumber`:

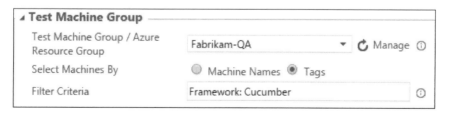

3. The **Agent Configuration** section accepts the credentials and the test agent service will run under it once installed. Create a variable for the test agent username and the test agent password from the **Variables** tab. Add the variables to the **Agent Configuration** section. Check the **Interactive Process** option to run the agent as an interactive process. The agent is installed as a Windows service if it's not requested to be run as an interactive process:

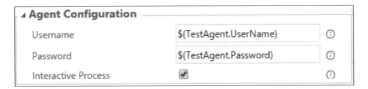

4. The **Advanced** section allows you to specify the location for the installer of the test agent. This is useful if you want to control the version of the agent getting installer. In the absence of a location, the latest version of the test agent is downloaded from the Internet. Check the option to enable data collection:

5. Save the build definition as `FabrikamTFVC Agent Deployment`. Queue a new build from this build definition. Once the build is complete, navigate to the `QA-App1.Fabrikam.lab` server. The test agent has successfully been installed as a Windows service.

How it works...

1. The build agent downloads the test agent installer from the Internet into a `temp` location. The installer is then pushed for installation into the remote `QA-App1.Fabrikam.lab` machine:

```
DistributedTests: Machine Group name: Fabrikam-QA
DistributedTests: Run as process: True
DistributedTests: Login Automatically: True
DistributedTests: Disable Screen saver: True
DistributedTests: Agent would be downloaded from http://go.microsoft.com/fwlink/?LinkId=536423
DistributedTests: Update test agent: True
DistributedTests: Run test agent as DataCollection only : True
```

2. The agent is installed as a Windows service on the machines in the Machine Group:

Distributing test execution on a Lab Machine Group

Earlier in this chapter, you learned how to create a Machine Group and deploy the test agent on selected machines in the Machine Group. The TFBuild framework ships a task to distribute the test execution across multiple test agents. In this recipe, you'll learn how to trigger a distributed test run across a farm of test runners deployed in a Machine Group.

Getting ready

Scenario: The FabrikamTFVC Team has over 2,000 automated coded UI tests that need to be executed as part of the functional testing workflow. FabrikamTFVC Team would like the ability to parallelize the test execution. In order to do this, the Team wants to deploy the Visual Studio test agent to all machines in the Fabrikam-QA Machine Group and then parallelize by distributing the test execution at the test assembly level:

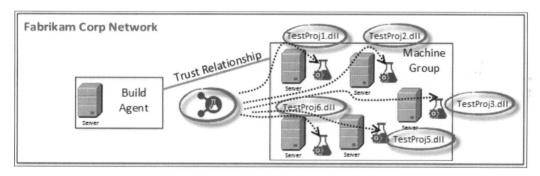

In this recipe, you'll be using the Fabrikam-QA Machine Group. If you don't already have Machine Group set up, follow the instructions in the *Creating and setting up a Machine Group* recipe. Since test agents need to be deployed as a prerequisite to the distribution of the tests, follow the steps in the *Deploying a test agent through the TFBuild task* recipe to learn how TFBuild can be used to deploy the test agent in a Machine Group.

How to do it...

1. Navigating to the build hub in the FabrikamTFVC Team Web Portal, click on **Edit** to open `FabrikamTFVC Agent Deployment` in edit mode.

2. Click on **+** to add a build step and from the **Add Task** window, select the **Build** tab and add the Visual Studio Build task. This task will be used to compile the test projects:

3. From the **Deploy** tab, add the **Windows Machine File Copy** task. This task will copy the test assemblies across to the machines the test need to be executed:

4. From the **Test** tab, add the **Visual Studio Test using Test Agent** task. This task will be used to manage the test distribution across the farm of test agents:

5. Click on close icon to close the **Add Task** window. The tasks in the build definition need to be ordered as:

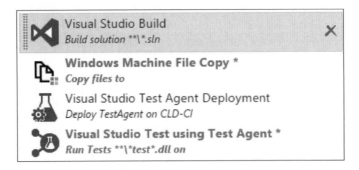

6. Configure the Visual Studio Build task to build the solution the functional tests are part of:

7. Configure the Windows Machine File Copy task to copy the test assemblies into a directory on the machines in the Machine Group. It is always recommended to parameterize the test locations with configuration variables. The preconfigured build variables can be used to construct the path to the assemblies on the build agent working folder that need to be copied across. If the **Clean Target** flag is checked, the build engine will delete the contents of the destination folder before copying the new files. The advanced section in this task also includes a flag to enable copying files in parallel and use this flag to allow the build system to copy the binaries across the machines on the Machine Group in parallel:

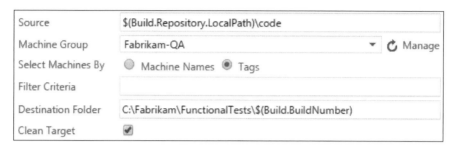

8. No changes need to be made to the Visual Studio test agent deployment task. The configuration set up in the *Deploying a test agent through the TFBuild task* recipe will carry out the test agent deployment across all machines in the Machine Group. The Visual Studio Tests using test agent task should immediately follow this task. Select the Fabrikam-QA Machine Group as the destination Machine Group, where the tests need to be executed. In addition to this, specify the test binaries location, the pattern of the test assemblies, the configuration, and the platform the tests need to be executed in. Check the code coverage flag in the **Advanced** section. You can inject the test settings file to optionally override the configuration in the test settings file through the **Override Test Run Parameters** field:

9. Save the changes to the build definition and queue a new build. Once the build completes, navigate to the build summary page; the logs for the Visual Studio Tests using test agent step shows the details of the test distribution:

```
##[debug]Importing cmdlet 'Invoke-DeployTestAgent'.
##[debug]Importing cmdlet 'Invoke-RunDistributedTests'.
##[debug]Getting the connection object
##[debug]UnregisterTestAgent script Path  =
##[debug]Calling Invoke-RunDistributedTests
##[debug]DistributedTests: Creating DTL client
```

How it works...

Let's look at the log files of the Visual Studio Test using a test agent task through the build summary. As illustrated in the preceding screenshot, the test DLLs have been distributed to multiple test agents in the group. The distribution is done at a DLL level rather than a test level. The test distribution significantly reduces the execution time if your tests are in multiple projects since each DLL is distributed to a test agent to execute.

It is also worth noting that the Windows Machine File Copy task successfully moves the files from the agent working directory across to the `C:\Fabrikam\FunctionalTests\$(Build.BuildNumber)` folder in the Machine Group:

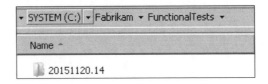

You'll learn more about the Windows Machine File Copy task in *Chapter 6, Releasing Your Application*, as it'll be used extensively for deployments in release management.

Triggering Selenium Web Tests on a Selenium Test Grid using TFBuild

The cost of testing can significantly increase if your software needs to support multiple devices and browsers. The rise in client-side scripting frameworks and responsive design technologies enable each browser to offer a unique immersive user experience. With the matrix of devices and browsers rapidly increasing, it is virtually impossible to cover the matrix with manual testing. There are a number of commercial and open source tools available for assisting with the development of test automation. Selenium is possibly the most widely used open source solution. TFS works better together with open source tools. In this recipe, you'll learn how to execute Selenium Tests from TFBuild.

Getting ready

Scenario: The FabrikamGit Team has automated functional tests using Selenium. The Team now wants to validate the functionality by running the tests in Chrome, Firefox, and Internet Explorer. The FabrikamGit Team would like to trigger the execution of these tests on a Selenium grid via TFBuild.

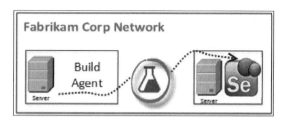

Follow the instructions in the blog post at `http://bit.ly/1PSjfWy` to set up a Selenium grid on a Windows machine. For the purposes of this recipe, we'll follow a simple setup that comprises of both the Selenium hub and node on the same machine:

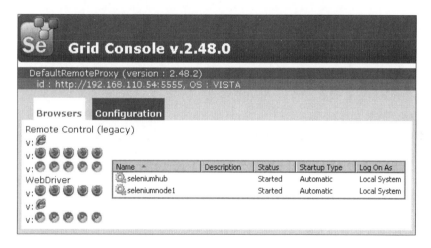

The course material provided with this book includes a Selenium Test Project. Download the `SeleniumHelloWorld.zip` folder; alternatively, you can use your own Selenium Test Project. Commit and publish `Selenium.Web.Test.sln` into the master branch in the FabrikamGit repository:

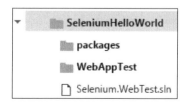

More information on how to commit and publish changes to a Git repository is available in the introduction section of *Chapter 2, Setting Up and Managing Code Repositories*. The SeleniumHQ website (`http://bit.ly/1YmqRDJ`) includes great C# tutorials for authoring Selenium Tests.

How to do it...

1. In the FarbikamGit Team Web Portal, navigate to **Build** hub. Click on the **+** icon to add a new build definition. Select the Visual Studio Build Template and click on **Create**. Navigate to the **Repository** tab in the build definition and map the repository to the master branch of the FabrikamGit repository:

2. In the build definition navigate to the **Build** tab, select the **Visual Studio Build** task. Set the name of the solution containing the Selenium Test Project. Ensure that the **Restore NuGet Packages** flag is checked:

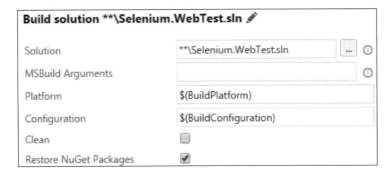

3. Select the Visual Studio Test task, enter the path to the test settings file, and inject the URL of the Selenium grid via the **Override TestRun Parameters** field:

4. Save the build definition as `FabrikamGitSelenium`. Queue a new build for this definition. Once the build execution completes, you can see the test results from the build summary view:

```
21:07.9759061Z Starting test execution, please wait...
21:22.8677541Z Passed   Selenium_ClickApplicationName_Firefox
21:29.3767143Z Passed   Selenium_ClickApplicationName_Chrome
21:38.2059993Z Passed   Selenium_ClickAbout_Firefox
21:43.5909377Z Passed   Selenium_ClickAbout_Chrome
21:49.8614017Z Passed   Selenium_ClickContact_Firefox
21:55.5099186Z Passed   Selenium_ClickContact_Chrome
```

How it works...

Let's start by understanding why the Selenium grid URL was injected in the Visual Studio Test task via the **Override TestRun Parameters** field. The solution contains Selenium Test Project and a `Run` settings file. This is the configuration file holding test settings used by the Test Project. The new build system provides the ability to overwrite the values in the `Test` settings file by directly passing the values through the **Override TestRun Parameters** field, in this specific case, the value of `SeleniumTestGridURL`. This value is used by the Selenium Test to execute the test:

```
<TestRunParameters>
  <Parameter name="GridHub" value="http://fab-selenium-grid.cloudapp.net:4440/wd/hub" />
</TestRunParameters>
```

Next, let's look at the build execution log file for this task; this provides a clear summary of the test executed, duration, and update on the result publishing:

```
21:55.6661446Z Test Run Successful.
21:55.6661446Z Test execution time: 41.6065 Seconds
21:55.9473514Z Publishing Test Results...
```

Last but not least, the TFBuild system automatically handles the publishing of test results back to the TFS, independent of the testing framework used:

As you can see in the preceding screenshot, the Selenium Test Project execution results can directly be viewed in the build summary section.

Integrating the Cloud Load Testing Service in TFBuild

"Tests at Amazon revealed: every 100 ms increase in load time of Amazon.com decreased sales by 1% (Kohavi and Longbotham 2007)."

Performance Testing can't be an afterthought! Mature software teams test for performance early in the development life cycle. The biggest entry barrier to performance testing is the high cost and low utilization of infrastructure required to generate sufficient load on the application. Today, a wide range of pay-as-you-go Cloud Load Test Services are available. Microsoft also offers a Load Test Service with Visual Studio Team Services. Each VSTS account receives 20,000 virtual user minutes of Load Test Quota free every month. In this recipe, you'll learn how to integrate the VSTS Cloud Load Test Service into your CI Pipeline in TFS.

Getting ready

Visual Studio Team Services is free for Teams of up to five people. You can create a free account at `http://bit.ly/1lANwhA`. In this recipe, we'll be using the account `https://tfs2015cookbook.visualstudio.com`.

For TFS to authenticate with the VSTS account using your identity, you will need to generate a personal access token in the VSTS account. Follow the instructions at `http://bit.ly/1I3kzVk` to generate a personal access token.

Now that we have the Cloud Load Test service in VSTS and personal access token, the Cloud Load Test service needs to be added as an endpoint in TFS. Adding an endpoint in TFS requires that you have **Edit project level information** permissions. You can acquire this permission by being added to the Team Project Administrator Group. Follow the instructions here to add the Cloud Load Test Service endpoint to TFS.

Navigate to FabrikamTFVC Team Administration Console. In the **Services** tab, click on the **+** icon to add a new endpoint. Select the **Generic** endpoint option and fill out the details as illustrated in the following screenshot. Name the endpoint CLD-VSTS.

How to do it...

1. Navigate to the **Build** hub in the FabrikamTFVC Team Web Portal. Edit the FabrikamTFVC CI build definition.

2. Click on the **+** icon to launch the **Add New Task** window. From the **Test** tab, select and add the **Cloud-based Web Performance Test** task:

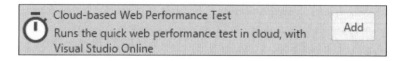

3. The Cloud Load Test Service was added as a generic endpoint in the Fabrikam Team Administration Console. Select the CLD-VSTS endpoint from the registered connection dropdown. Enter the endpoint you would like to run the test against. Specify the location to generate the load from:

4. Click on **Save** and trigger queue a new build. Once the build execution completes, the results of the load test execution is available as part of the build result:

```
2015-07-07T22:22:05.0439607Z [Message]This run was requested by 'Tarun Arora' using the Visual Studio Online Account 'Geeks'.
2015-07-07T22:22:05.0439607Z [Message]This load test will run using 1 agent cores. Learn more about agent core allocation her
2015-07-07T22:22:05.0449612Z [Message]This run will use 250 virtual-user minutes. To learn more about usage limits, refer  ht
2015-07-07T22:22:05.5599666Z ##[warning][Exception] 2 occurrences of ['','','LoadTestErrorLimitExceededException'] : More tha
2015-07-07T22:22:05.5609674Z ##[warning][HttpError] 536 occurrences of ['Scenario1','WebTest1','403 - Forbidden'] : 403 - For
2015-07-07T22:22:05.5619671Z ##[warning][ValidationRuleError] 528 occurrences of ['Scenario1','WebTest1','ValidateResponseUrl
2015-07-07T22:22:05.5729660Z ##[warning][ThresholdMessage] 3 occurrences of ["Agent0","Processor","% Processor Time","0"] : T
2015-07-07T22:22:05.5739671Z ##[warning][ThresholdMessage] 3 occurrences of ["Agent0","Processor","% Processor Time","_Total"
2015-07-07T22:22:05.5749675Z ##[warning][ThresholdMessage] 1 occurrences of ["Agent0","Processor","% Processor Time","_Total"
2015-07-07T22:22:05.5759667Z ##[warning][ThresholdMessage] 1 occurrences of ["Agent0","Processor","% Processor Time","0"] : T
2015-07-07T22:22:05.5829670Z The load test completed successfully.
2015-07-07T22:22:05.5869677Z Run-id for this load test is 1 and its name is 'LoadTest1.loadtest'.
```

How it works...

You can start to load test your application with simple configuration. It is easy to get started and utilize the free Cloud Load Test Virtual User Minutes available in your VSTS account. TFBuild also includes a Cloud-based Load Test task that allows you to run multistep performance tests.

Analyzing test execution results from the Runs view

In Team Foundation Server 2015, the test execution results of both manual and automated testing are surfaced in the **Runs** page. This page is a new addition to the **Test** hub in Team Web Portal. The **Runs** page offers a unified experience for analyzing the results of test executed using any framework. In this recipe, you'll learn how to analyze and action the test execution results in the **Runs** view in Team Web Portal.

How to do it...

1. Navigate to the **Test** hub and click on **Runs** to load the **Runs** page. The **Runs** page displays the recent test runs. At first glance, you can see the test execution status, test configuration, build number, number of failed tests, and the pass rate:

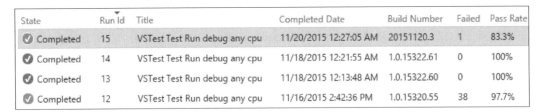

State	Run Id	Title	Completed Date	Build Number	Failed	Pass Rate
✓ Completed	15	VSTest Test Run debug any cpu	11/20/2015 12:27:05 AM	20151120.3	1	83.3%
✓ Completed	14	VSTest Test Run debug any cpu	11/18/2015 12:21:55 AM	1.0.15322.61	0	100%
✓ Completed	13	VSTest Test Run debug any cpu	11/18/2015 12:13:48 AM	1.0.15322.60	0	100%
✓ Completed	12	VSTest Test Run debug any cpu	11/16/2015 2:42:36 PM	1.0.15320.55	38	97.7%

2. Navigate to the **Filters** view by clicking on the **Filters** tab. The query is defaulted to display the test runs from the last 7 days. Amend and add new clauses to show only the automated test runs for today:

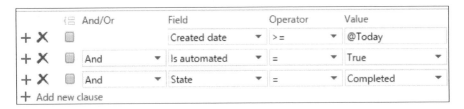

	And/Or	Field	Operator	Value
+ ✗ ▢		Created date	>=	@Today
+ ✗ ▢	And	Is automated	=	True
+ ✗ ▢	And	State	=	Completed
+ Add new clause				

3. The query narrows down the test execution results to just one run:

4. Double-click on test run ID to open the test run for analysis. This view shows the run summary along with charts to visualize the test results by properties, traits, configuration, failures types, and resolution. Any attachments associated to the test run are also available in this view:

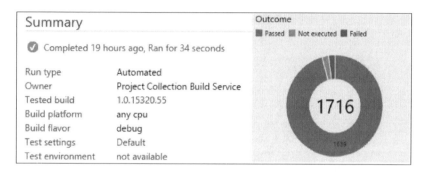

5. Navigate to the **Test results** tab to see the list of all tests executed as part of this test run. Prior to TFS 2015, you would have had to download the TRX file and open it in Visual Studio to get to this information. This view provides the next level of detail among other things. You can see the test execution duration and failure error messages:

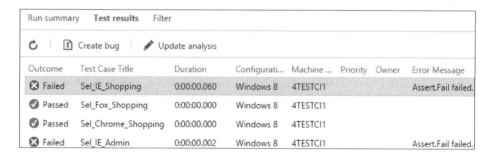

6. Select multiple tests and click on **Create Bug** to create a bug-type Work Item. Clicking on **Update Analysis** lets you add comments to the test results. You can also double-click on a test to go the next level of detail on its test execution:

UPDATE ANALYSIS
Analysis owner
🧑 Tarun Arora
Failure type
New Issue
Resolution
Configuration issue
Comment
The IE configuration is causing the integration tests to fail.

How it works...

This functionality gives you a unified test analysis experience irrespective of the framework you choose to execute your tests in. In summary, you can query all test runs available in your Team Project, drill down into a specific test run to get a summary view of that run, visualize test runs using charts, query/filter the test results within a run, drill down to a specific test result, download attachments, and last but not least, analyze test failures and file bugs.

Exporting and importing test cases in Excel from TFS

While test cases in TFS can be accessed from Microsoft Test Manager as well as Team Web Access, you may still find stakeholders wanting to access the test cases from Excel. As a matter of preference, a few of your stakeholders may find it easier to document test cases in excel. While TFS does not offer an out-of-the-box feature to export and import test cases in Excel, it offers a good **Software Development Kit** (**SDK**) that can be used to create tools that enable such functionality. In this recipe, you'll learn how to use "test case export to excel" and "Test Case Migrator Plus (open source community tools)" to export test cases into Excel and import test cases from Excel into TFS.

Getting ready

Download and install the following utilities on your machine:

▶ **Test case export utility**: https://tfstestcaseexporttoexcel.codeplex.com

▶ **Test case import utility**: http://tcmimport.codeplex.com

You'll need elevated permissions to install these utilities. The machine where these utilities are installed needs a version of Excel installed. These utilities do not need to be installed on the TFS application tier.

How to do it...

Exporting test cases from TFS

1. On starting the **Test Cases Export** utility, you'll be prompted to connect to TFS. Once connected, you'll see a list of test plans and test suits associated to that plan. Select the test suite and the file location for export and fill out the export output location and filename as illustrated in the following screenshot:

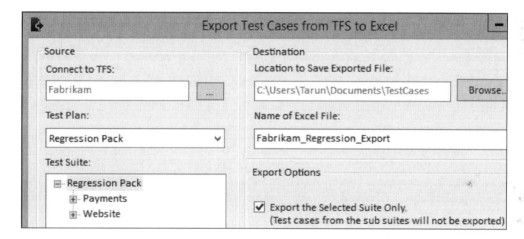

2. The export process gives you the following options:

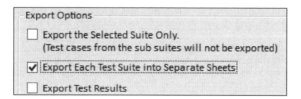

3. Select the **Export Each Test Suite into Separate Sheets** option to export each test suite into a separate sheet. In the preceding example, regression pack, payments, and website will be exported in three separate sheets in the workbook.

4. Once the export completes, open the spreadsheet from the export location to view the results of the export.

Importing test cases from TFS

1. Start the **Test Case Migrator Plus** utility to launch the test case import wizard.

2. Select the data source from the **Source** tab. The input format can either be **Excel Workbook** or **MHT/Word**. In this recipe, we'll be using the input source format as **Excel Workbook**. Key in the output folder location. Once the workbook has been parsed, you'll see the list of columns in the selected worksheet. Click on **Next** to configure the **Destination** settings:

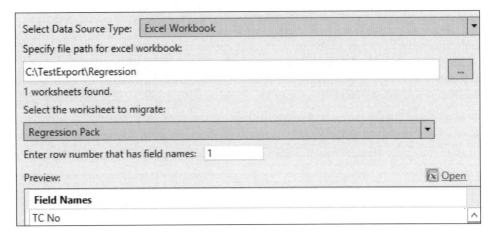

3. From the **Destination** tab, enter the destination details such as Team Project and Work Item type to import the test cases to. From the **Settings** tab, choose to create a new settings file and click on the **Next** button (the settings file will persist your selections for future imports). From the **Field** mapping tab, map the columns in the spreadsheet to the Work Item. For example, the **Title** field in the spreadsheet maps to the title field of the Work Item.

4. From the **Links mapping** tab, you can optionally enable linking between Work Items using the **Miscellaneous** tab to specify how the data is read from the source Excel file. Click on **Save and Migrate** to start the migration process based on the settings configured through the wizard. This will trigger the import process; progress on the update is shown on the user interface:

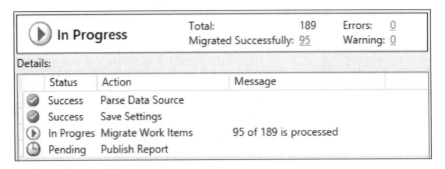

5. Once the import has been completed, exit the wizard by clicking on the **Close** icon button. The import utility processes the worksheet and generates a report in the same location as the source worksheet. The import settings file is also generated in the same location. The import settings file stores the settings specified during the import process. The settings file can be used for future imports:

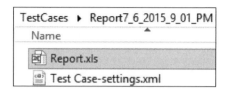

6. Open the `Report.xls` file and all successfully imported test cases will be listed in the **Passed** sheet. Any test cases that have issues during import will be listed in the warning sheet, and any test cases that couldn't be imported will be listed in the failed sheet.

7. To view the imported test results, navigate to the FabrikamTest hub in Team Web Portal. You'll see the new plans appear in the test plan dropdown. The following screenshot illustrates a test suite and a linked test case in Team Web Portal:

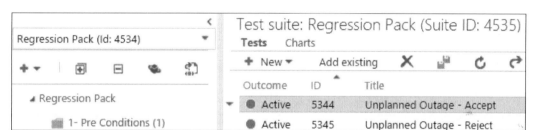

How it works...

This, by no means, is a Test Case Migration solution, but it is worth pointing out that if you are using other Test Case Management tools that support extracting test cases into Excel, you could use these tools to import the artifacts into TFS.

There is more

While we are on the subject of test suites, it is worth highlighting that TFS 2015 now supports assigning multiple people to a test suite. This capability can be invoked by right-clicking on a test suite in test hub and choosing **Assign Individuals** from the context menu. As illustrated in the following screenshot, the new form allows assigning multiple testers to the test suite:

Assign all the test cases in this test suite to be run by multiple testers. For example, you can assign the tests to all your user acceptance testers. Then send them an email to let them know that the tests are ready to be run.

Select testers

If you want to have multiple users run the same test cases in this test suite, add these users to this list. Tests are created from all the test cases for each tester.

| Aaron Bjork✕ | Charles Sterling✕ | Chris Patterson✕ | Claude Remillard✕ | Gopinath CH✕ |

| Display Name or Microsoft Account 🔎 | Browse | Check name |

If at a later time you decide to remove a tester from this list for this suite, then the tests that were created for this tester are removed.

Send email

☑ Send email to the testers

This will iterate through the test suite and create test cases for each individual. An e-mail with the link to the test cases is e-mailed out to the individuals. This is a great way to enable multiple individuals to test using the same test suite, giving you the ability to track the test activity of each individual in isolation.

Copying and cloning test suites and test cases

TFS offers two types of copy operations for test suites and test cases, namely, **copy** and **clone**. Copy uses a mechanism called shallow copy that simply creates a reference to the artifact. If any amendment is made to the artifact, it reflects into all its references. Clone uses a mechanism called deep copy; the new artifacts have no reference back to its origin and is not impacted by any updates made to the original artifact. A common scenario for using shallow copy is when testing using the same scripts across multiple iterations. On the other hand, a common scenario for deep copy is creating a regression test script by copying several existing test suites and test cases. In this recipe, you'll learn how to use the copy and clone functionality.

Getting ready

In this recipe, we'll be using Microsoft Test Manager. Microsoft Test Manager is installed with Visual Studio Enterprise or Visual Studio Test Professional. Launch Microsoft Test Manager and connect to the FabrikamTFVC Team Project.

How to do it...

Copying (shallow copy)

1. In Microsoft Test Manager, from the **Plan** tab, select a static test suite that will hold the new copy.

2. From the toolbar, click on the **Create test suites by referencing existing test cases** button.

3. From the dialog, select the test plan and test suites that you want to copy and click on **Create Suite**.

Clone (deep copy)

1. In the Microsoft Test Manager, from the **Organize** tab, select a test plan.

2. From the toolbar, click on the **Clone** button.

3. From the dialog, select one or more test suites that you want to clone. You can optionally choose to clone requirements that are associated with the selected test suite.

4. Enter the name of the destination test plan and set the associated Area Path and Iteration Path.

5. Next, click on the **Clone** button to trigger the clone operation. The clone log appears showing updates of the clone process.

 Cloning test cases is supported between Team Projects, but only in the same Team Project Collection.

You can also use the /clone switch with tcm.exe from command line to clone test cases and test suites. In the following sample, you'll notice that the /clone requirements is being used to clone the requirements. The value of the field Area Path and Iteration Path in the destination will be overridden with the specified value:

```
tcm suites /clone
/collection:http://tfs2015:8080/tfs/DefaultCollection
    /teamproject:FabrikamTFVC /destinationteamproject:FabrikamGit
    /clonerequirements
    /suiteid:234 /destinationsuiteid:567
    /overridefield:"Iteration Path"=" FabrikamGit\sprint3"
    /overridefield:"Area Path"=" FabrikamGit\catalog"
```

How it works...

When you clone a test suite, the following objects get copied from the source test plan to the destination test plan:

Test plan object	Notes
Test case	Each new test case retains its shared steps. A link is made between the source and new test cases. The new test cases do not have test runs, bugs, test results, and build information.
Shared steps referenced by cloned test cases	Any shared steps referenced by the source test cases are maintained in the cloned test cases at destination.
Test suite	The following data is retained: ▸ Names and hierarchical structure of the test suites ▸ Order of the test cases ▸ Assigned testers ▸ Configurations
Action recordings linked from a cloned test case	Any action recording links are maintained in the clone test case.
Links and attachments	Any links and attachments in the source are also available in the cloned test case.
Test configuration	The test configuration is reapplied in the destination test plan.

Exporting test artifacts and test results from the test hub

TFS test artifacts comprise of test plans, test suites, and test cases, and of course, test results. It is common to have to export the test artifacts for purposes of sharing and reporting. Back in the days of TFS 2013 Test Scribe delivered as a Visual Studio Extension, it was the only way to export these artifacts from TFS. Test hub now boasts the e-mail or print test artifacts functionality that allows you to easily share test artifacts with stakeholders. The feature is simple to use and can be triggered from several places within the test hub in Team Web Portal. In this recipe, you'll learn how to export the test artifacts from the test hub.

How to do it...

1. Browse to the FabrikamTFVC Team web access and navigate into **Test** hub. To export at the test plan level, select the test plan, and then click on the **Email or print test artifacts** button from the toolbar:

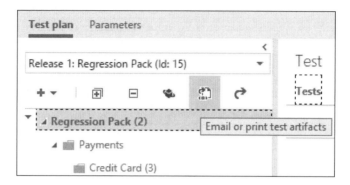

2. To export at the test suite level, select the test suite open the context menu and chose the **Export** option:

3. Whether you choose to export from test plan or test suite, in both cases, you will get a new form to select "what" and "how". The "what" in this case being the artifacts. The "how" in this case being e-mail or print. A few items are worth highlighting in the following screenshot. The **Latest test outcome** option has been added in Update 1, selecting this option also exports the test results. Choosing **Selected suite + children** recursively exports all children of the selected suite:

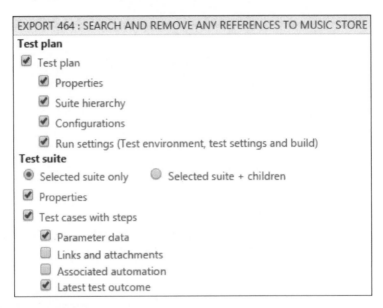

How it works...

Clicking on print or e-mail starts the process of generating the extract; this may take up to a few seconds to complete depending on the quantity and size of the artifacts being exported. Once the export has been completed, a form will pop up to show you the preview of the export. You can also edit and format the values from the preview form. Since we have chosen the e-mail option, the form has a field that allows us to choose the e-mail address of the person we would like the export to be sent out to:

TEST SUITE: 71: AS THE BUSINESS PERSON, I WANT TO TEST FUNCTIONALITY (SUITE ID: 299)	
To	Display Name or Microsoft Account 🔍 Browse | Check name
Subject	Test suite: 71: As the business person, I want to test functionality (Suite ID: 299)
B *I* U ꝋ ꝋ ꞉꞊ ꞉꞊ ꞊꞉ ꞊꞉	

Test plan 293: PartsTestPlan

As illustrated in the following screenshot, the export also includes the test steps:

Test Case 1032: Create ticket - get customer profile

STEPS

#	Action	Expected value	Attachments
1	Login to the system		
2	Click on Create New Ticket		
3	Enter Title, Description and Severity		
4	Click on Select customer	This action should bring up another dialog showing existing customers	
5	Search by customer last name, first name and select appropriate customer	This should filter customers with given last name and first name	
6	Click on "Create"	This action should create the ticket and show ticket details back to the customer	

PARAMETERS

LINKS

ID	WorkItemType	Link type	Title
1030	Product Backlog Item	Tests	Create new service ticket

There is more...

It is possible to customize the format of the export by modifying the underlying template used by TFS during the export/print process. The following points are to be kept in mind before customizing the template:

You should create a backup of the original template, for example, copy and rename it to `TestSuite-Original.xsl`. If not, when you upgrade TFS, the changes you made in the `TestSuite.xsl` file may get overwritten. The export does not support customization per project; the style changes will affect all projects in your TFS instance.

Follow the steps listed here to add your company logo to the export:

1. Log on to the TFS application tier and navigate to the following path. Add your company logo (`companylogo.png`) in the `C:\Program Files\Microsoft Team Foundation Server 14.0\Application Tier\Web Services\_static\tfs\12\_content` folder path.

2. Modify the `TestSuite.xsl` file in the `C:\Program Files\Microsoft Team Foundation Server 14.0\Application Tier\Web Services\_tfs_resources\TestManagement\v1.0\Transforms\1033` folder.

3. Open the `TestSuite.xsl` file in the notepad and add the following lines of code to include your company logo into the export template:

```
<div style="align:center;">
<img src="../../_static/tfs/12/_content/companylogo.png" />
</div>
```

4. The results of the customization can be tested by generating an export through the test hub in Team Web Portal.

Charting testing status on Dashboards in Team Portal

The charting tools in Team Web Portal provide a great way to analyze and visualize test case execution. The charts created through the charting tools can be pinned to custom Dashboards. Both charts and Dashboards are fantastic information radiators to share the test execution results with Team members and stakeholders. In this recipe, you'll learn how to pin the test execution results on a custom Dashboard in Team Portal.

Getting Started

Follow the steps in the Configuring Dashboards in Team Project recipe in *Chapter 1, Team Project Setup*, to create a custom Dashboard for testing.

How to do it...

1. Navigate to the **Test** hub in FabrikamTFVC Team Web Portal. The **Test Plan** page gives you a list of test suites and a list of test cases for the selected suite. The **Charts** tab gives you a great way to visualize this information. Click on the **+** icon and select **New test result** charts. Select a bar chart and group by **Outcome**; this renders the test case outcome in the bar chart. Click on **OK** to save the chart. Right-click on the newly created chart and pin the chart to the testing Dashboard:

2. Now, click on the **+** icon and select the **New test case** chart. Test case chart types support trend charts and the supported trend period is from 7 days to up to 12 months. Select the stacked area chart type and chose to stack by **State**. This will allow you to visualize the state of the test cases over time. Click on OK to save the chart, right-click on the chart and pin it to the Dashboard:

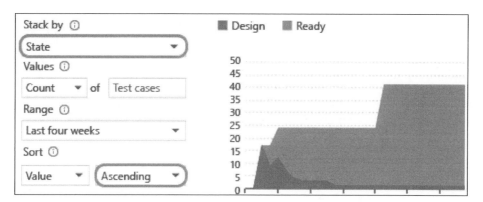

How it works...

The charts are calculated using the Work Item data in the transactional database. When Work Items are updated, the charts reflect the updates immediately. To learn more about the charting functionality in Team Web Portal refer to the walkthrough at `http://bit.ly/1PGP8CU`.

6
Releasing Your Application

"Continuous Deployment can be thought of as an extension to Continuous Integration, aiming at minimizing lead time"

–Agile Allianz

In this chapter, we will cover the following:

- ▶ Creating a release definition in Team Web Portal
- ▶ Mapping artifacts to a release definition
- ▶ Configuring a release definition for the continuous deployment
- ▶ Adding and configuring environments in a release definition
- ▶ Configuring security for release definitions
- ▶ Configuring global and local variables for a release
- ▶ Deploying an Azure website using release management
- ▶ Deploying the IIS Web Application using release management
- ▶ Tracking a release in release management

Introduction

So far in the book, we have talked about planning, developing, testing, and building software. Software teams spend weeks and months developing and testing software; however, software can only reap its worth when it reaches the hands of the people it's meant for. Release management is an enabler for that:

> *"Release management is the process of managing, planning, scheduling, and controlling a software build through different stages and environments; including testing and deploying software releases."*

> *—Wikipedia*

On June 3rd, 2013, Microsoft acquired the InRelease product from InCycle software. The InRelease product was rebranded as Microsoft Release Management and integrated into Team Foundation Server 2013. Microsoft Release Manager gave Microsoft a position in the growing release management market. While Release Manager shipped along with Team Foundation Server, it required separate installation and setup. Though various improvements were made to improve the integration between the two products, they still felt disjointed at several places. The WPF-based desktop client was clunky and limiting. Release Manager did not support non-.NET applications and could not be used on non-Windows platforms. It was clear that Release Manager was only a stop-gap solution and would need to be replaced by a proper solution.

Microsoft has recently released the web-based Release Management solution in Visual Studio Team Services. While the new solution has not been released in Team Foundation Server 2015 Update 1, it is expected to debut in TFS 2015 in either Update 2 or Update 3. No further investment is expected to be made in the old Release Management Solution, and it will inevitably be replaced by the new web-based Release Management Solution. With this in mind, this chapter is entirely focused on the new web-based Release Management Solution. To try out the recipes in this chapter, you'll need to create a Visual Studio Team Services account; follow the instructions at `http://bit.ly/1N50I7j`.

 Recipes in this chapter are based on the new web-based Release Management Solution. The new web-based Release Management Solution is expected to be available in Team Foundation Server in Update 2 or Update 3. To try out the recipes in this chapter, create a Visual Studio Team Services account (`http://bit.ly/1N50I7j`).

The new web-based Release Management Solution is very well integrated into the product. No separate installation or configuration is required to start using the new Release Management Solution. The security infrastructure of the Release Manager is different from the previous version, in that it did not manage its own groups and permissions. New permissions are introduced in VSTS for release management, such as **Create release definitions**, **Create releases**, and **Manage approvers**. Default values for these permissions are set for specific groups at the Team Project level. These permissions can then be overridden for the groups or individual users, for a specific release definition or for a specific environment within a release definition.

Both Team build and release management share the same agent—pool and queue infrastructure. Unified agent infrastructure reduces administration and setup overhead. The tasks used to orchestrate the actions are also shared between build and release. This significantly reduces the learning curve for release management. The new solution is web based, open, extensible, and fully cross-platform. The underlying framework between Team build and release management is the same, so you get the same real-time console output in release management as you get with Team build. The release definitions support change revision and different functionality similar to that in the build definitions. Release management supports draft releases similar to the draft build functionality in Team build. With so much in common between build and release management, the only difference is the build also has access to deployment tasks, you may ask how are the build and release management different?

The line between build and release management is blurred because both share so much in common. The key difference is that deployment is just one of the activities performed in the release management. As illustrated in the following image, the new release management solution allows creating release pipelines. A release pipeline can consist of one or more environments. Each environment can have one or more physical or virtual deployment targets. Environments provide pre-release and post-release approval workflow as well as tasks for testing and deployment:

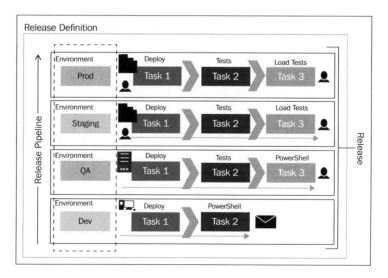

The software deployed through Release Manager can be injected from Team build, Jenkins, Team City, FTP, and so on. With artifacts shared across all environments in the release pipeline, it truly lets you build once and deploy everywhere.

To lower the entry barrier, Release Manager provides out-of-the-box Deployment Templates. The Deployment Template adds the set of tasks required for the type of deployment in an environment. You still need to configure the tasks, but pre-adding the tasks gives you a head start in your release configuration. The framework also allows you to clone or save your configured environments as templates. Again, the intention is to speed up release configuration and maximize reuse across release definitions. Release management is expected to soon supplement the REST API gallery with Release Management REST APIs. This will allow you to integrate release management into other parts of the release workflow used in your organization or simply extend the release management capabilities where you find them lacking.

You will kick off the chapter by learning the different capabilities in the new web-based release management solution; in the later recipes, we'll cover deployment scenarios for Azure and on-premise web applications. Last but not least, we'll understand the release tracking and reporting capabilities available in release management.

Creating a release definition in Team Web Portal

In this recipe, you'll learn how to create a new release definition using an empty Deployment Template. You'll also learn about the different functions available in a release definition.

Getting ready

To create a new release definition, you need to be a member of the Release Administrators Group. These permissions are also available to the Project Administrators Group.

How to do it...

1. Navigate to the **Release** hub in FabrikamTFVC Team Project:

2. Click on the **+** icon to create a new release definition. There are preconfigured Deployment Templates to choose from. In this recipe, we'll start with the **Empty** template. Unlike the other templates, the **Empty** template creates a blank release definition without any pre-added tasks:

3. Name the release definition `FabrikamTFVC Web Release`:

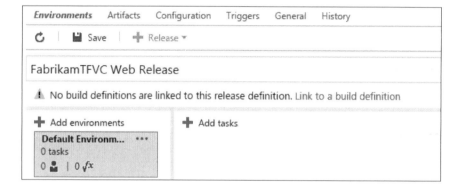

4. Navigate to the **General** tab and change the release number format from `Release-$(rev:r)` to `Rel-$(System.TeamProject)-$(rev:r)`. The releases generated from this definition will have a release name in the format `Rel-FabrikamTFVC-1`:

5. Click on the **Save** button to save the release definition. In this recipe, we've created a blank release definition. We'll walk through the different functions of a release definition in the next *How it works...* section.

How it works...

In this recipe, we started off from an empty release template. The Deployment Template window provides an option to start from a pre-configured release template. The pre-configured Deployment Template adds an environment and all necessary release tasks to the default environment, only leaving the task configuration to you. As illustrated in the following screenshot, the **Azure Website Deployment** template adds a default environment and two tasks, namely, **Azure Web App Deployment** and **Visual Studio Test**. In the long term, you'll start seeing more pre-configured Deployment Templates being made available out of the box:

Let's now understand the functions in the **Environments** tab of the FabrikamTFVC Web release definition:

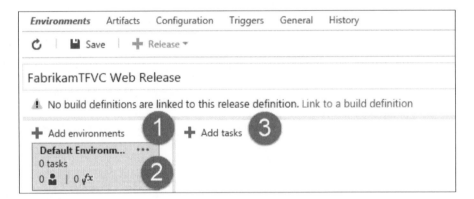

> ▸ **Add environments**: This is the collection of server(s) where your application needs to be deployed. Clicking on the **Add environments** icon also launches the Deployment Template window. The deployment window gives you the ability to add an environment and related tasks for deploying the application in that environment.

> ▸ **Default Environment**: This is a logical container holding the tasks required to release an application in the environment. As illustrated in the following screenshot, an environment supports a level of configuration. We'll be covering the functions supported by an environment in detail in the *Adding and configuring environments in a release definition* recipe:

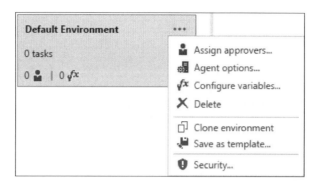

- ▸ **Add tasks**: This is simply a step in the release process to an environment. A set of pre-created tasks are already available out of the box. The gallery also provides scripting tasks to enable you to perform operations that may not necessarily be available in the pre-created tasks. The framework is fully extensibility; refer to the *Creating a new build task using the TFBuild Extensibility framework* recipe in *Chapter 4, Building Your Application*, to learn how you can add your own tasks. Both build and release hub shared a common task gallery. This allows you to use the tasks from the build process in the release process too. You'll learn more about tasks as we start configuring them in the later recipes in this chapter.

Navigate to the **General** tab. This tab allows you to specify the release name format. The names of releases for a release definition are, by default, sequentially numbered. The first release is named `Release-1`, the next release is `Release-2`, and so on. You can change this naming scheme by editing the release name format mask. The field supports the use of predefined (listed in the following table). You can also use custom variables; we'll be covering more on variables in the *Configuring global and local variables for a release* recipe:

Variable	Description
`Rev:rr`	An auto-incremented number with at least the specified number of digits.
`Date/Date:MMddyy`	The current date, with the default format MMddyy. Any combinations of M/MM/MMM/MMMM, d/dd/ddd/dddd, y/yy/ yyyy/yyyy, h/hh/H/HH, m/mm, s/ss are supported.
`System.TeamProject`	The name of the Team Project to which this build belongs.
`Release.ReleaseId`	The ID of the release is unique across all releases in the project.
`Release. DefinitionName`	The name of the release definition to which the current release belongs.

Variable	Description
`Build.BuildNumber`	The number of the build contained in the release. If a release has multiple builds, this is the number of the build that triggered the release in the case of continuous deployment or the number of the first build in the case of a manual trigger.
`Build.DefinitionName`	The definition name of the build contained in the release. If a release has multiple builds, this is the definition name of the build that triggered the release in the case of continuous deployment or the definition name of the first build in the case of a manual trigger.
`Artifact.ArtifactType`	The type of the artifact source linked with the release. For example, this can be Team build or Jenkins.
`Build.SourceBranch`	The branch for which the build in the release was queued. For Git, this is the name of the branch in the form `refs/heads/master`. For Team Foundation Version Control, this is the root server path for the workspace in the `form$/teamproject/branch`. This variable is not set in the case of Jenkins artifact sources.
`Custom variable`	The value of a global configuration property defined in the release definition.

The **History** tab shows you the list of changes made to a release definition since its creation. You also have the ability to differentiate the changes between the two revisions of changes to a release definition. The **Artifacts** tab allows you to map the different artifacts that need to be deployed as part of the release definition; you'll be learning about the functions of the **Artifacts** tab in the *Mapping artifacts to a release definition* recipe. The **Configuring** tab allows you to configure variables for your release definitions; you'll learn about the functions of the **Configuration** tab in the *Adding and configuring environments in a release definition* recipe. The **Triggers** tab enables you to configure the release as a continuous deployment by setting the trigger as a continuous integration. This configuration triggers the release process whenever there is a change to the underlying artifacts mapped to the release definition. You'll learn more about this in the *Configuring a release definition for a continuous deployment* recipe.

Mapping artifacts to a release definition

The release definition allows you to deploy an application into multiple environments. The files and installers required to deploy an application are referred to as artifacts. At present, release management understands artifacts from Team build, Jenkins, and on-premises TFS. A release definition can have one or more artifacts. This flexibility is extremely useful for Teams building software in modules that are pulled together to form a release. In this recipe, you'll learn how to map the output from a Team build definition into a release definition.

Getting ready

To edit a release definition, you need to be a member of the Release Administrators Group. These permissions are also available to the Project Administrators Group.

Scenario: FabrikamTFVC Team has two build definitions, namely, `FabrikamTFVC.Website` and `FabrikamTFVC.Services`. Website and services are two components of the same application; these components need to be rolled out together in the release. To enable this scenario, the FabrikamTFVC Team needs to map the installers from `FabrikamTFVC.Website` and `FabrikamTFVC.Services` into the release definition FabrikamTFVC Web:

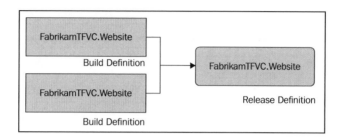

You can follow the steps in the *Creating a continuous integration build definition in TFBuild* recipe of *Chapter 4, Building Your Application*. Follow the steps in the *Creating a release definition in Team Web Portal* recipe, to create the FabrikamTFVC Web release definition.

How to do it...

1. Navigate to the **Release** hub in FabrikamTFVC Team Project and edit the release definition FabrikamTFVC Web. As illustrated in the following screenshot, the release definition prompts you to link a build definition to this release:

2. Click on the link to build definition hyperlink, set the artifact type as **Build**, and choose the **FabrikamTFVC.Services** build definition. The text at the bottom tells you the artifacts being published by this build definition. Click on **OK** to finish mapping the `FabrikamTFVC.Services` build definition to FabrikamTFVC Web release definition:

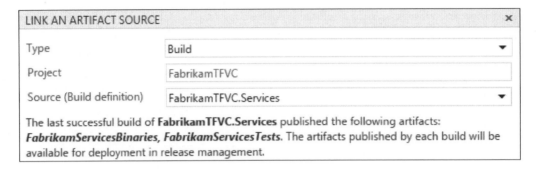

3. Now, navigate to the **Artifacts** tab; you'll see that the **FabrikamTFVC.Services** build definition shows up as an artifact source for this release definition:

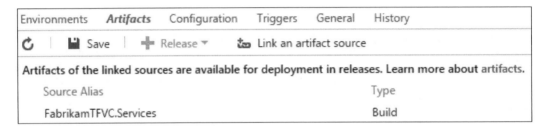

4. Click on **Link an artifact source** to map the build definition of **FabrikamTFVC. Website** to this release definition. Once done, you'll see both **FabrikamTFVC.Services** and **FabrikamTFVC.Website** show up as an artifact source for this release definition. Click on **Save** to commit the changes to the build definition:

How it works...

The artifacts in a release definition allow you to truly build once and deploy everywhere. The artifacts are mapped at the release definition level and are available to all environments in a release definition.

When queuing a release, you have an option to select the version of the build to be used in the release. As illustrated in the following screenshot, you can choose the version of the builds used in this release. These artifacts are available across all selected environments. The version of the artifact cannot be changed once a release has been triggered from a release definition:

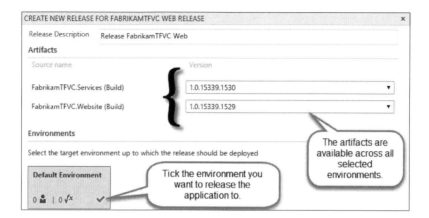

As illustrated in the preceding screenshot, you can directly trigger a release from a build. Choosing release from the build opens up the queue release option allowing you to choose the version of other artifacts and the environments that the build needs to be deployed to. You can enjoy this truly integrated experience when you choose Team build as the artifact for the release definition:

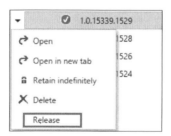

When a release is triggered, the selected versions of the artifacts are downloaded into the agent working directory. Tasks running within that environment can then deploy the artifacts. The artifact download behavior can be customized; you can skip the download of the artifact to the agent for a particular environment. This can be done by setting the **Skip artifacts download** flag in the **General** settings of an environment:

There is more...

Release management currently supports Team build, Jenkins, on-premises TFS, and other sources as valid artifact sources. The source needs to be added as a service endpoint from the Team Administration Console. As illustrated in the following screenshot, you must create a service endpoint for Jenkins using the Jenkins endpoint and specifying connectivity details. Once the Jenkins connection endpoint has been successfully added, you can choose Jenkins as an artifact type in the release definition:

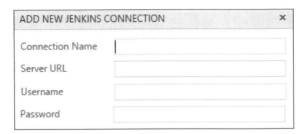

Release management also supports adding other artifact sources. This option is suitable if you want to connect to sources such as Team City, NuGet repository, or file share.

Configuring a release definition for a continuous deployment

A continuous deployment is a software engineering approach in which Teams deploy incremental changes to software as they are committed to a repository. It aims at building, testing, and releasing software faster and more frequently. A release definition already stores details of systems generating the artifacts that need to be deployed. A release definition can be configured to trigger a release when a new version of the artifact is available. In this recipe, you'll learn how to configure the release definition to trigger a new release when a new artifact version is available.

Getting ready

To edit a release definition, you need to be a member of the Release Administrators Group. These permissions are also available to the Project Administrators Group.

Scenario: The FabrikamTFVC Team has mapped **FabrikamTFVC.Website** and **FabrikamTFVC. Services** to the release definition of FabrikamTFVC Web. The Team now wants the FabrikamTFVC release definition to automatically trigger a new release when a new successful build is available for **FabrikamTFVC.Services**.

How to do it...

1. Navigate to the **Release** hub in the FabrikamTFVC Team Project and edit the release definition FabrikamTFVC Web. Click on the **Triggers** tab to configure the triggers for this release definition:

2. Check the **Continuous deployment** checkbox and select **FabrikamTFVC.Services** as the trigger for artifact source label. Also select the environments you would like the release to be automatically deployed to. It is a common scenario to continuously deploy all changes to a selected environment; however, release management gives you the option to select one or more environments for continuous deployment. Click on **Save** to commit the changes:

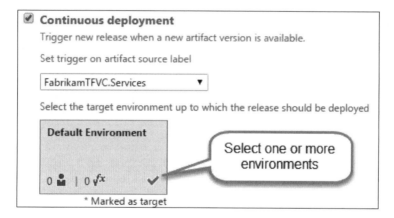

3. Navigate to the **Build** hub and queue a new build for **FabrikamTFVC.Services**. Once **FabrikamTFVC.Services** is completed successfully, a release from the release definition FabrikamTFVC Web is triggered. A new release will not trigger if the **FabrikamTFVC.Services** option fails:

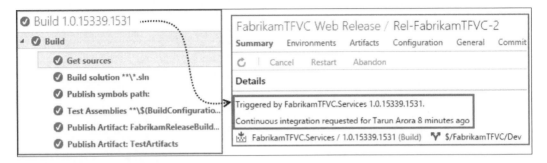

How it works...

The FabrikamTFVC release definition is now configured to detect when a new artifact is available in the **FabrikamTFVC.Services** build definition. Under the hood, this configuration sets up a queue between the build and release definition. A successful built-in **FabrikamTFVC. Services** generates an event; as soon as the receiver in FabrikamTFVC Web release definition receives this event, it triggers a new release.

The release will trigger sequentially in all the selected environments. At present, you cannot set up triggers to automatically deploy to multiple environments in parallel. It is expected that in future, REST APIs will be available to trigger releases remotely from other systems.

There's more...

While **FabrikamTFVC.Services** does not need to be a continuous integration build, even if it is manually triggered, as long as a new successful build artifact is produced by the build the release will be trigged. You can optionally set the build as continuous integration from the **Build** hub as illustrated in the following screenshot:

Adding and configuring environments in a release definition

A release definition is composed of a collection of environments. An environment is a logical container that holds information on where a release needs to be deployed and how it needs to be deployed. The environment can be a collection of server(s) on premises, in the cloud, multiple clouds, or an app store. The steps used to deploy the application on each environment can be the same or different. The deployment steps in an environment are described using tasks. In this recipe, you'll learn how to add and configure environments.

Getting ready

To edit a release definition, you need to be a member of the Release Administrators Group. These permissions are also available to the Project Administrators Group.

Scenario: The FabrikamTFVC Team has a collection of servers categorized as development, QA, staging, and production environments. The Team wants the ability to deploy the application across all environments in a single release process. Each environment has different owners and approvers. The Team wants the release definition to be configured such that developers can approve the release into the development environment; the QA approves all releases in the QA environment. Both the QA and Release Manager approve releases in staging (pre-production). The Release Manager approves production releases:

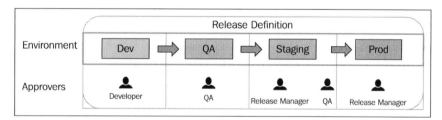

How to do it...

1. Navigate to the **Release** hub in FabrikamTFVC Team Project and edit the release definition FabrikamTFVC Web. Rename the default environment to **Development**:

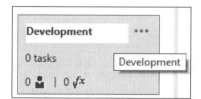

2. Launch the context menu by clicking on the ellipsis to configure the development environment. From the context menu, choose **Assign approvers...**:

3. This window allows you to configure the approvers for pre-deployment and post-deployment approval as well as set up an overall environment owner and choose to enable e-mail notifications. Click on **OK** to save the configured changes. This screen allows adding both individual user accounts as well as groups as approvers and owners:

4. You can now click on the **+** icon to add deployment tasks to the development environment. Adding and configuring tasks will be covered in future recipes.

5. From the development environment, launch the context menu by clicking on the ellipsis. From the context menu, choose **Save as template...**:

6. Give the Deployment Template a name and description as illustrated in the following screenshot:

7. Click on the **+** icon to add an environment. This will launch the Deployment Template window. As illustrated in the following screenshot, you'll see a new **Custom** tab. This tab will list all Custom Templates saved by the Team. Select and add this template; it will add a new environment with the approval configuration setup in step 3:

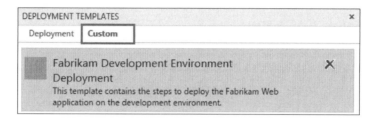

8. Now, add a new environment for QA, staging, and production, and set the approvers as indicated in the diagram in the *Getting ready* section of this recipe. As illustrated in the following screenshot, each environment has symbols that provide useful information:

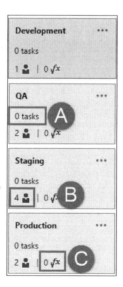

    ❑ This shows the count of tasks in an environment. At present, there are 0 tasks in this QA environment.

    ❑   This shows the count of approvers in an environment. At present, there are four approvers set up for the staging environment.

    ❑   This shows the count of variables in an environment. At present, there are 0 variables set up for the production environment.

9. Click on the ellipsis in the environment to launch the context menu. From the context menu, select **Clone Environment**. This will clone the selected environment into a new environment. This is great when you want to copy an existing environment without saving it as a template.

10. Security can also be configured at the environment level. Select an environment and launch the security configuration from the context menu. This screen allows you to configure permissions specific to the environment such as which groups can delete a release environment, edit a release environment, manage release approvers, and administer the release permissions:

ACCESS CONTROL SUMMARY
Shows information about the permissions being granted to this identity

Administer release permissions	Inherited allow
Delete release environment	Inherited allow
Edit release environment	Inherited allow
Manage release approvers	Inherited allow

11. The agent used for deploying an environment can also be configured at the environment level. Select **Agent options...** from the environment context menu:

The **Agent options** window has various configuration options such as whether artifacts should be downloaded, which agent to use, and agent demands. The **Variables** tab allows you to specify the variables for this environment:

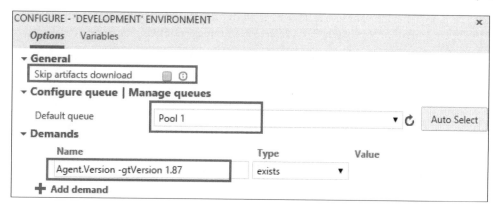

Having the ability to configure the agent per environment is extremely useful if the environment you are trying to deploy the application to is in a secure network that is only accessible to a special agent. You can use the configure queue option to select the queue that has the agent you need to use for this deployment.

12. Click on **Save** to commit the changes. Queue a new release for this release definition by clicking on the **+** icon:

How it works...

This queues a new release for the release definition FabrikamTFVC Web. As illustrated in the **Environments** column, the release represents each environment with a line. The icon pre-fixed before the first gray line shows that the release in this environment is pending approval:

Double-click on the release to navigate to the log **Summary** tab for this release. You can see that the release is pending approval for deployment into the **Development** environment:

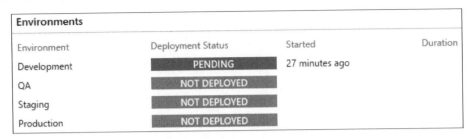

The **Development** environment was configured for pre-approval before deploying the application. The environment was also configured to send out e-mail notification. As per the configuration, the environment sends out an e-mail notification:

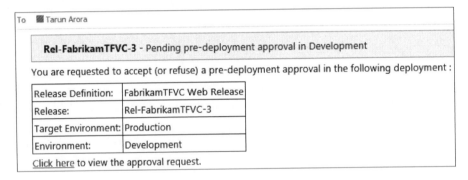

The release is kicked off once the release pre-approval is granted:

When multiple approvers are specified, each of the approvers will be notified in sequence. All the listed approvers must approve the deployment before it continues. If you specify a group as an approver, the entire group is notified when there is a pending approval. However, only one user in the group needs to approve or reject the deployment.

The summary view gives you an overall summary of the release:

Environments			
Environment	Deployment Status	Started	Duration
Development	SUCCEEDED	35 minutes ago	00:34:41
QA	PENDING	less than a minute ago	

The **Logs** view gives you a full break down of all actions performed in an environment:

Step	Details	Agent: Hosted Agent
⊿ Development		1 2015-12-05T16:30:46.0611702Z
⊘ Pre-deployment approval	👤	2 2015-12-05T16:30:46.0651896Z
⊿ ⊘ Deploy		3 2015-12-05T16:30:47.1299721Z
		4 2015-12-05T16:30:47.1459781Z
⊘ Download artifacts		5 2015-12-05T16:30:47.1490040Z
		6 2015-12-05T16:30:47.1499719Z
⊘ Post-deployment approval	👤	7 2015-12-05T16:30:47.1679709Z
		8 2015-12-05T16:30:47.1879820Z
⊿ QA		9 2015-12-05T16:30:47.1889911Z
		10 2015-12-05T16:30:47.7881476Z
Pre-deployment approval	⏱	11 2015-12-05T16:30:48.4118123Z

This is great for identifying the bottlenecks in your release process. We'll cover release tracking in more detail in the *Tracking a release in release management* recipe.

Configuring security for release definitions

Like other modules in TFS, release management also uses the role-based permission model for security. Permissions define the authorizations that can be granted or denied to users and groups. In this recipe, you'll learn about the different levels at which security can be applied for release management.

Getting ready

To administer the permissions for release management, you need to have **Administer release permissions** set to **Allow**. This is, by default, set to **Allow** for members of the Project Administrators and Release Administrators Group:

Administer release permissions	Allow

How to do it...

1. Navigate to the **Release** hub in FabrikamTFVC Team Project. From the **All release definitions** context menu, choose **Security...** to open the permission dialog. This will allow you to administer the permissions for all release definitions in the Team Project:

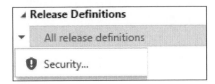

The permissions dialog shows groups, users, and permissions. The permission dialog can be used to change permissions for groups as well as add new users and groups to these groups:

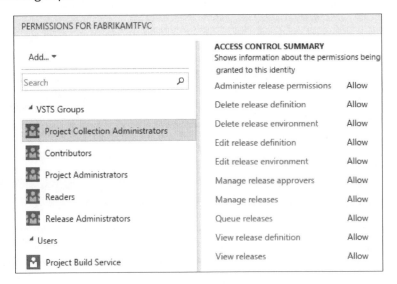

2. In the previous step, we saw how to manage security for **All release definitions**. To manage the security for a specific release definition, open the context menu for this release definition and choose **Security...** from the context menu:

The permissions dialog allows you to manage the permissions for existing, new users, and groups for this specific release definition.

3. So far, we have seen how to apply security to all release definitions and a specific release definition. Release management also allows applying security on environments within a release definition. Edit FabrikamTFVC Web release definition from the **Environment** context menu and select **Security...**:

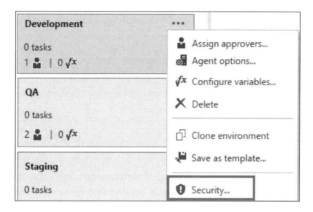

The permissions dialog allows you to manage the permissions for existing, new users, and groups for this specific environment.

How it works...

Release management contains a hierarchical role-based permission model. The following table summarizes the permissions and the hierarchy to which it can be applied:

Permission	Description	Scope
Administer release permissions	Can change any of the other permissions	Project, release definition, and environment
Delete release definition	Can delete release definition(s)	Project and release definition
Delete release environment	Can delete environment(s) in release definition(s)	Project, release definition, and environment
Edit release definition	Can create and edit release definition(s), configuration variables, triggers, and artifacts	Project and release definition
Edit release environment	Can edit environment(s) in release definition(s)	Project, release definition, and environment

Permission	Description	Scope
Manage release approvers	Can add or edit approvers for environment(s) in release definition(s)	Project, release definition, and environment
Manage releases	Can edit the configuration in releases, and can start, stop, or restart release deployments	Project and release definition
Queue releases	Can create new releases	Project and release definition
View release definition	Can view release definition(s)	Project and release definition
View releases	Can view releases belonging to release definition(s)	Project and release definition

The default values for all of these permissions are set for all Team Project collection and Team Project groups. For example, Project Collection Administrators, Project Administrators, and Release Administrators are given all of the preceding permissions by default. Project Contributors are given all permissions except **Administer release permissions**. Project Readers, by default, are denied all permissions except **View release definitions** and **View releases**.

Configuring global and local variables for a release

Variables are used to store values that need to be passed into tasks during the release. There are various advantages of using variables over hardcoding these values directly in tasks:

- ▶ Variables support encrypting values in a way that they cannot be seen or changed by users of a release definition
- ▶ Storing values in variables helps avoid duplication
- ▶ Variables can be shared across all environments
- ▶ Variables can be shared across all tasks within a specific environment

In this recipe, you'll learn how to configure release and environment variables for a release definition.

Getting ready

To edit a release definition, you need to be a member of the Release Administrators Group. These permissions are also available to the Project Administrators Group.

Scenario: The FabrikamTFVC Team uses Azure blob storage for storing files that are needed by the FabrikamTFVC Web release definition. The Team would like the ability to access the blob storage connection details from across the release definition. The Team also need to store the connection string details that are required by one of the tasks in the environment. The value for the connection string is different per environment. The Team would like to store these values securely so that the connection string details are not available in plain text:

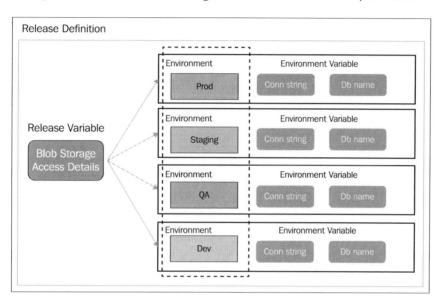

How to do it...

1. Navigate to the **Release** hub in FabrikamTFVC Team Project and edit the release definition FabrikamTFVC Web. Click on the **Configuration** tab. The **Configuration** tab allows you add variables that can be shared across the release definition:

2. Click on the **+** icon to add a variable. Add the connection details for the Azure blob storage as illustrated in the following screenshot. Click on the padlock icon next to the property. The values of such properties are stored securely and cannot be viewed by users once they are saved. During a deployment, the release management service decrypts those values that are referenced by the tasks and passes them to the agent over a secure HTTPS channel:

3. Navigate to the **Environment** tab, click on the ellipsis in the **Development** environment, and select **Configure variables...** from the context menu:

4. Click on the **+** icon to add a variable. Add the connection string details and click on the padlock icon to hide the connection string. Add another variable for storing the database name. Follow this step to configure these variables for all other environments:

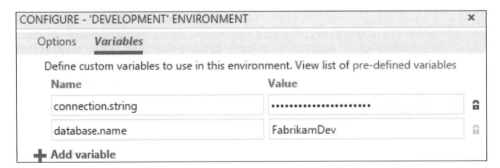

5. Now, navigate to the **Configuration** tab and change the variable type from the top right-hand side to **Environment variables**:

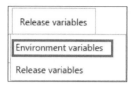

6. This shows a list of all the environment variables and their values for all environments:

	Development	QA	Staging	Production
connection.string	********	********	********	********
database.name	FabrikamDev	FabrikamQA	FabrikamPP	Fabrikam

7. You can filter out the environments that you do not want to see the environment variables for by selecting the checklist next to the view list:

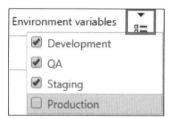

How it works...

In this recipe, we configured variables at release and environment levels. Variables that are defined at the release level are available to all tasks across all environments in the release definition. Variables that are defined at the environment level are only available to tasks within this environment; these variables cannot be accessed by other environments. Using the view type option in the configuration view, you can view both release as well as environment variables. You can click the padlock icon next to the property to hide the value of the property. The values of such properties are stored securely and cannot be viewed by users once they are saved. During a deployment, the release management service decrypts the values that are referenced by the tasks and passes them to the agent over a secure HTTPS channel. You can reference the variables in the task using the $(variablename) format. Apart from using custom variables, you can also use the built-in variables; a full list of built-in variables can be found at http://bit.ly/1ON0Usg.

Deploying an Azure website using release management

In this recipe, you'll learn how to deploy an Azure website from a release definition.

Getting ready

To create a release definition, you need to be a member of the Release Administrators Group. These permissions are also available to the Project Administrators Group.

Scenario: The **FabrikamTFVC.Website** build definition produces a web package as an artifact. The FabrikamTFVC Team wants to deploy the web package to an Azure website:

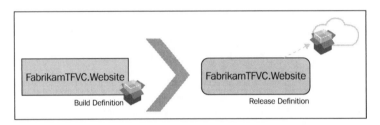

Ensure you have an active Azure Cloud subscription. Download your Azure publish settings file from `https://manage.windowsazure.com/publishsettings`. Set up an Azure website. In this recipe, we'll be using `https://fabrikamTFVC-dev.azurewebsites.net/`.

Navigate to the FabrikamTFVC Team Administration Console. Click on the **Services** tab and create a new endpoint. From the services endpoint context menu, select **Azure**. Change the connection type to **Certificate Based**. Copy the details from the Azure publish settings file and populate the Azure endpoint connection details. Click on **Save** to create the Azure endpoint:

ADD NEW AZURE CONNECTION	
◯ Credentials ⦿ Certificate Based ◯ Service Principal Authentication	
Connection Name	Azure Subscription (Tarun)
Subscription Id	a08894e3-0748-4859-83aa-8eb8b38b1307
Subscription Name	Tarun's MSDN Enterprise Subscription
Management Certificate	MIIKFAIBAzCCCdQGCSqGSIb3DQEHAaCCCcUEggnBMIIJvTCCBe4GCSqGSI b3DQEHAaCCBd8EggXbMIIF1zCCBdMGCyqGSIb3DQEMCgECoIIE7jCCBO owHAYKKoZIhvcNAQwBAzAOBAhnUGGuM9HatAICB9AEggTIA+gbWopl

Navigate to the **Build** hub in the FabrikamTFVC Team Project. Edit the FabrikamTFVC build definition, if you don't already have this build definition refer to the *Creating a continuous integration build definition in TFBuild* recipe in *Chapter 4, Building Your Application* to learn how to create a build definition. In the Visual Studio Build Task, configure the following `MSBuild Arguments`:

```
/p:DeployOnBuild=true /p:WebPublishMethod=Package
/p:PackageAsSingleFile=true /p:SkipInvalidConfigurations=true
```

Configure the **Copy and Publish Build Artifacts** task to publish the contents of the web deployment package. This can be done by setting the following configuration:

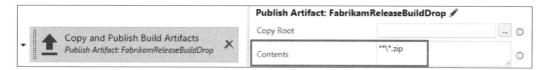

Save the changes and queue a build. Once the build successfully completes, you can see the web deployment package from the artifact explorer:

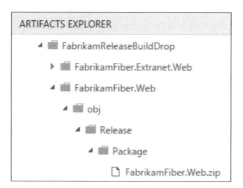

Now, we have a working Azure subscription and an Azure website (`https://fabrikamTFVC-dev.azurewebsites.net`). We have an Azure service endpoint as well as a build definition generating a web deployment package as an artifact.

How to do it...

1. Navigate to the **Release** hub for the FabrikamTFVC Team. Click on the **+** icon to create a new release definition. Select the **Azure Website Deployment** Template:

2. The **Azure Website Deployment** templates adds a default environment with the **Azure Web App Deployment*** and **Visual Studio Test** tasks:

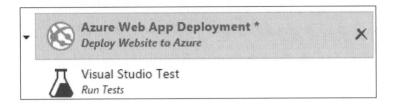

3. Select **Azure Web App Deployment*** task and configure the values as illustrated in the following screenshot. Select the Azure subscription configured as a service endpoint. Select the location where the web app `FabrikamTFVC-dev` was created. Specify the path to the web deployment package within the artifact repository:

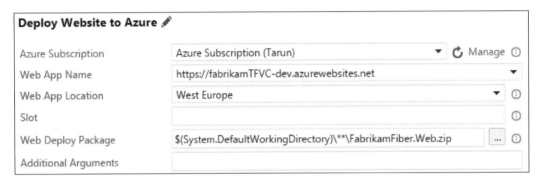

4. Click on **Save** to commit the changes to this release definition. Create a new release.

How it works...

The release agent uses the Azure service endpoint to securely publish the web deployment package to the `FabrikamTFVC-dev` website. The log tab in the release shows the full summary of processing:

```
2015-10-27T16:55:56.8177850Z Executing the powershell script: C:\LR\MMS\Services\Mms\TaskAgentProvisioner\Tools
2015-10-27T16:56:31.7335304Z Looking for Azure PowerShell module at C:\Program Files (x86)\Microsoft SDKs\Azure
2015-10-27T16:56:33.8222272Z AzurePSCmdletsVersion= 0.9.8
2015-10-27T16:56:34.4373014Z Get-ServiceEndpoint -Name 3658cca8-0289-4ec6-8bca-4b8968c279b6 -Context Microsoft.
2015-10-27T16:56:34.4553020Z subscription= MSDN Ultimate
2015-10-27T16:56:34.4563015Z Get-X509Certificate -CredentialsXml <xml>
2015-10-27T16:56:34.8022985Z azureSubscriptionId= 5a829588-b66c-4f42-83e5-a56a525e04b5
2015-10-27T16:56:34.8022985Z azureSubscriptionName= MSDN Ultimate -
2015-10-27T16:56:34.8062985Z azureServiceEndpoint= https://ms.portal.azure.com/
2015-10-27T16:56:34.8152977Z Set-AzureSubscription -SubscriptionName MSDN
2015-10-27T16:56:34.9602969Z Select-AzureSubscription -SubscriptionId
2015-10-27T16:56:35.1692969Z ConnectedServiceName= 3658cca8-0289-4ec6-8bca-4b8968c279b6
2015-10-27T16:56:35.1702966Z WebSiteName=
2015-10-27T16:56:35.1712961Z Package= C:\a\92c4c5056\**\FabrikamFiber.Web.zip
```

The service endpoint has two permission groups, namely, **Endpoint Administrators** and **Endpoint Readers**. Individuals who need to manage this build definition should also be part of the Endpoint Administrators Group, others can be part of the Endpoint Readers Group:

Deploying the IIS Web Application using release management

In this recipe, you'll learn how to deploy the IIS Web Application using release management.

Getting ready

Scenario: The FabrikamTFVC Team has a collection of servers in the `Fabrikam.lab` domain that they need to perform IIS Web Application Deployment on.

Where does it need to be installed?

As illustrated in the following figure, the servers are in the same domain `Fabrikam.lab`. The IIS Web Application Deployment needs to take place on two servers, namely, `QA-Web1.Fabrikam.lab` and `QA-Web2.Fabrikam.lab`:

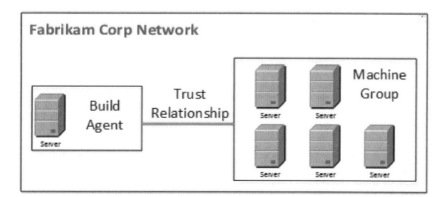

The agent uses WinRM protocol to connect to the machines in the Machine Groups. WinRM needs to be enabled on a machine as a prerequisite before it can be added into the Machine Group. Follow the *Creating and setting up a Machine Group* recipe in *Chapter 5, Testing Your Application*, to set up the Fabrikam-QA Machine Group. The machines in the Machine Group the website will be deployed to need to meet the following prerequisites:

- ▶ Web Deploy 3.5 or higher
- ▶ IIS Web should already be installed and configured
- ▶ .NET 2 and .NET 4 should be registered with IIS using `aspnet_iisreg -i`

What needs to be installed?

To deploy a web application on IIS, the Web Deployment Package needs to be available locally on the destination machines. You can either manually copy the Web Deployment Package on the destination machine or make it available on a UNC that is reachable from the destination machines. In this recipe, we will configure the build definition to generate the Web Deployment Package and copy it across to all destination machines.

Navigate to the **Build** hub in the FabrikamTFVC Team Project. Edit the `FabrikamTFVC.Website` build definition. If you don't already have this build definition, refer to the *Creating a continuous integration build definition in TFBuild* recipe in *Chapter 4, Building Your Application*, to learn how to create a build definition.

As illustrated in the following screenshot in the Visual Studio Build task, configure the following MSBuild arguments:

```
/p:DeployOnBuild=true /p:WebPublishMethod=Package
/p:PackageAsSingleFile=true /p:SkipInvalidConfigurations=true
/p:PackageLocation="$(build.StagingDirectory)"
```

We will now use the **Copy And Publish Build Artifacts** task to upload the contents of `$(build.stagingDirectory)` as an artifact. The copy root is being set to `$(build.stagingDirectory)` since the Visual Studio Build task has MSBuild arguments specifying the Web Deployment Package to be copied to the `$(build.stagingDirectory)`. The `**\*` search pattern is used to copy all the contents of `$(build.stagingdirectory)`:

We will now use the Windows Machine File Copy task to copy the contents of the $(build.stagingDirectory) to the target machines too. The machine names specified in the machine file need to have been configured for WinRM. Specify either a local folder on the destination server or a UNC that's accessible from the destination server. Check the option **Clean Target** to have the older binaries in the destination folder location overwritten with new binaries. Also, check the **Copy Files in Parallel** option to speed up the copy operations across multiple machines. From the **Variables** tab, add two variables, namely, machine.username and machine.password for holding the login details for the machines you intend to have the files copied on to:

Copy files $(build.stagingDirectory) 🖉		
Source	$(build.stagingDirectory)	⋯ ⓘ
Machines	QA-Web1.Fabrikam.lab:5985 QA-Web2.Fabrikam.lab:5985	ⓘ
Admin Login	$(machine.username)	ⓘ
Password	$(machine.password)	ⓘ
Destination Folder	C:\Temp\FabrikamTFVC.Website	ⓘ
⊿ **Advanced Options**		
Clean Target	✔	ⓘ
Copy Files in Parallel	✔	ⓘ

Queue a build; once the build is successfully completed, navigate to the Artifacts Explorer. You should see the website binaries as illustrated in the following screenshot:

ARTIFACTS EXPLORER	✕
⊿ 🗄 FabrikamWebsiteBinaries	
📄 FabrikamFiber.Extranet.Web.deploy-readme.txt	
📄 FabrikamFiber.Extranet.Web.deploy.cmd	
📄 FabrikamFiber.Extranet.Web.SetParameters.xml	
📄 FabrikamFiber.Extranet.Web.SourceManifest.xml	
📄 FabrikamFiber.Extranet.Web.zip	
📄 FabrikamFiber.Web.deploy-readme.txt	
📄 FabrikamFiber.Web.deploy.cmd	
📄 FabrikamFiber.Web.SetParameters.xml	
📄 FabrikamFiber.Web.SourceManifest.xml	
📄 FabrikamFiber.Web.zip	

The same files should now be available locally on the destination machines in the `C:\Temp\FabrikamTFVC.Website` folder.

In this recipe, we'll create a new release definition specifically for deploying IIS Web Application and App Pool. To create a release definition, you need to be a member of the Release Administrators Group. These permissions are also available to the Project Administrators Group.

How to do it...

1. Navigate to the **Release** hub in the FabrikamTFVC Team Project. Add a new release definition. Select an empty Deployment Template and name the definition FabrikamTFVC Web Server release definition. Rename the default environment to QA and add the IIS Web Application Deployment task to this environment:

2. In the **QA** environment, click on the ellipsis and select **Configure variables...** from the context menu:

3. Add two variables, namely, `machine.username` and `machine.password` for this environment holding the login details for the machines where IIS needs to be deployed:

4. Now to configure the IIS Web Application Deployment task, first specify the machines and the login details. We'll use the `machine.username` and `machine.password` variables defined in the previous step. Since we are in a closed domain group where WinRM is configured to use HTTP, select **HTTP**:

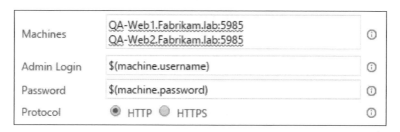

5. Now, specify the location of the web deployment package. Since the web deployment package was copied using the machine file, copy the task using the build definition. You can directly specify the local destination machine location here. Optionally, you can specify the web deploy parameter file and override parameters to replace the website properties such as application name, connection string, database details, and so on, in the web configuration. Alternatively, you can also use the PowerShell script after the deployment to carry out the value replacements:

6. Check the **Create or Update Application Pool** option and specify the application pool name, .NET version, pipeline mode, and identity for the application pool:

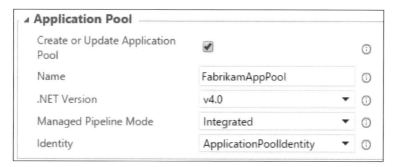

7. Click on **Save** and trigger a release for this release definition. Wait for the release to complete. The summary view will show you the result of the release execution:

Environments			
Environment	Deployment Status	Started	Duration
QA	SUCCEEDED	an hour ago	00:00:29

How it works...

First, let's check the results of the deployment on the destination machines. As illustrated in the following screenshot, **FabrikamAppPool** has been created as per the specifications in the configuration:

Name ▲	Status	.NET Framework Version	Managed Pipeli...	Identity	Applications
ASP.NET v4.0	Started	v4.0	Integrated	ApplicationPoolIdentity	0
ASP.NET v4.0 Classic	Started	v4.0	Classic	ApplicationPoolIdentity	0
Classic .NET AppPool	Started	v4.0	Classic	ApplicationPoolIdentity	0
DefaultAppPool	Started	v4.0	Integrated	ApplicationPoolIdentity	2
FabrikamAppPool	Started	v4.0	Integrated	ApplicationPoolIdentity	1

The web deployment package has also been installed under the default website with the website binaries copied in the `C:\inetpub` folder:

The task uses the standard web deployment package functionality to deploy to IIS. Using WinRM allows the release management agent to orchestrate this workflow remotely. You can read more about the parameters and functionality of web deployment at `http://bit.ly/1XT0yTq`.

There is more

The IIS Web Application Deployment task also has a **Create or Update Website** section. This gives you far more granular control on specifying how the website is structured. You can use this to change the physical path of the website, configure the bindings to be used, as well as the protocol and ports along with host names:

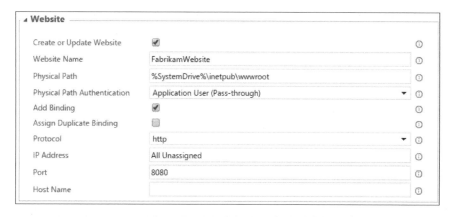

Tracking a release in release management

It is common to want to see the list of releases by status, check the status of a current release, track the approvals for a release, investigate the failures in logs, and view the details of the agent processing the release. In this recipe, you'll learn about all the release tracking features available in release management.

How to do it...

1. Navigate to the **Release** hub for the FabrikamTFVC Team. The landing page shows you a list of all release definitions. This is a quick way to see the status of releases. The view surfaces information about the status as well as the release definition, environments, build, branch, start time, and created by. Releases triggered using the continuous deployment configuration have an icon in the first column:

2. This view can be filtered by the status of the releases. From the top-right corner, change the **State** dropdown to **Rejected**; this will narrow the list down to rejected releases:

3. Switch over to the **Overview** tab. This will help you visualize the status of all the release definitions. As illustrated in the following screenshot, the last release for the **Fabrikam Website Release Pipeline** definition failed while FabrikamTFVC Web Release was successful in the **Development** environment, it failed in the **QA** environment and no deployments have been attempted in **Staging** and **Production** using this pipeline. You can click on the ellipsis next to the release definition name to queue a new release, edit the definition, or manage the security for the release definition:

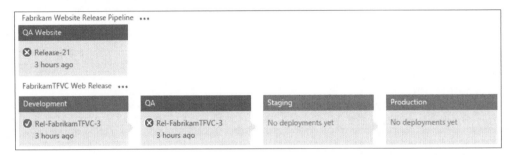

Fabrikam Website Release Pipeline showing the status of the Release-21 in the QA environment; FabrikamTFVC Web Release Pipeline showing the status of the Rel-FabrikamTFVC-3 across the environments

4. Locate **Release-11** and double-click on it to view the release. This opens the release summary view by default. The summary view shows you the details of the release, environments, issues, work Items, and test results. You can also restart or abandon the release from this view:

5. To dig into the issue further, either click on the error message or navigate to the log view. The log view lets you browse the logs by environment and task making it easier to investigate reasons for failure:

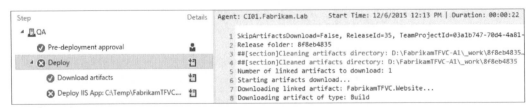

6. You can hide the logs and narrow down the view to approvals or tasks only by changing the options from the top right:

7. The **Commits** and **Work Items** views in the release show you information about the code changes and Work Items associated to the artifacts processed as part of this release:

| Summary | Environments | Artifacts | Configuration | General | Commits | Work Items | Logs |

8. Now, navigate to the **Team Project Collection Administration** page in Team Portal. Click on **Agents** queues to see a list of builds and agents grouped by queue. The following screenshot illustrates all the builds and releases processed by the Fabrikam CI01 agent queue. You can directly browse to the failing builds and releases by clicking on the definition or name of the hyperlink:

How it works...

Release management gives you the ability to track the releases and narrow down the reasons for failure by drilling in through the various levels of hierarchy. Though there is no charting capability to pin the release status to the Dashboard yet, this area is set to review a good amount of investment over the next few releases; hopefully, enhancements to visualize the release pipelines will be taken care of as part of these investments.

7
Managing Team Foundation Server

"It's hardware that makes a machine fast... It's software that makes a fast machine slow."

–Craig Bruce

In this chapter, we will cover the following:

- ▶ Diagnosing builds in TFS
- ▶ Analyzing the TFS database and configuring test retention policies
- ▶ Using Activity and Job Monitoring logs to diagnose TFS issues
- ▶ Changing update frequency and forcing a rebuild of the TFS Warehouse
- ▶ Configuring TFS Cache settings
- ▶ Managing CodeLens in TFS
- ▶ Continuous synchronization with TFS Proxy server
- ▶ Creating a TFS database back up schedule
- ▶ Cleaning up dead workspaces and shelvesets in TFS

Introduction

We are entering the era of self-driven cars; you may ask, "why can't products just maintain themselves?" The Product Teams deliver high-quality software yet the real-world usage of a feature can significantly differ from its anticipated usage. The building blocks the product operates on and the ecosystem of frameworks that rely on the product keep evolving too. TFS does not have a very high administration over head. The administration needs are somewhat proportional to the level of usage. Smaller Teams may be able to administer TFS within the day-to-day activities of individuals on the Team, while larger Teams may need a dedicated TFS administrator.

The key tasks that need to be performed by a TFS administrator can broadly be divided into three categories: **Update**, **Maintain**, and **Optimize**:

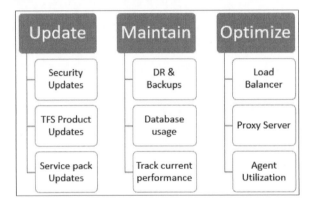

Let's explain each of these tasks in detail:

Update: It is very important to keep the environment secure, and for this reason, all security updates that the MBSA tool identifies as "Critical" should be applied within 48 hours. The product updates are roughly rolled out every quarter. Each product update contains bug fixes, performance enhancements, and new features. Quarterly updates rarely have breaking changes; this also reduces the effort in testing the upgrade. The product updates should also be applied as soon as possible. It is also recommended to keep the underlying OS and SQL Server updated to the latest available service packs.

Maintain: There needs to be a clear strategy for disaster recovery and backup restore. The TFS database usage should be closely monitored to find any unexpected growth patterns. It is recommended that the TFS Perfmon counters be used to benchmark the performance of the server and reevaluated overtime regularly, especially during upgrades. More information on TFS Perfmon counters is available at `http://bit.ly/1SijysU`. Maintaining TFS also involves day-to-day cleanup activities such as managing permissions, build drop locations, test attachments, workspaces, shelvesets, and so on.

Optimize: By monitoring the TFS usage using the Activity logs, you can identity requirements for scalability. Load balancing the TFS application tier is usually the first step to provide resilience and scale to the TFS setup. If Teams are working in a low bandwidth location, installing a TFS proxy server can significantly improve the experience. By closely monitoring the build and release agent utilization, you can supplement the build queues with additional agents. This can help bring down the queue times for builds and releases.

If your organization has systems center setup, there is now a management pack available for Visual Studio Team Foundation Server 2015 that can be downloaded from `http://bit.ly/1lgcEJN`. If you have recently upgraded from TFS 2013 or any of the earlier versions, then it's worth reading up about enabling TFS 2015-specific features on existing Team Projects (`http://bit.ly/1P6IbLu`). There is a wealth of documentation available on MSDN (`http://bit.ly/1R4Uh79`) covering key administration concepts with samples and walkthroughs. In addition to that, this article (`http://bit.ly/1QGxVcQ`) talks at length about all things TFS administrators should focus on. TFS administration and management is a fairly big topic. In this chapter, we'll focus on some of the key administration and management activities that every TFS administrator should perform.

Diagnosing builds in TFS

Development Teams use TFBuild for validating code changes and inspecting code quality and running tests. Builds are a critical part of any software development life cycle. As a TFS administrator, you may need to inspect issues with a build agent or diagnose a specific build definition. In this recipe, we'll learn how to diagnose build agents and build definitions.

Getting ready

Download TFBuild Agent from the TFS Administration Console. For more information on how to download the TFBuild Agent, refer to the *Configuring TFBuild Agent, Pool, and Queues* recipe in *Chapter 4, Building Your Application*. You need to have collection administration permissions to configure a TFBuild Agent. To create or edit a build definition, you need to be a member of the Build Administrators Group.

How to do it...

1. The best place to start when diagnosing agent issues is to look at the agent trace logs. The agent trace logs are stored in the `_diag` folder in the agent working directory.

2. If there is nothing obvious in the agent trace logs, as a next step you should run an HTTP Trace against the agent. This can be done using an HTTP Proxy tool. If you are on Windows, you can use Fiddler; for other platforms, you can use Charles Proxy. Refer to `http://bit.ly/1P6dqGt` on how to set up and capture an HTTP Trace.

3. When capturing an HTTP Trace, the agent needs to be run in interactive mode. Browse to the location where the TFBuild Agent has been downloaded. Unzip the TFBuild Agent. Open a command prompt in administrator mode and set the working directory to the unzipped location of the TFBuild Agent. As illustrated here, run the `ConfigureAgent` command:

```
c:\>cd C:\Users\Tarun\Downloads\agent
C:\Users\Tarun\Downloads\agent>.\ConfigureAgent.cmd_
```

The `ConfigureAgent` command will prompt to configure the agent for a few details. When prompted for `Would you like to install the agent as a Windows Service` key in *N*, this will run the agent as an interactive process rather than installing the agent as a service:

```
Would you like to install the agent as a Windows Service (Y/N) (default is N) N_
```

All agent activity will show up in verbose in the command prompt. This will likely provide clues to diagnose problems with the agent.

4. When troubleshooting problems with the build definition, its best to run the build definition in verbose mode. In verbose mode, the agent produces very detailed logs; investigating the logs is usually the best way to identify problems causing the unexpected behavior. To run the build definition in verbose mode, create a new variable `System.Debug` and set the value of this variable to `true`:

How it works...

An HTTP Trace can contain credentials, so avoid sharing HTTP Traces publically. TFS currently does not support personal access tokens, so as a work-around, you can create a temporary account for the purposes of capturing the trace; alternatively, sanitize the trace logs before sharing with other Teams for investigation.

Analyzing the TFS database and configuring test retention policies

As the TFS usage increases over time, the TFS instances can build up very large volumes of data files, builds, releases, Work Items, and so on. For the most part, this is a very good thing – a big part of the value of many **Application Lifecycle Management (ALM)** features, after all, is maintaining a reliable history of the various artifacts involved in a producing software. At some point, however, there are implicit and explicit costs involved in maintaining older data, such as performance impacts and increased time spent on upgrades, in addition to the increased disk space requirements. In this recipe, you'll learn how to analyze the TFS database size and set up test retention policies for a Team Project.

Getting ready

It is not recommended to query the live instance of TFS transactional database directly. Restore a backup of the TFS transactional database on an alternate instance of SQL and execute the queries in this recipe on that instance instead of the live instance.

To administer the test retention policies for a Team Project, you need to be a member of the Team Project Administrator Group.

How to do it...

Let's first analyze the TFS databases to understand the storage distribution:

1. Open SQL Server Management Studio. Connect to the SQL instance the TFS transactional database has been restored to, open a new query window and run the following T-SQL code to get the database size for TFS databases:

```
use [master]
select DB_NAME(database_id) AS DBName, (size/128) SizeInMB
FROM sys.master_files with (nolock)
where type=0  and
substring(db_name(database_id),1,4)='Tfs_' and
DB_NAME(database_id)<>'Tfs_Configuration' order by size
desc
GO
```

You will get the following output after executing the preceding code:

DBName	SizeInMB
Tfs_DefaultCollection	421837
Tfs_TPC2	89093
Tfs_Warehouse	33321

2. Scope the connected database in the SQL Server Management Studio to the `TFS_DefaultCollection` column. Execute the following T-SQL to identify the distribution of storage within this collection:

```
SELECT Owner =
        CASE
                WHEN OwnerId = 0 THEN 'Generic'
                WHEN OwnerId = 1 THEN 'VersionControl'
                WHEN OwnerId = 2 THEN 'WorkItemTracking'
                WHEN OwnerId = 3 THEN 'TeamBuild'
                WHEN OwnerId = 4 THEN 'TeamTest'
                WHEN OwnerId = 5 THEN 'Servicing'
                WHEN OwnerId = 7 THEN 'WebAccess'
                WHEN OwnerId = 8 THEN 'ProcessTemplate'
                WHEN OwnerId = 9 THEN 'StrongBox'
                WHEN OwnerId = 10 THEN 'FileContainer'
                WHEN OwnerId = 11 THEN 'CodeSense'
                WHEN OwnerId = 255 THEN 'PendingDeletion'
            END,
        SUM(CompressedLength) / 1024 as TotalSizeInKB
FROM tbl_FileReference fr
JOIN tbl_FileMetadata fm
on fr.PartitionId = fm.PartitionId
AND fr.ResourceId = fm.ResourceId
WHERE fr.PartitionId = 1
GROUP BY OwnerId
ORDER BY 2 DESC
```

The storage is categorized into the areas of ownership. This should help identity the hot spots at a high level.

3. The following query will show you the next level of details on the individual areas of ownership:

```
use Tfs_DefaultCollection
select  SUBSTRING(a.filename,len(a.filename)-
CHARINDEX('.',REVERSE(a.filename))+2,999)as Extension,
sum(fm.compressedlength)/1024 as SizeInKB from
tbl_Attachment as a
inner join tbl_FileReference as fr on a.TfsFileId=
fr.fileid
join tbl_FileMetadata fm on fr.PartitionId = fm.PartitionId
and fm.ResourceId = fr.ResourceId
group by SUBSTRING(a.filename,len(a.filename)-
CHARINDEX('.',REVERSE(a.filename))+2,999)
order by sum(fm.compressedlength) desc
```

4. From the analysis so far, we narrowed down that `TeamTest` is the biggest occupier in the database. The breakdown shows that this is because of the large volume of test runs, results, and attachments from manual and automated tests. To configure test retention policies for the FabrikamTFVC project, navigate to the FabrikamTFVC Administration Console in Team Web Portal and browse to the **Test** tab. As illustrated in the following screenshot, set the manual and automated test retention policies:

Retention

Days to keep automated test runs, results, and attachments	30 ▼
If you retain a build indefinitely, the related test results are kept, even if they're older than the specified number of days.	
Days to keep manual test runs, results, and attachments	365 ▼
Manual test results are kept when a build is deleted. To keep these results for a limited time, select the number of days.	

How it works...

Test retention policies is a new addition to TFS 2015. Test retention policies allow you to individually manage the retention policies for automated and manual tests. The default configuration is set to retain indefinitely. In this recipe, we've configured the automated test execution runs, results, and attachments to be deleted in 30 days and the manual test execution runs, results, and attachments to be deleted in 365 days. The retention policies are automatically processed by a job in TFS.

> **Warning**
>
> Removing any files should be done with caution and *never directly from the database*. As always, before you modify, update, or delete, take a full backup of the databases.

There is no provision to configure the test retention policies centrally. For this reason, the test reason policies need to be configured for each Team Project individually.

The test retention policies are just one of the ways to control the size of your TFS database. TFS also supports build retention policies; this has been discussed at length in the *Using the build retention policy to automate build deletion* recipe in *Chapter 4, Building Your Application*. In addition to this, you can free up more space by destroying deleted version control branches, Team Projects, files, and XAML builds. Refer to `http://bit.ly/1PMhuvB` to know how this can be accomplished.

Using Activity and Job Monitoring logs to diagnose TFS issues

TFS logs both the activity and the job execution data in the backend database. TFS has a built-in job agent that runs on the application tier and logs diagnostic information about jobs and processes. Having visibility of poor performing and failed jobs, along with diagnostic information, helps narrow down potential problems faster. The diagnostics page in TFS comprises of Activity logs and Job Monitoring logs. In this recipe, you'll learn how to use the diagnostics page in TFS.

Getting ready

To use the diagnostics page, you need to be a member of the TFS Administrators Group. Validate access by browsing `http://tfs2015:8080/tfs/_oi/`:

How to do it...

1. To access Activity log navigate to `http://tfs2015:8080/tfs/_oi/_diagnostics/activityLog`. The page can take a little longer to load if you are accessing it for the first time.

2. This page basically presents the data in the `tbl_Command` table. As illustrated in the following screenshot among other things, the page contains a list of commands, applications, status, start time, time taken for execution, execution status, identity, IP address, unique identifier, user agent, command identifier, execution count, authentication, and response code:

Id	Application	Command	Status	Start Time	Execution Time	Identity Name	IP Address
18580	Web Access	Git.index	0	11/19/2015 4:18 PM	425611	TFS2015\Tarun	10.0.0.4
18579	CustomerI...	CustomerIntelligenceEven...	0	11/19/2015 4:18 PM	5749	TFS2015\Tarun	10.0.0.4
18578	Git	GitItems.GetItem	0	11/19/2015 4:18 PM	166194	TFS2015\Tarun	10.0.0.4
18577	Git	GitPushes2.GetPushes	0	11/19/2015 4:18 PM	164427	TFS2015\Tarun	10.0.0.4

3. Double-click on an item in the list to see more details. As illustrated in the following image, the details for the reconcile workspace command shows you the rich next level of details of the operation:

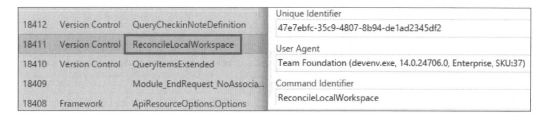

4. The **Activity Log** page also allows filter and export operations. Since the data in the `tbl_command` table is only retained for 14 days, you can export the data in the Activity log incrementally to a separate repository to keep this valuable information for historic trend analysis.

5. Click on the **Job Monitoring** tab to navigate to the **Job Monitoring** view. Alternatively, you can directly browse `http://tfs2015:8080/tfs/_oi/_jobMonitoring`. The **Job Monitoring** view has three more submenus: **Job Summary**, **Job Queue**, and **Job History**:

6. Let's first look at the **Job Summary** view. The summary view shows a graphical representation of the total runtime for each job. Being able to visualize job execution time relative to other jobs helps identify potential problems. As you can see in the following screenshot, the TFS Periodic Identity Synchronization and Incremental Analysis Database sync job takes longer to process as compared to optimize databases job:

7. To get more details on Incremental Analysis Database sync job, click on the blue bar next to the job name. This will navigate you to the **Job History** tab. The **Job History** tab has two graphs, one showing the job execution time for all jobs and the other showing the details for Incremental Analysis Database sync job. Seeing the two charts together helps you compare the contribution one has on the other. The following figure illustrates the graph for the execution of Incremental Analysis Database sync job. Looking at the chart, you can work out that the job on the 07/25 is out of pattern and has taken significantly longer than usual. However, the queue time metric on the chart shows that the delay is contributed by the prolonged average queue time:

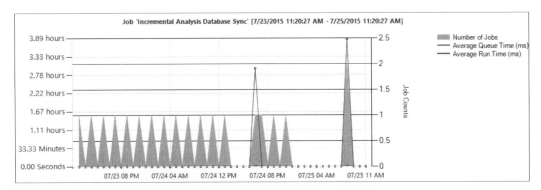

8. Navigate back to the **Job Summary** view; this view also has a pie chart that shows the split between **Succeeded**, **Blocked**, and **Disabled** jobs. Clicking on any will navigate you to the **Job History** view and provide job-level details on each type:

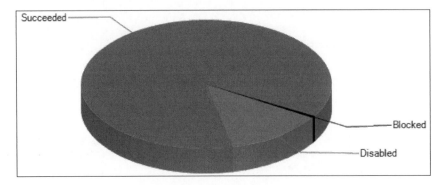

9. Last but not least, the **Job Summary** page has a chart for number of job runs. The chart displays the number of times a job has run combined with the result types for that particular job. Click on any of the bars in the chart to display details on those jobs. Hovering over the chart provides further information:

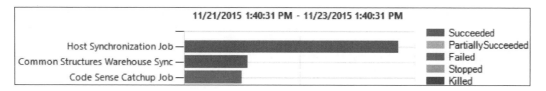

10. Next, navigate to the **Job Queue** tab. The chart in this tab describes the job queue; it provides the counts for each queue type. Click on the bar to see the job details associated to each queue type:

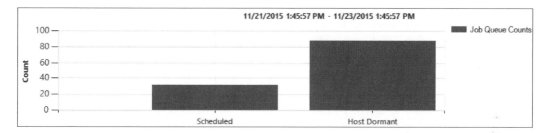

How it works...

It is recommended that you do not directly query the TFS Transactional database. Any changes made to the database can significantly impact the functioning of TFS. While some changes may not show the impact immediately, the changes can cause disruption during upgrades. Prior to the introduction of the diagnostics page, there was no alternate but to query the database directly to retrieve and analyze the data from the `command` and `actions` table. The diagnostics page makes it easier to access this valuable dataset.

All built-in TFS jobs track their activity in the `command` table. The logging is internally handled by the framework in TFS. There is a very interesting article that talks about the built-in jobs and the execution interval; you can read more about this at `http://bit.ly/1kPSbfg`.

Changing update frequency and forcing a rebuild of TFS Warehouse

The reporting warehouse in TFS is a traditional data warehouse that consists of a relational database and an analysis services database. The data warehouse aggregates all the operational data, such as version control, Work Item tracking, build, and test. The warehouse corresponds to the `Tfs_Warehouse` relational database. The cube corresponds to the SQL Server Analysis Services database `Tfs_Analysis`. The default rebuild frequency for the TFS Warehouse is 2 hours. In this recipe, you'll learn how to manually change the TFS Warehouse refresh frequency from 2 hours to 1 hour. You'll also learn how to force a rebuild of the TFS Warehouse cube.

TFS Warehouse refresh is default to 2 hours; if you reduce the interval to less than the default of 2 hours, processing of the data warehouse will consume server resources frequently. If your TFS Server has large volumes of data, reducing the refresh frequency may adversely affect the performance of the server.

Getting ready

To work through this recipe, you'll need to ensure the following:

▸ The TFS deployment you are working with a TFS Warehouse configured. You can validate this by checking the **Reporting** tab of TFS Administration Console:

Warehouse Database:	Configured and Jobs Enabled
Status:	Idle
Server:	TFS2015
Database:	Tfs_Warehouse

▸ You must be a member of the Team Foundation Administrators security group or you must have the server-level administer warehouse permission set to **Allow**.

▸ The Microsoft Team Foundation Server Application Pool must be running for the Warehouse Control Web Service:

Virtual Path	Physical Path	Application Pool
/tfs	C:\Program Files\Microsoft Team Foundation Server 14.0\Application Tier\Web Services	Microsoft Team Foundation Server Application Pool (v4.0.30319)

How to do it...

1. Log into Team Foundation Server Application Tier and validate that the Warehouse Control Service is available by browsing `http://localhost:8080/tfs/TeamFoundation/Administration/v3.0/WarehouseControlService.asmx`. Revisit the *Getting ready* section if you don't see the Warehouse Control Web Service as illustrated in the following screenshot:

WarehouseControlWebService

Team Foundation Warehouse Control web service
The following operations are supported. For a formal definition, please review the **Service Description**.

- **BringAnalysisProcessingOnline**

2. In the `WarehouseControlWebService` page, look for the `changesetting` web method. Click on this to navigate to the definition of this function. This method has two input parameters, namely, `settingId` and `newValue`. In the `settingId` textbox, type `RunIntervalSeconds`. This property holds the warehouse rebuild frequency. In the `newValue` textbox type `3600`, `3600` here represents 3600 seconds (1 hour), that is, the new value for the property `RunIntervalSeconds`:

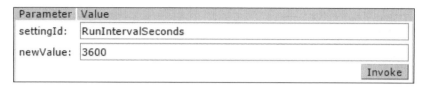

Parameter	Value
settingId:	RunIntervalSeconds
newValue:	3600
	Invoke

3. Click on **Invoke**. This will redirect you to the response page. The response page will list the result of the action. In this case, the message confirms that the run interval value has been successfully updated to 3600 seconds:

```
▼<string xmlns="http://schemas.microsoft.com/TeamFoundation/2005/06/Services/Controller/03">
  The setting RunIntervalSeconds has been successfully changed to 3600.
</string>
```

4. In this step, we'll see how to force the rebuild of the warehouse. Navigate back to the Warehouse Control Web Service and select the **ProcessWarehouse** web method. This method has two input parameters, namely, **collectionName** and **jobName**. In the **collectionName** textbox, enter **defaultcollection**. This is the TFS collection you want to force the rebuild for. Don't pass any values in the **jobName** textbox:

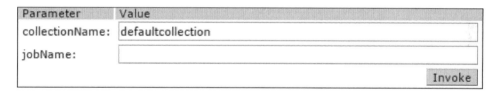

Parameter	Value
collectionName:	defaultcollection
jobName:	
	Invoke

You can optionally leave the **collectionName** textbox empty. This will force the rebuild of all Team Project Collections.

5. Clicking on **Invoke** will redirect you to the response page. The response page will list the result of the action. The service returns `True` when it successfully starts the processing of the warehouse and `False` if it is not successful. A value of `False` indicates that the warehouse is currently being processed:

```
<boolean xmlns="http://schemas.microsoft.com/TeamFoundation/2005/06/Services/Controller/03">true</boolean>
```

How it works...

Forcing a TFS Warehouse rebuild isn't something you need to do on a regular basis. However, a TFS Warehouse and cube rebuild is required if you move, restore, rename, and fail over the data tier of TFS. The warehouse rebuild is required to see refreshed reports if you move, attach, detach, or delete a Team Project Collection.

There is more

The `RebuildWarehouse` command is available via command-line utility as well. More details on how to use the `RebuildWarehouse` command can be found at `http://bit.ly/1HjaQdp`.

Configuring TFS Cache settings

The TFS application tier maintains a file cache in order to speed up the file download process to the end user by serving the files from the cache, rather than getting them afresh from the database each time. The cache grows over time and can start to dent the available storage space on the application tier. The cache uses a good percentage of the available space; in case your main drive does not have a lot of available space, you will ignorantly not benefit from the caching facility. Moving the TFS Cache to a separate directory enables you to free up the storage on the main drive and plan a more relaxed backup or recovery procedure for the new drive. It is possible that you may see some performance gains by changing the cache directory to its own directory. In this recipe, you'll learn how to change the TFS Cache directory to a different directory.

Getting ready

You need permission to log into the TFS application tier.

How to do it...

1. Log into the TFS application tier. Navigate to the installation folder for TFS. The default install location is `C:\Program Files\Microsoft Team Foundation Server 14.0`.

2. The TFS's `web.config` is available in the folder location `C:\Program Files\Microsoft Team Foundation Server 14.0\Application Tier\Web Services`. Take a backup of the `web.config` file before making any changes. Open the `web.config` file and search for the key `dataDirectory`:

```
<!-- Application Tier file cache folder, used by the AT proxy and other components as a file system cache -->
<add key="dataDirectory" value="C:\TfsData\ApplicationTier\_fileCache" />
```

3. Change the value of the data directory from the default to the new location. For this recipe, a new drive W has been set up for TFS Cache. Repoint the cache to W:\ TfsData\ApplicationTier_fileCache and save the changes in the config file:

```
<!-- Application Tier file cache folder, used by the AT proxy and other components as a file system cache -->
<add key="dataDirectory" value="W:\TfsData\ApplicationTier\_fileCache" />
```

4. In addition to this, you can optionally add a PercentageBasedPolicy key, which would dictate what percentage of the free space can be consumed by the cache. This key only accepts whole number values:

```
<add key="PercentageBasedPolicy" value="70"/>
```

Alternatively, the FixedSizeBasedPolicy key can be used. The value for this key is the total allowed space to the cache. For example, setting this to 500 would mean the cache only has 500 MB of available space for storage. If both FixedSizeBasedPolicy and PercentageBasedPolicy keys are specified, the value of FixedSizeBasedPolicy takes precedence.

How it works...

Saving web.config will restart the application pool and the changes will be effective immediately. Carry out a get operation on version control and TFS will cache a copy of the files served back to the client as a result of the get operation in the new location.

Managing CodeLens in TFS

CodeLens is a Microsoft Visual Studio feature that shows you information about your code directly in the code editor. Before CodeLens, one had to dig through several different windows for information such as method references, tests linked to a method, the last change to a line of code, or the code churn to a class. Since all of this information is in TFS, you would just expect it to be available in one place. CodeLens just does that by putting this information literally at your fingertips within the code editor. CodeLens supports both TFVC and Git repositories. CodeLens now supports C#, VB, C++, SQL, and JavaScript files. You can learn more about CodeLens and other quality and diagnostic tools available in Visual Studio at http://bit.ly/1NNbtJ6.

This book focuses on TFS, you are probably wondering why Visual Studio-specific features are being discussed. TFS is responsible for preparing the information served by CodeLens in Visual Studio. TFS has specific jobs for code indexing, and the information produced off that is stored in the TFS database. In this recipe, you'll learn how to manage the TfsConfig CodeIndex command to check the indexing status of a Team Project Collection, enable/disable indexing, find large files, and ignore them from indexing, review ignore list, and destroy code index.

Getting ready

In order to use the CodeIndex command, you need to be a member of the Team Foundation Administrators Security Group. This command can only be invoked from the TFS Application tier; for this reason, you need to have login permissions to the TFS Application tier.

How to do it...

1. Log on to TFS Application tier and open a command prompt in the elevated mode.

2. Run the following command to see the indexing status for the default collection:

    ```
    TFSConfig CodeIndex /indexingStatus /collectionName:"default
    collection"
    ```

3. Start indexing all changesets:

    ```
    TFSConfig CodeIndex /setIndexing:on /collectionName:"default
    collection"
    ```

4. Stop indexing previously created changesets and start indexing new changesets only:

    ```
    TFSConfig CodeIndex /setIndexing:keepupOnly /
    collectionName:"default collection"
    ```

5. Run the following command to list the top 50 files that have a size greater than 10 KB in the default collection:

    ```
    TfsConfig CodeIndex /listLargeFiles /fileCount:50 /minSize:10 /
    collectionName:<CollectionName>
    ```

6. Run the following command to exclude a specific file from indexing and add it to the ignored file list:

    ```
    TFSConfig CodeIndex /ignoreList:add "$/Fabrikam Web Site/Catalog.
    cs" /collectionName:"default collection"
    ```

7. Run the following command to see all the files that aren't indexed:

    ```
    TFSConfig CodeIndex /ignoreList:view
    ```

8. Run the following command to clear previously indexed data and restart indexing:

    ```
    TFSConfig CodeIndex /reindexAll /collectionName:"default
    collection"
    ```

9. Run the following command to delete the code index with confirmation:

    ```
    TFSConfig CodeIndex /destroyCodeIndex /collectionName:"default
    collection"
    ```

How it works...

The `TfsConfig` command gives you the ability to manage the `CodeIndex` functions. Refer to `http://bit.ly/1NNcwZi` for more details on the individual commands.

Continuous synchronization with the TFS Proxy server

It is not uncommon today to have geographically distributed Teams accessing TFS from remote locations. Remote users may suffer from latency of the connection between their location and the location where TFS is hosted. The Team Foundation Proxy Server comes to the rescue here. There is a common misconception about TFS Proxy caching all requests. However, the proxy server only caches the `Get` operation for TFVC-based version control. The proxy server does not carry out a continuous synchronization or replication operation, instead it caches the item on first request. While the first caller from the remote location will still face the latency in their `get` operation, all future requests will get the data as if it was being accessed locally. Today, developers are encouraged to check in code frequently. This means geographically distributed Teams operating in low network bandwidth regions will notice a lag when performing a get operation on source control. In this recipe, you'll learn how to precache the data in TFS Proxy to improve the overall performance of the proxy.

Getting ready

This recipe requires that you have a TFS Proxy Server setup. Follow the steps at `http://bit.ly/1lfGDS7` to configure a TFS Proxy Server if you don't already have one. Supplement your proxy server with an additional drive. In this recipe, we'll be using `D:\TFS\Workspace` as the additional directory.

Scenario: A part of the distributed Team that is working in a remote location does not have great network bandwidth. Operations that require code download from the TFS server are generally slow. The Team has installed the TFS Proxy Server in their remote location; however, they still face a lag when downloading the incremental changes in the source code. The Team would like a proactive solution that downloads the incremental code changes to the proxy server, so when the Team performs a `Get` operation on TFS, the proxy server can serve the content from the local cache rather than needing to make a round trip to TFS.

How to do it...

1. Log into the TFS Proxy Server machine. Browse to the `D:\TFS\Command` directory and create a new file called `PreGetTfsProxy.bat`.

2. Copy the following code into to the `PreGetTfsProxy.bat` file and save the changes:

```
@echo off
set local
set TFSPROXY=http://localhost:8081
echo Forcing Pre-cache of files using TFS VC proxy at
%TFSPROXY%
cd D:\TFS\Workspace
"%PROGRAMFILES%\Microsoft Visual Studio
14\Common7\IDE\TF.exe" get
del /F /S /Q d:\ tfs\workspace\*.*
echo Pre-cache complete.
end local
```

3. Test the script by double-clicking on `PreGetTfsProxy.bat` to run the script. If the script is set up correctly, the `D:\TFS\Workspace` location should now be populated with the source code from TFS.

4. Set up a Windows scheduled task to run the `PreGetTfsProxy.bat` file once every 10 minutes. You can tune the frequency of execution of this job to best suit the landscape of your organization.

How it works...

Installing Team Foundation Server Proxy Server installs the Team Foundation Server command-line tools. The core function of the TFS Proxy Server is to locally cache any files requested from TFS, so any subsequent calls for that file can be served directly by the proxy server. By saving a round trip out to the TFS Server, the proxy server can significantly reduce the lag noticed when performing the Get operation. TFS Proxy Server does not perform a workspace synchronization operation, instead it only caches the files requested from the TFS Server. In this recipe, we created a temporary workspace on the proxy server and scheduled the execution of Get operation through a Windows-scheduled task to proactively fetch the incremental code changes. This will, in turn cause the proxy server to cache the changes on the proxy server proactively. While the approach is simple, it is effective in synchronizing the changes from source control locally on the proxy server.

The TFS Proxy Server can significantly reduce the time taken to perform a Get operation. Perfmon is a very useful tool to measure the system performance using performance counters. Follow the walkthrough in `http://bit.ly/1SZEN2T` to measure the times for the Get operation with and without the proxy server. It is generally recommended to baseline the performance gained by the proxy server. This should be revalidated after TFS upgrades.

Creating a TFS database back up schedule

"If you fail to plan, you are planning to fail!" –Benjamin Franklin

No one wants to be the administrator of a server that goes down without a complete set of backups in place. TFS Database sits at the core of the product; the database is the repository of the data you interact with using Web Portal, Visual Studio, and Microsoft Test Manager. In this recipe, you'll learn about the database backup capability available with in TFS.

Getting ready

To configure the backup schedule, you will need to be a member of the TFS Administrator Group, a member of SQL Server Administrator Group, and (if your deployment uses SharePoint Products) a member of the Farm Administrators Group.

The TFS Service Account must have a SQL Server perform backup and create maintenance plan permissions set to allow on each instance of the SQL Server that hosts the databases that you want to back up. You need a network share to store the database backup. The service account needs full control permission on the network share, folder, or storage device where the backups will be kept.

How to do it...

1. Log into the Team Foundation Server Application tier and open the Team Foundation Server Administration Console. Navigate to the **Scheduled Backups** screen by clicking on **Scheduled Backups** from the navigation panel on the left:

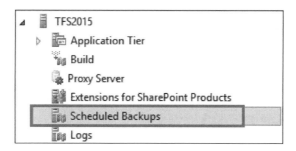

2. As illustrated here, specify the network backup path and duration to 30 days:

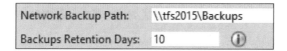

The **Advanced** section allows you specify the file extension for the backup and the transactional backup file:

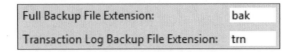

| Full Backup File Extension: | bak |
| Transaction Log Backup File Extension: | trn |

You can optionally choose a unique extension name and configure that to be exempted from the antivirus scan. The general industry wide accepted extension for backups are `bak` for the full backups, `diff` for differential backups, and `trn` for transactional backups.

3. The next screen allows you to specify the reporting databases. Check the option to include the reporting database in the backup schedule. This will allow you to back up the reporting databases along with the TFS Database backups.

4. Reporting services needs an encryption key for accessing reports after the database restore, set an encryption key password in the reporting key page and click on **Next**.

5. You can optionally choose to backup SharePoint databases as well by checking the **Include SharePoint databases in the backup schedule** option.

6. Click on next to go to the **Alerts** screen. The **Alert** screen can be used to specify the backup scheduled alert settings. You can choose to alert the user on the success or failure of the backup job:

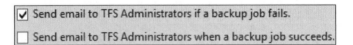

| ☑ Send email to TFS Administrators if a backup job fails. |
| ☐ Send email to TFS Administrators when a backup job succeeds. |

7. The schedule backup page allows you to choose from **Nightly**, **Manual**, and **Custom** schedule. The **Custom** schedule gives you more control to set a schedule for the full backup, a differential backup schedule, and the interval for the transactional backup.

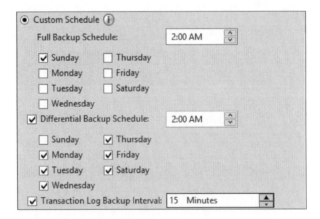

8. Confirm the settings on the review page and click on **Next** to trigger the validation checks. Now that the validation has successfully passed, you can click on the **Configure** button to configure the backup per the settings:

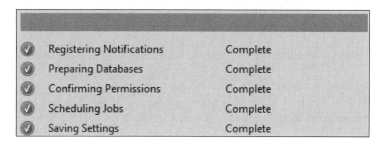

✓ Registering Notifications	Complete
✓ Preparing Databases	Complete
✓ Confirming Permissions	Complete
✓ Scheduling Jobs	Complete
✓ Saving Settings	Complete

9. Navigate to `\\tfs2015\backup` and you'll find the `BackupSets.xml`, `BackupSettings.xml`, and strong key for the reporting server. Make a copy and store these in a safe location.

10. You can trigger an ad hoc backup by clicking on the **Take Full Backup Now** link from the Team Foundation Server Administration Console:

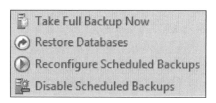

Updates on the backup processing are displayed in a pop-up window. Once the backup completes, you can find the full set available in the network share.

How it works...

Knowing the classification and criticality of the data as well as the recover goals of the organization are really useful in working out a backup and recovery strategy for the organization. Certain organizations may have very specific backup needs, which may not be possible to configure via the built-in "schedule backup". The website `http://bit.ly/1IbxBLd` discusses these use cases in length.

Visual Studio ALM Rangers have some great guidance on disaster recovery planning for TFS. You can read more about it at `http://bit.ly/1Lwgx2y`.

Cleaning up unused workspaces and shelvesets in TFS – in progress

It is common for TFVC users to create workspaces to temporarily download files or simply forget to delete unused shelvesets. As a Team Foundation Server Administrator, you will benefit from reducing this clutter. The `tf.exe` command-line utility has commands for administrating workspaces and shelvesets. In this recipe, you'll learn how to use the `tf.exe` utility to delete unused workspaces and shelvesets.

Getting ready

To modify or delete an existing workspace or shelveset, you must have the global administer workspaces permission set to **Allow**.

How to do it...

1. Launch the developer command prompt in the elevated mode.

2. The following command will delete the `Win2k12R2_John` workspace, which belongs to default collection in TFS. Refer to `http://bit.ly/1P6mo6t` for more examples on how to use the workspace switch with the `tf.exe` command:

   ```
   tf workspace /delete /collection:"http://tfs2015:8080/tfs/
   defaultcollection" workspacename:"Win2k12R2_John"
   ```

3. Similar to the workspace delete, the shelveset delete follows a similar command pattern. The following command will delete the `Fabrikam_Delta` workspace from the default collection in TFS. Refer to `http://bit.ly/1lHChUk` for more examples

   ```
   tf shelve /delete shelvesetname:"Fabrikam_Delta" /
   collection:"http://tfs2015:8080/tfs/defaultcollection"
   ```

How it works...

The TFS command-line utility (`tf.exe`) is installed along with the installation of the Visual Studio. The TFS command-line utility includes switches for various TFS operations that empower TFS Administrators to script these routine operations. You can read more about these operations at `http://bit.ly/1P6mo6t`.

The build server is the biggest consumer of workspaces. Build definitions that have not been used for a while will retain the workspace and consume large amounts of storage in doing so. Identifying and manually deleting these dead workspaces is a painstaking task. TFS Workspace cleaner is an open source utility hosted on CodePlex that helps you free up storage by deleting workspaces unused in a number of days. You can learn more about this utility at `http://bit.ly/1LxFDhv`.

8

Extending and Customizing Team Foundation Server

"First, solve the problem. Then, write the code."

–John Johnson

In this chapter, we will cover the following topics:

- ▶ Acquiring the TFS object model from the NuGet Gallery
- ▶ Using Team Project Picker to connect to TFS programmatically
- ▶ Determining the version of TFS using the TFS object model
- ▶ Retrieving TFS permissions programmatically using the TFS object model
- ▶ Getting the Process Template name for a Team Project programmatically
- ▶ Getting build details programmatically using the REST API
- ▶ Getting a list of Git repositories programmatically using the REST API
- ▶ Getting a Work Item by ID programmatically using the REST API
- ▶ Adding a Team field to the Product Backlog Item to an existing Team Project
- ▶ Adding multi-item select control in the Work Item form

Introduction

TFS provides integrated tooling for software application delivery and life cycle management. It is not uncommon for organizations to have different tools for managing different parts of the life cycle, for example, Jira for Agile Project Management, TeamCity for builds, Jenkins for release management, and ServiceNow for service management. Customers expect to be able to integrate and share information between different systems. Team Foundation Server has a fairly large ecosystem of tools and services it integrates with. The following screenshot shows some of the partners from the TFS ecosystem, you can find the complete list at `https://vsipprogram.com/Directory`:

It is virtually impossible to provide out-of-the-box integration with every other system; to bridge the gap, TFS provides a very rich library that allows you to retrieve, edit, update, insert, and delete data in TFS. The API makes these operations secure and auditable. Today, TFS has two extensibility technologies, as shown in the following screenshot:

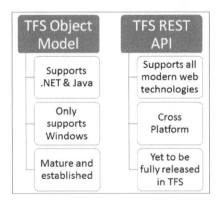

Let's explain these two extensibility technologies in detail:

- **The TFS object model**: The TFS object model supports both .NET and Java platforms and has been offered in the product from as early as TFS 2005. The object model library has been enriched with more functionality over releases. Extensions built using the object model can be integrated into Visual Studio and Team Explorer or can be used as standalone tools. The object model has the following limitations:
  - It does not support Team Web Portal extensibility
  - It does not support non-Windows operating systems
  - It does not support client-side extensions for mobile devices

- **The RESTful services**: The RESTful services first debuted in TFS 2013. The RESTful services are JSON-based REST services, primarily focused on bridging the limitations of the TFS object model. The services enable Team Web Portal extensibility, extensions for non-Windows platforms, and client-side extensions for mobile devices. The RESTful services can also be called from within the TFS object model. This is quite powerful as this enables you to build extensibility for features that do not support any extension points within the TFS object model. For example, Team Rooms is a web-only feature that has no extensibility points within the TFS object model. The Team Rooms Visual Studio Extension (`http://bit.ly/1TeNIO7`) has been built using the Team Rooms REST APIs with the TFS object model.

The TFS object model and RESTful services open up limitless opportunities for extensibility. While RESTful services can be used in conjunction with TFS object model today, the RESTful services aren't quite ready for extending Team Web Portal in TFS. The RESTful services use OAuth for authentication and authorization. TFS does not have an OAuth token provisioning capability. As a work-around, it is possible to use alternate credentials for authenticating with the REST APIs. Organizations may be reluctant to enable alternate credentials since it requires basic authentication to be enabled on the instance of IIS hosting TFS. Recipes in this chapter using REST APIs have been implemented using alternate credentials. Follow the instructions here to enable alternate credentials: `http://bit.ly/1IhEQH1`.

Since TFS does not have an OAuth token provisioning capability, it is not possible to build Team Web Portal extensions for TFS. The OAuth token provision capability is expected to be released in TFS 2015 in future updates. The RESTful extensibility model is the same between TFS and VSTS. Since VSTS has an OAuth token provisioning system, you can use the RESTful services in VSTS to start building extensions for Team Web Portal in VSTS. The RESTful services are the foundation to the marketplace capability recently introduced in VSTS. It is expected that this capability will be available in TFS in future updates. You can learn more about the VSTS marketplace at `http://bit.ly/1Q6afgw`.

Apart from covering extensibility, we'll be learning about the possibilities of customization in TFS. TFS provides a customization framework that enables customization at the Team Project level. Customizations to Team Projects are applied through Process Templates. A Process Template is a collection of XML files that hold instructions for artifacts and the processes that need to be applied to a Team Project. To give you an example, the Process Template holds instructions for security groups, areas, iterations, Work Items, and backlogs. The template also applies the workflow and behavior these artifacts exhibit, for example, a Bug Work Item in CMMI template has a ready-for-testing state, the Bug Work Item in the Scrum Template does not. While TFS comes preloaded with the Scrum, Agile, and CMMI Process Templates, TFS supports customizing of existing Process Templates and creating new Process Templates to best meet the needs of your Team. A Process Template consists of nine plugins; each plugin executes a set of tasks during the Team Project setup. The following diagram illustrates the plugins and the object files that can be customized:

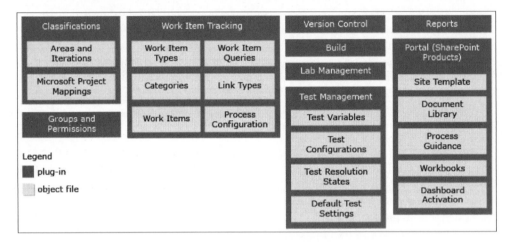

The current Process Template structure and tooling is limited in various ways:

▶ **Tooling**: To edit a Process Template, you need to install the Process Template Editor. This editor can only be installed by installing the TFS power tools (`http://bit.ly/1jJkEmt`). The Process Template Editor is strongly linked to the version of TFS. The editor can only be launched via Visual Studio. The editor does not support non-Windows platforms.

▶ **Complexity**: To edit a Process Template, you need to have good working knowledge of Process Templates and Team Projects. The Process Template Editor is rudimentary; it does not provide any validation or the means to test the changes being made.

▶ **Maintainability**: If the Process Template for a Team Project has been modified, TFS does not upgrade that product to the latest features automatically. Features need to be manually enabled on such projects.

To remove the limitations of the current Process Template customization tooling, a new process customization experience is being developed in Team Web Portal. The new experience will be web based to make it available on non-Windows devices. The new experience will simply modify the process by providing a rich guided experience for common tasks. The new tooling will enable Team Projects to be automatically updated with new functionality after upgrades. To enable this, all system fields in the Process Templates will be locked and won't be customizable. The new tooling has been released in preview in VSTS. You can learn more about it at `http://bit.ly/1OxP31n`. The new tooling is expected to be released in TFS 2015 in one of the future updates. The recipes in this chapter are based on customizing the Process Templates using the Process Template Editor.

To recap, the extensibility recipes in this chapter are based on the TFS object model and RESTful services with alternate credentials. The customization recipes in this chapter are based on the Process Template Editor. Both extensibility and customization are undergoing a great change. While the changes to both have been released in VSTS, they aren't available in TFS 2015 Update 1. These changes are expected to be available in TFS 2015 in future updates.

Acquiring TFS object model from the NuGet Gallery

If you have used the TFS object model before, you will acknowledge that acquiring the DLLs and the dependencies is a cumbersome process. The TFS DLLs need to be picked out from the install directory. The licensing framework does not allow the distribution of these DLLs. This means anyone working with the code either needs all dependencies installed or needs to manually add the DLLs into project references. In TFS 2013, a standalone installer was introduced that deployed all TFS object model binaries on the machine. While this simplified the setup, it did add an extra step for the developers. This complicates not only the development, but also the build and test process.

NuGet has become the Standard Package Manager for the Microsoft development platform including .NET. The NuGet client tools provide the ability to produce and consume packages. The NuGet Gallery is the central package repository used by all package authors and consumers. It seems natural to offer the object model as a package through NuGet. With the Team Foundation Server 2015, the object model can now directly be acquired through NuGet. Additionally, the licensing policies have been amended to allow distribution of the package. In this recipe, you will learn how to acquire the TFS object model through NuGet.

Getting ready

This recipe requires Visual Studio 2015. If you do not have Visual Studio installed, you can use the freely available Visual Studio Community edition available at `https://www.visualstudio.com/en-us/downloads/download-visual-studio-vs.aspx`.

How to do it...

1. Open Visual Studio, create a new project of type Windows Console Application, and name the project `asPlayPit`.

2. From the Solution Explorer, right-click on the project and choose **Manage NuGet Packages**. This will load the NuGet package search window within the Visual Studio.

3. Search and add the `Microsoft.TeamFoundationServer.Client` and `Microsoft.TeamFoundationServer.ExtendedClient` packages.

4. Installing these packages will also install the dependant packages. Once the package installation has completed successfully, from the Solution Explorer expand the references section in the `PlayPit` project. You'll see that all TFSs and dependency DLLs have been successfully added as project reference.

How it works...

In Team Foundation Server 2015, Team Explorer is now installed as a VSIX package. There are two ramifications of this:

▶ The Team Explorer install location will likely be different for each install

▶ The TFS assemblies are not in the **Global Assembly Cache** (**GAC**) anymore

If you are developing an extension, your extension will not be able to resolve TFS references on its own since TFS DLLs are no longer in the GAC. It is, therefore, recommended that you add a reference to TFS NuGet packages in your project to resolve these dependencies. The primary reason for moving the TFS DLLs out of GAC is to reduce the complexities in managing multiple versions of the product and their dependencies.

Adding the packages through NuGet creates a `package` folder at the solution level. All packages added are also stored in this folder. As you can see in the following screenshot, the TFS and related packages that were installed as part of this recipe have been downloaded into this folder:

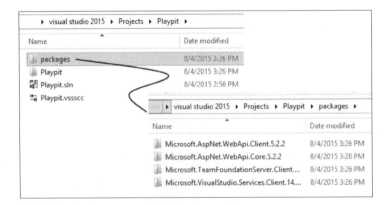

When checking in code, these packages will be checked into source control too. The benefit here is that anyone working on the code does not have to worry about the references. The **auto restore NuGet Packages** option can be enabled at the solution level. This will restore all NuGet references on other developer machines at compile time (this does not require packages to be checked into source control). It also applies during the build and test workflow, and significantly reduces the overhead on development setup. The license terms have been changed so that you can now redistribute the TFS 2015 client OM with your application. Refer to `http://bit.ly/1jkoSQj` for more details on the packages, their content, and purpose.

Using Team Project Picker to connect to TFS programmatically

The TFS object model exposes a few options for connecting to Team Foundation Server. The **Team Project Picker** (**TPP**) is one of the options; the advantage of using the project picker is that the user sees a TFS connection dialog that they are familiar with. The user can specify the TFS Server details and authenticate using this dialog. In this recipe, you'll learn how to use the TPP to authenticate and connect to TFS programmatically.

Getting ready

Follow the steps in the *Acquiring TFS object model from the NuGet Gallery* recipe to create a project in Visual Studio and add the TFS NuGet packages to this project.

How to do it...

1. Copy the following code into the `Program.cs` class in the newly created project:

```
// Global Variables
private static TfsTeamProjectCollection _tfs;
private static ProjectInfo _selectedTeamProject;

// Connect to TFS Using Team Project Picker
public static void ConnectToTfsUsingTeamProjectPicker()
{
// The user is allowed to select only one project
var tfsPp = new
TeamProjectPicker(TeamProjectPickerMode.SingleProject,
false);

tfsPp.ShowDialog();

        // The TFS project collection
        _tfs = tfsPp.SelectedTeamProjectCollection;
```

```
if (tfsPp.SelectedProjects.Any())
    {
// The selected Team Project
    _selectedTeamProject = tfsPp.SelectedProjects[0];
    }
}
```

2. From `Main`, make a call to the `ConnectToTfsUsingTeamProjectPicker` method. As soon as the `tfsPp.ShowDialog()` statement is triggered, the TPP pops up. As illustrated in the following screenshot, the project picker allows you to configure the TFS server, collection, and project interactively:

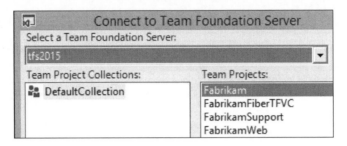

How it works...

The `TeamProjectPicker` class accepts the `TeamProjectPickerMode` and `DisableCollectionChange` as parameters. In the preceding snippet, we are forcing the `TeamProjectPicker` class to be launched in single-project mode, that is, only one Team Project can be selected. The false value is used to override, disabling the Team Project Collection change option available in the picker. The rest of the code is simply reading and storing the name of the selected Team Project in a global variable.

You can alternatively pass the `TeamProjectPicker.MultiProject` value to allow the user to pick multiple Team Projects. You can also disable the change project collection dropdown by passing the `true` value for the `DisableCollectionChange` parameter.

Determining the version of TFS using the TFS object model

If you are building an extension using the TFS object model that is going to target multiple versions of TFS, you would most likely want to programmatically figure out the version of the TFS Server you are currently pointing at. Some of the API services introduced in the later version of TFS aren't available in earlier versions of TFS. Unfortunately, the API does not expose a property or function that will give you the exact version of TFS. In this recipe, you'll learn how to determine the TFS version programmatically.

Getting ready

Follow the steps in the *Acquiring TFS object model from the NuGet Gallery* recipe to create a project in Visual Studio. Name the project `DetermineTFSVersion` and add the TFS NuGet packages to this project.

How to do it...

1. Copy the following code into the `Program.cs` class in the newly created project.

2. In the `Main` method, add the following code:

```
var server = new TfsTeamProjectCollection(new
Uri("http://tfs2015:8080/tfs"));
server.EnsureAuthenticated();
var serverVersion = server.ServerDataProvider.ServerVersion;
Console.WriteLine("Server Version: {0}", serverVersion);
Console.ReadKey();
```

3. The server version will be printed in the console output, as shown in the following output:

```
Server Version: Dev14.M89-Part7
```

How it works...

While the output of this program does not necessarily give you the full assembly version of TFS, it helps you work out the version of the product. In the following screenshot, you can see that the TFS version in the TFS Administration Console is showing up as `14.0.24706.0` while the program returns `Dev14.M89-Part7`:

```
Server Version: Dev14.M89-Part7
```

Let's go through the code to understand what is being done:

▸ The `TfsTeamProjectCollection` class is used to initialize a new connection to the server. The server details in this case are passed as a URI to the class. There are other ways to establish a connection with the TFS Server, as discussed earlier in this chapter in the *Using Team Project Picker to connect to TFS programmatically* recipe.

▸ The `EnsureAuthenticate` method is called to invoke the authentication connection process if the connection hasn't already been authenticated before.

▸ Once the connection has been authenticated, the `ServerVersion` property nested in the `ServerDataProvider` class holds the value of the TFS Server version.

▶ The value of the `ServerVersion` property is printed to the console using the console `WriteLine` method. The console's `Readkey` method is used to pause the console so the result of `ServerVersion` being printed to the console output can be read.

There is an alternate approach to identify the version of TFS programmatically; the TFS location service returns a list of services available in TFS. The list and version of the services can be used to identify the version of TFS. More information on this approach is available at `http://bit.ly/21loYX8`.

Retrieving TFS permissions programmatically using the TFS object model

TFS administrators are often required to publish and review user permissions. In this recipe, you will learn how to use the TFS object model to programmatically generate the security groups, members, permissions, and security settings of users in Team Projects in TFS.

Getting ready

Follow the steps in the *Acquiring TFS object model from the NuGet Gallery* recipe to create a project in Visual Studio and add the TFS NuGet packages to this project.

How to do it...

1. **Connect to TFS programmatically**: As a first step, a connection to the TFS needs to be established. This can be done using the following snippet:

```
var tfs = TfsTeamProjectCollectionFactory
            .GetTeamProjectCollection(new
            Uri("http://tfs2015:8080/tfs"));
tfs.EnsureAuthenticated();
```

2. **Get an instance of the version control server service**: The version control server service exposes an interface with a set of methods to work with TFS version control component programmatically:

```
// Version control service exposes methods to work with TFS
version control
var vcs = tfs.GetService<VersionControlServer>();

// Since we'll be reporting groups for all team projects,
imp to get all team projects
var teamProjects = vcs.GetAllTeamProjects(false);
// Narrow down to the FabrikamTFVC Team Project
var teamProject = teamProjects.FirstOrDefault(p=>p.Name ==
"FabrikamTFVC");
```

3. **Application groups**: The `IGroupSecurityService` interface is used to retrieve a list of group membership for a Team Project:

```
// Group Security service exposes methods to get groups,
users and security details
var sec = tfs.GetService<IGroupSecurityService>();

Identity[] appGroups =
sec.ListApplicationGroups(teamProject.ArtifactUri.
AbsoluteUri);
```

This information can be retrieved through the Team Explorer by navigating into the **Settings** page and clicking on the **Group Membership** hyperlink. Clicking on the **Group Membership** hyperlink will navigate you to the security page in Team Web Portal. The left-hand side of the following screenshot shows the groups in the security page for FabrikamTFVC project and the right-hand side of the screenshot shows the results returned programmatically:

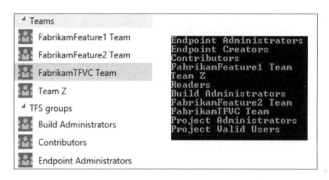

4. **Get members within the application groups**: Each application group comprises of either users or further AD groups. The following code snippet loops through the members of the application groups and gets the identity of each member:

```
foreach (Identity group in appGroups)
{
Identity[] groupMembers =
sec.ReadIdentities(SearchFactor.Sid, new string[] {
group.Sid }, QueryMembership.Expanded);

foreach (Identity member in groupMembers)
                {
Console.WriteLine(member.DisplayName);
if (member.Members != null)
                    {
foreach (string memberSid in member.Members)
                    {
```

```
                          Identity memberInfo =
                          sec.ReadIdentity
                          (SearchFactor.Sid, memberSid,
                          QueryMembership.Expanded);
        var userName = memberInfo.Domain + "\\" +
        memberInfo.AccountName;
        Console.WriteLine(string.Format("          {0}",
        memberInfo.AccountName));
                          }
                    }
                }
        }
```

The program now not only returns the name of the group, but also the members in each of the nested groups:

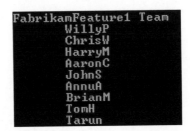

5. **Get the user membership settings**: The user in the application group either inherits the permissions or is directly assigned the permissions. The following code snippet uses the `GetPermissions` method in the version control service to work out the user membership setting:

```
var actualPermission = vcs.GetPermissions(new string[] {
TeamProject.ServerItem }, RecursionType.Full);
foreach (var memberOf in memberInfo.MemberOf)
    {
        // Get information about the members
}
```

This information can be retrieved through Team Explorer by navigating into the **Settings** page and clicking on the **Security** hyperlink. The **Security** hyperlink launches the security page in Team Web Portal:

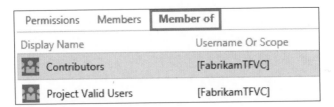

6. **Version control permissions**: Individual user permissions on version control can be retrieved using the `GetEffectivePermissions` method in the version control service:

```
var permissions = vcs.GetEffectivePermissions(userName,
teamProject.ServerItem);

foreach (var permission in permissions)
{
versionControlPerTmissions.Add(new
VersionControlPermission(){Name = permission});
}
```

This returns the version control permission for each user in the group. As illustrated in the following screenshot, the user `Tarun` is a member of the `Project Valid Users` group and has the `Manage Branch` permission:

```
[Project Valid Users] Tarun
                Read
                PendChange
                Checkin
                Label
                Lock
                ReviseOther
                UnlockOther
                UndoOther
                LabelOther
                AdminProjectRights
                CheckinOther
                Merge
                ManageBranch
```

Getting the Process Template name for a Team Project programmatically

In this recipe, you'll learn how to get the name of the Process Template used to create a Team Project.

Getting ready

Follow the steps in the *Acquiring TFS object model from the NuGet Gallery* recipe to create a project in Visual Studio and add the TFS NuGet packages to this project.

How to do it...

1. First, connect to TFS programmatically. As a first step, a connection to the TFS needs to be established. This can be done using the following snippet:

```
var tfs = TfsTeamProjectCollectionFactory
            .GetTeamProjectCollection(new
            Uri("http://tfs2015:8080/tfs"));
tfs.EnsureAuthenticated();
```

2. To obtain the Process Template details for a Team Project, we need an instance of the VersionControlServer service and the Now instance to get ICommonServerService. The VersionControlServer service is used to get the project details, specifically, it is AbsoluteUri that we are after. AbsoluteUri for the Team Project is used by ICommonServerService to identify the project properties such as the Process Template name:

```
// Get an instance of the VersionControlServer
var vcs = server.GetService<VersionControlServer>();
// Get an instance of the ICommonStructureService
var ics = server.GetService<ICommonStructureService>();
ProjectProperty[] ProjectProperties = null;

// Get the team project by name
var teamProject= vcs.GetTeamProject("FabrikamTFVC");

string ProjectName = string.Empty;
string ProjectState = string.Empty;
int templateId = 0;
ProjectProperties = null;

// Get the project properties using the
ICommonStructureServer
ics.GetProjectProperties(teamProject.ArtifactUri.AbsoluteUri,
out ProjectName, out ProjectState,
out templateId, out ProjectProperties);

// Output all the project properties
foreach (var pp in ProjectProperties)
{
Console.WriteLine(string.Format("{0} - {1}", pp.Name,
pp.Value));
}
```

Executing this returns the list of properties and their values. As you can see in the following screenshot, the `Scrum` template has been used to create the FabrikamTFVC Team Project. The `SourceControlGitEnabled` and `SourceControlTfvcEnabled` properties tell you source control capabilities in the Team Project:

```
Process Template - Scrum
SourceControlCapabilityFlags - 1
SourceControlGitEnabled - True
SourceControlTfvcEnabled - True
```

How it works...

Use the Process Template Manager to download the Scrum Process Template from TFS. From the download location, open the `Classification.xml` file from under the `Classification` folder. The API basically renders the contents of `Classification.xml`:

```xml
<properties>
    <property name="MSPROJ" isFile="true" value="Classification\FieldMapping.xml"/>
    <property name="Process Template" value="Scrum"/>
</properties>
```

You can add more properties and values to the `Classification.xml` file and use this version of the template to create Team Projects. The `GetProjectProperties` method in the `ICommonStructureServer` service will return the newly added properties. In addition to this, you can use the `UpdateProjectProperties` method in `ICommonStructureService` to update the values of these properties.

Getting build details programmatically using the REST API

In this recipe, you'll learn how to get a list of builds with details in a Team Project using the `BuildHttpClient` REST APIs.

Getting ready

As alluded to in the chapter introduction, Team Foundation Server 2015 does not yet have OAuth token provisioning capability; for this reason, the only way to consume the REST API is using alternate credentials. Alternate credentials uses basic authentication as the authentication protocol. When using basic authentication, the user credentials are sent to the server in plain text. This type of setup simply isn't acceptable in a professional environment. Follow the instructions at `http://bit.ly/1Nfe8e0` to set up a self-signed certificate to configure SSL for TFS. With SSL, the traffic between the client and TFS is encrypted.

If you simply want to play around with the REST API without getting into the complexities of the setup, then API Sandbox is a great place to start: `https://apisandbox.msdn.microsoft.com`. The API Sandbox is wired up to a sample Visual Studio Team Services account, it gives you pre-configured code samples to try out the capabilities offered by the API, you can additionally connect to your Visual Studio Team Services instance too. While API Sandbox does not offer the capability to connect an on-premise TFS instance, it allows you to call older versions of the API by specifying the version of the API in the version parameter in the constructed service URL. An alternate to the API Sandbox is Postman (`http://bit.ly/11044iU`). Postman is available as a free extension in the Chrome store. It's a fantastic utility to build, test, and document APIs faster. You can trigger all REST operations by directly passing the server URLs and parameters right from within Postman. This enables you to connect to on-premise TFS instance too; this is very useful to try the APIs against real data.

Download the `RESTDemo` solution provided with the course material. The solution contains three projects, namely, `GetBuildDetails`, `GetGitRepos`, and `GetWorkitemById`. Open the `RESTDemo` solution in Visual Studio. In this recipe, we'll be going through the `GetBuildDetails` project to get a list of builds with details from a Team Project.

How to do it...

1. In the `RESTDemo` solution, set `GetBuildDetails` as the startup project:

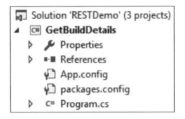

2. Run the `GetBuildDetails` project, this will launch a console, enter the TFS server URL, and press *Enter*:

```
This program gets the Git repositories in the given team project using REST API
Press Control + C anytime to quit

Enter the url of your TFS server including collection name.
NOTE: Ensure that you have enterd https URL to TFS. This is necessary for connec
ting to TFS using username and password.
E.g: https://tfs2015/tfs/defaultcollection
https://tfs2015:8080/tfs/defaultcollection
```

3. Enter the username and password of the user you want to connect to TFS with and press *Enter*:

```
Please enter the username to connect
Tarun
Please enter password
********
```

4. Enter the project name you would like to retrieve the build details from:

```
Enter the name of Team Project you want to fetch Builds from
FabrikamTFVC
Please wait...
```

5. The console outputs the list of builds in FabrikamTFVC along with the details of the build, such as the name of the build definition, the build number, result, requested by, start time, and finish time of the build:

```
Done..Found 82 builds
*** Details ***
Definition: FabrikamTFVC CI
BuildNumber: 1.0.15325.228
Result: Failed
Requsted By: Tarun Arora
StartTime: Sat, Nov 21 2015 03:20:25
FinishTime: Sat, Nov 21 2015 03:21:26
```

How it works...

We'll go through the code in the `GetBuildDetails` project to understand the working of the code. To connect and get the data from TFS, the project requires TFS API binaries. The project uses the `Microsoft.TeamFoundationServer.ClientNuGet` package to get the right binary references:

```
Microsoft.TeamFoundation.Build2.WebApi
Microsoft.TeamFoundation.Chat.WebApi
Microsoft.TeamFoundation.Common
Microsoft.TeamFoundation.Core.WebApi
Microsoft.TeamFoundation.Discussion.WebApi
Microsoft.TeamFoundation.Policy.WebApi
Microsoft.TeamFoundation.SourceControl.WebApi
Microsoft.TeamFoundation.Test.WebApi
Microsoft.TeamFoundation.TestManagement.WebApi
Microsoft.TeamFoundation.Work.WebApi
Microsoft.TeamFoundation.WorkItemTracking.WebApi
Microsoft.VisualStudio.Services.Common
Microsoft.VisualStudio.Services.WebApi
```

From the Solution Explorer, open the `Program.cs` file in the `GetBuildDetails` project. The program gets the TFS Server URL, username, and password details as an input from the user. The password is asterisked on the console by replacing the entered characters into asterisk form before printing out to the console. An instance of `VssBasicCredential` is created with the username and password. This information is then passed into `BuildHttpClient`. When an instance of the `BuildHttpClient` class is created, the constructor takes the server URL and credentials. The `BuildHttpClient` object validates the connection to TFS as part of the instantiation process:

```
var tfsServerUrl = Console.ReadLine();
var userName = Console.ReadLine();
var password = GetConsolePassword();
var projectName = Console.ReadLine();
var credentials = new VssBasicCredential(userName, password);
BuildHttpClient buildClient = new BuildHttpClient(new
Uri(tfsServerUrl), credentials);
```

The `BuildHttpClient` class contains the `GetBuildsAsync` method. The Team Project name is passed as a parameter to the `GetBuildsAsync` method:

```
var builds = buildClient.GetBuildsAsync(projectName).Result;
```

The function returns a list of build. The build entity contains all build properties, as seen in the following screenshot:

```
public Build();

...public string BuildNumber { get; set; }
...public BuildController Controller { get; set; }
...public DefinitionReference Definition { get; set; }
...public List<Demand> Demands { get; set; }
...public DateTime? FinishTime { get; set; }
...public int Id { get; set; }
...public bool? KeepForever { get; set; }
```

The program then loops through the list of builds and prints the properties to the console. You can get more details about the build REST API at `https://www.visualstudio.com/integrate/api/build/overview`.

Getting a list of Git repositories programmatically using the REST API

In this recipe, you'll learn how to get a list of Git repositories in a Team Project programmatically using the `GitHttpClient` REST API.

Getting ready

Refer to instructions in the *Getting ready* section of the *Getting build details programmatically using the REST API* recipe for setup details. Download the `RESTDemo` solution provided with the course material. In this recipe, we'll be going through the `GetGitRepos` project to get a list of Git repositories with details from a Team Project.

How to do it...

1. In the `RESTDemo` solution, set `GetGitRepos` as the startup project:

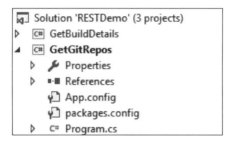

2. Run the `GetGitRepos` project, this will launch a console. Enter the TFS Server URL and press *Enter*:

```
This program gets the Git repositories in the given team project using REST API
Press Control + C anytime to quit

Enter the url of your TFS server including collection name.
NOTE: Ensure that you have enterd https URL to TFS. This is necessary for connec
ting to TFS using username and password.
E.g: https://tfs2015/tfs/defaultcollection
https://tfs2015:8080/tfs/defaultcollection
```

3. Enter the username and password of the user you want to connect to the TFS with and press *Enter*:

```
Please enter the username to connect
Tarun
Please enter password
********
```

4. Enter the project name you would like to retrieve the build details from:

```
Enter the Team Project name you want to fetch Git repositories from
FabrikamGit
Please wait...
```

5. The console outputs the list of Git repositories in FabrikamGit project along with the details of the repositories such as its ID, name, and remote URL:

```
Done..Found 8 repositories
*** Details ***
Id: 2712f261-918a-55zf-ae98-4a1bb7826tta
Name: FabrikamGitWeb
RemoteUrl: http://tfs2015:8080/tfs/defaultcollection/_git/FabrikamGit
```

How it works...

We'll go through the code in the `GetGitRepos` project to understand the working of the code. To connect and get the data from TFS, the project requires TFS API binaries; the project uses the `Microsoft.TeamFoundationServer.ClientNuGet` package to get the right binary references:

```
■·■ Microsoft.TeamFoundation.Build2.WebApi
■·■ Microsoft.TeamFoundation.Chat.WebApi
■·■ Microsoft.TeamFoundation.Common
■·■ Microsoft.TeamFoundation.Core.WebApi
■·■ Microsoft.TeamFoundation.Discussion.WebApi
■·■ Microsoft.TeamFoundation.Policy.WebApi
■·■ Microsoft.TeamFoundation.SourceControl.WebApi
■·■ Microsoft.TeamFoundation.Test.WebApi
■·■ Microsoft.TeamFoundation.TestManagement.WebApi
■·■ Microsoft.TeamFoundation.Work.WebApi
■·■ Microsoft.TeamFoundation.WorkItemTracking.WebApi
■·■ Microsoft.VisualStudio.Services.Common
■·■ Microsoft.VisualStudio.Services.WebApi
```

From the Solution Explorer open the `Program.cs` file in `GetGitRepos` project. The program gets the TFS Server URL, username, and password details as an input from the user. The password is asterisked on the console by replacing the entered characters into asterisk form before printing out to the console. An instance of `VssBasicCredential` is created with the username and password. This information is then passed into the `GitHttpClient`. An instance of the `GitHttpClient` class is created, the constructor takes the server URL and credentials. The `GitHttpClient` class validates the connection to TFS as part of the instantiation process:

```
var tfsServerUrl = Console.ReadLine();
var userName = Console.ReadLine();
```

```
var password = GetConsolePassword();
var projectName = Console.ReadLine();
var credentials = new VssBasicCredential(userName, password);

GitHttpClient gitClient = new GitHttpClient(new Uri(tfsServerUrl),
credentials);
```

The `GitHttpClient` class contains the `GetRepositoriesAsync` method. The Team Project name is passed as a parameter to this method:

```
var gitRepositories = gitClient.GetRepositoriesAsync(projectName,
true).Result;
```

The function returns a list of `GitRepository`. The `GitRepository` entity contains all `GitRepository` properties:

```
...public string DefaultBranch { get; set; }
...public Guid Id { get; set; }
...public ReferenceLinks Links { get; set; }
...public string Name { get; set; }
...public TeamProjectReference ProjectReference { get; set; }
...public string RemoteUrl { get; set; }
...public string Url { get; set; }
```

The program then loops through the list of `GitRepositories` and prints the properties to the console. You can get more details about the Git REST API at `https://www.visualstudio.com/integrate/api/git/overview`.

Getting a Work Item by ID programmatically using the REST API

In this recipe, you'll learn how to get details of a Work Item programmatically using the `WorkItemTrackingHttpClient` REST API.

Getting ready

Refer to instructions in the *Getting ready* section of the *Getting build details programmatically using the REST API* recipe for setup details. Download the `RESTDemo` solution provided with the course material. In this recipe, we'll be going through the `GetWorkItemById` project to get the details of a Work Item.

How to do it...

1. In the `RESTDemo` solution, set `GetWorkItemById` as the startup project:

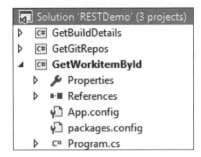

2. Run the `GetWorkItemById` project, this will launch a console, enter the TFS server URL, and press *Enter*:

```
This program gets the details of the work item given using TFS REST API
Press Control + C anytime to quit

Please enter the TFS server url including the collection name.
NOTE: Ensure that you have enterd https URL to TFS. This is necessary for connec
ting to TFS using username and password.
E.g: https://tfs2015/tfs/defaultcollection
https://tfs2015:8080/tfs/defaultcollection
```

3. Enter the username and password of the user you want to connect to TFS with and press *Enter*:

```
Please enter the username to connect
Tarun
Please enter password
********
```

4. Enter the Work Item ID you would like to query the API for:

```
Please enter the workitem id
26
```

5. The console outputs the details of the Work Item such as the Team Project it belongs to, its type, title, state, and created by:

```
*** Details of WorkItem: 26 ***
Team Project: FabrikamTFVC
Type: Product Backlog Item
Title: Set up a Multi Value Selector Control
State: New
Created By: Tarun
```

How it works...

We'll go through the code in the `GetWorkItemById` project to understand the workings of the code. To connect and get the data from TFS, the project requires TFS API binaries; the project uses the `Microsoft.TeamFoundationServer.ClientNuGet` package to get the right binary references:

```
Microsoft.TeamFoundation.Build2.WebApi
Microsoft.TeamFoundation.Chat.WebApi
Microsoft.TeamFoundation.Common
Microsoft.TeamFoundation.Core.WebApi
Microsoft.TeamFoundation.Discussion.WebApi
Microsoft.TeamFoundation.Policy.WebApi
Microsoft.TeamFoundation.SourceControl.WebApi
Microsoft.TeamFoundation.Test.WebApi
Microsoft.TeamFoundation.TestManagement.WebApi
Microsoft.TeamFoundation.Work.WebApi
Microsoft.TeamFoundation.WorkItemTracking.WebApi
Microsoft.VisualStudio.Services.Common
Microsoft.VisualStudio.Services.WebApi
```

From the Solution Explorer, open the `Program.cs` file in the `GetWorkItemById` project. The program gets the TFS server URL, username, and password details as an input from the user. The password is asterisked on the console by replacing the entered characters into asterisk form before printing out to the console. An instance of `VssBasicCredential` is created with the username and password. This information is then passed into `WorkItemTrackingHttp Client`. An instance of the `WorkItemTrackingHttpClient` class is created, the constructor takes the server URL and credentials. The `WorkItemTrackingHttpClient` class validates the connection to TFS as part of the instantiation process. As you would have noticed, in this sample we did not have to ask for the Team Project name, that's because Work Item IDs are scoped at the Team Project Collection level. This means a Work Item ID is unique at a Team Project Collection level, since the TFS Server URL contains the collection name this information does not need to be requested separately:

```
var tfsServerUrl = Console.ReadLine();
var userName = Console.ReadLine();
var password = GetConsolePassword();
var credentials = new VssBasicCredential(userName, password);

WorkItemTrackingHttpClient witClient =
new WorkItemTrackingHttpClient(new Uri(tfsServerUrl),
new VssBasicCredential(userName, password));
```

The `WorkItemTrackingHttpClient` class contains the `GetWorkItemAsync` method. The Work Item ID is passed as a parameter to this method.

```
var workItem =
witClient.GetWorkItemAsync(Convert.ToInt32(workitemId)).Result;
```

The function returns an object of type `WorkItem`. The `WorkItem` class contains information about the Work Item fields along with information about the relation and revision:

```
...public IDictionary<string, object> Fields { get; set; }
...public int? Id { get; set; }
...public IList<WorkItemRelation> Relations { get; set; }
...public int? Rev { get; set; }
```

The program then prints the values of the fields to the console:

```
Console.WriteLine($"Team Project:
workItem.Fields["System.TeamProject"]}");
Console.WriteLine($"Type:
{workItem.Fields["System.WorkItemType"]}");
Console.WriteLine($"Title: {workItem.Fields["System.Title"]}");
Console.WriteLine($"State: {workItem.Fields["System.State"]}");
Console.WriteLine($"Created By:
{workItem.Fields["System.CreatedBy"]}");
```

You can get more details about the Work Item REST API at `https://www.visualstudio.com/integrate/api/wit/overview`.

Adding a Team field to the Product Backlog Item to an existing Team Project

The original purpose of the Area Path field was to logically group Work Items based on the functional or technical area they belong to before this field got hijacked as the Team Backlog Path. If you intend to use the Area Path for functional or technical grouping of the Work Items, you will need a new field to allocate the Work Items to Teams within a Team Project. In this recipe, you'll learn how to add a Team field to a Team Project by modifying an existing Process Template.

Getting ready

A Process Template can be downloaded using the Process Template manager. To do this, navigate to the Team Explorer's **Settings** page. Select the **Process Template Manager** hyperlink from the **Team Project Collection** view:

The out-of-the-box Process Templates in TFS have been locked for editing. This has been done by adding a known GUID to the Process Template. This ID helps identify the out-of-the-box Process Template from others. If you intend to customize a Process Template, then it is advisable to modify the GUID of the out-of-the-box Process Template to a different GUID. As illustrated in the following screenshot, this can be done by downloading the Process Template and chaining the GUID to a different value:

```
<name>Scrum</name>
<description>This template is for teams who follow the Scrum framework.</description>
<version minor="1" major="14" type="6B724908-EF14-45CF-84F8-768B5384DA45"/>
```

Modifying an existing Team Project can lead to corruption of data, it is, therefore, advisable that you create a Test Project using the updated Process Template before trying out the changes highlighted in this recipe. You need to be a member of the Project Administrators Group to make these changes to the Team Project.

Download and install the TFS Power Tools (http://bit.ly/1jJkEmt), this will install the Process Editor extension.

How to do it...

1. Create a `ProcessTemplateRecipe` directory and a new file `TeamGlobalList.xml`. Copy and save the following text in the `TeamGlobalList` file:

```xml
<?xml version="1.0" encoding="utf-8"?>
<gl:GLOBALLISTS
xmlns:gl="http://schemas.microsoft.com/VisualStudio/2005/
workitemtracking/globallists">
    <GLOBALLIST name="Teams">
        <LISTITEM value="Unassigned"/>
        <LISTITEM value="Fabrikam Feature 1"/>
        <LISTITEM value="Fabrikam Feature 2"/>
        <LISTITEM value="Fabrikam Feature 3"/>
        <LISTITEM value="Fabrikam Feature 4"/>
    </GLOBALLIST>
</gl:GLOBALLISTS>
```

2. Open Visual Studio, and launch the Process Editor from the **Tools** menu. From the context menu, select **Import Global List**:

3. To upload the `TeamGlobalList.xml` file, navigate to the directory and select `TeamGlobalList.xml`. To validate the upload, choose **Open Global List** from the server:

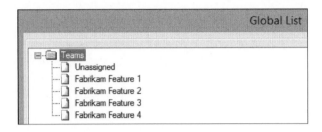

4. Open WIT from server by selecting this option from the **Process Editor** menu. Select the FabrikamTFVC Team Project and the Product Backlog Item type Work Item:

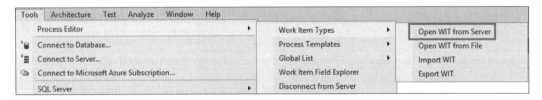

5. The Process Editor launches the Product Backlog Item type Work Item in a graphical interface:

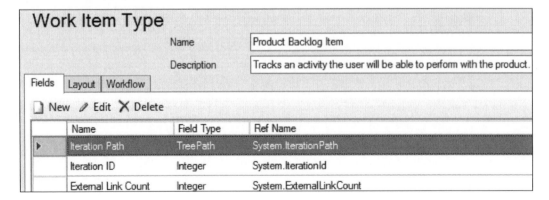

6. The **New** button is used to add a new field to the Work Item type. Click on **New** and enter the details as illustrated in the following screenshot:

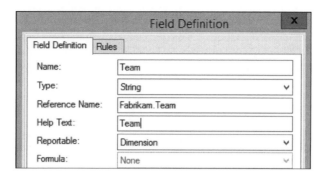

7. From the **Rules** tab, click on **New**, choose **Allowed Values**. Click on **New** and choose the Team's global list created earlier:

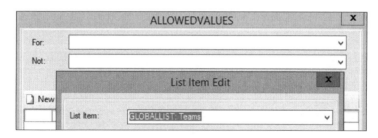

8. Navigate to the **Layout** tab and create a new control for Team under the **Status Group** column. Configure the Team control as illustrated in the following screenshot:

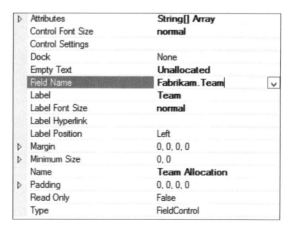

9. Click on the preview form button to load the preview of changes in the Work Item form. Click on **Save** in the **Work Item Type** form to apply the changes.

How it works...

To test the changes, create a new Work Item of type **Product Backlog Item**. The form now includes the **Team** field. The changes are applied to the Work Item form in Visual Studio and Team Web Portal:

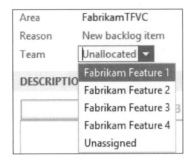

By choosing to add the field as a dimension, it now supports being reporting using the TFS warehouse. This is great if you intend to use this field for reporting.

The Process Templates support customization not only at the Work Item form level, but also at other levels such as security groups, project defaults, version control, and reports. MSDN has comprehensive guidance and walkthroughs on how to apply this customization; read more about it at http://bit.ly/1lmwLGr.

Adding multi-item select control in the Work Item form

Natively, the Work Item forms in Team Project do not support multivalue fields. While there isn't native support for multivalue fields in the Process Template, there is an open source multivalue field control that allows you to achieve exactly this. In this recipe, you'll learn how to set up and use the multivalue field control in an existing Team Project.

Getting ready

Download and install the custom Work Item Control from CodePlex http://witcustomcontrols.codeplex.com. The download includes a web extension and an extension for Visual Studio. The Visual Studio extension needs to be installed on all machines you intend to use the multivalue control from in Visual Studio. You do not need to install this control on machines where you intend to use this control in Web Portal only. You need to be a member of the Project Administrator Group to make these changes.

In this recipe, we'll be extending the Team Global List field set up earlier in the chapter in the *Adding a Team field to the Product Backlog Item to an existing Team Project* recipe.

How to do it...

1. Launch the Team Web Portal extensions console by browsing `http://tfs2015:8080/tfs/_admin/_extensions`:

2. Click on the **Install** button to upload the multivalue field control extension in the Web Portal. Select and add the extension from the download location:

3. Enable the extension once it has been uploaded. This will activate this extension across the TFS instance:

4. Open Visual Studio and launch the Process Editor, choose **Open WIT from server** from the context menu. Connect to the FabrikamTFVC Team Project and open the Product Backlog Item Work Item Type. In the previous recipe, a **Team** field was added and associated to a control of type `FieldType`. Navigate to the **Layout** tab, locate the **Team** field, and change the type of the control to `MultiValueControl`. Click on **Save** to apply the changes:

How it works...

To test the changes, create a new Work Item of type Product Backlog Item using the Team Web Portal. As illustrated in the following screenshot, the **Team** field shows a checkbox next to each Team name that allows you to select multiple items. Select multiple values and save the changes to the Work Item. The values set in the Work Item can also be queried from the **Work Item Query** window:

You will also see the multivalue selector option in the Product Backlog Item Work Item form when you open it in Visual Studio on a machine that has the multivalue selector control installed.

Index

W

Thank you for buying
Microsoft Team Foundation Server 2015 Cookbook

About Packt Publishing

Packt, pronounced 'packed', published its first book, *Mastering phpMyAdmin for Effective MySQL Management*, in April 2004, and subsequently continued to specialize in publishing highly focused books on specific technologies and solutions.

Our books and publications share the experiences of your fellow IT professionals in adapting and customizing today's systems, applications, and frameworks. Our solution-based books give you the knowledge and power to customize the software and technologies you're using to get the job done. Packt books are more specific and less general than the IT books you have seen in the past. Our unique business model allows us to bring you more focused information, giving you more of what you need to know, and less of what you don't.

Packt is a modern yet unique publishing company that focuses on producing quality, cutting-edge books for communities of developers, administrators, and newbies alike. For more information, please visit our website at www.PacktPub.com.

About Packt Enterprise

In 2010, Packt launched two new brands, Packt Enterprise and Packt Open Source, in order to continue its focus on specialization. This book is part of the Packt Enterprise brand, home to books published on enterprise software – software created by major vendors, including (but not limited to) IBM, Microsoft, and Oracle, often for use in other corporations. Its titles will offer information relevant to a range of users of this software, including administrators, developers, architects, and end users.

Writing for Packt

We welcome all inquiries from people who are interested in authoring. Book proposals should be sent to author@packtpub.com. If your book idea is still at an early stage and you would like to discuss it first before writing a formal book proposal, then please contact us; one of our commissioning editors will get in touch with you.

We're not just looking for published authors; if you have strong technical skills but no writing experience, our experienced editors can help you develop a writing career, or simply get some additional reward for your expertise.

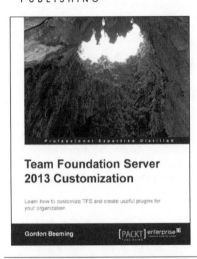

[PACKT] enterprise 88
professional expertise distilled
PUBLISHING

Team Foundation Server 2013 Customization

ISBN: 978-1-78217-714-2   Paperback: 102 pages

Learn how to customize TFS and create useful plugins for your organization

1. This book accelerates the understanding of TFS extension points.

2. Learn how to create a JavaScript web access plugin.

3. Discover the tips and tricks of customizing TFS.

Instant Team Foundation Server 2012 and Project Server 2010 Integration How-to

ISBN: 978-1-84968-854-3   Paperback: 54 pages

Successfully perform and understand how to integrate your Team Foundation Server 2012 and Project Server 2010

1. Learn something new in an Instant! A short, fast, focused guide delivering immediate results.

2. Learn to plan and successfully implement your Team Foundation Server and Project Server integration.

3. Easily install or upgrade your Team Foundation Server extensions for Project Server.

4. Understand and implement permissions to ensure security.

Please check **www.PacktPub.com** for information on our titles

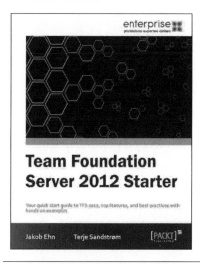

Team Foundation Server 2012 Starter

ISBN: 978-1-84968-838-3   Paperback: 72 pages

Your quick start guide to TFS 2012, top features, and best practices with hands on examples

1. Learn something new in an Instant! A short, fast, focused guide delivering immediate results.

2. Install TFS 2012 from scratch.

3. Get up and running with your first project.

4. Streamline release cycles for maximum productivity.

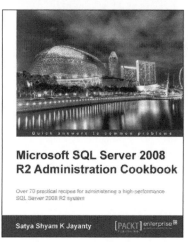

Microsoft SQL Server 2008 R2 Administration Cookbook

ISBN: 978-1-84968-144-5   Paperback: 468 pages

Over 70 practical recipes for administering a high-performance SQL Server 2008 R2 system

1. Provides Advanced Administration techniques for SQL Server 2008 R2 as a book or eBook.

2. Covers the essential Manageability, Programmability, and Security features.

3. Emphasizes important High Availability features and implementation.

Please check **www.PacktPub.com** for information on our titles